An Education System
Worthy of Malaysia

Books by M. Bakri Musa

The Malay Dilemma Revisited: Race Dynamics in Modern Malaysia
(1999)

Malaysia in the Era of Globalization
(2002)

An Education System Worthy of Malaysia

M. Bakri Musa

Writers Club Press

New York Lincoln Shanghai

An Education System Worthy of Malaysia

Writers Club Press
an imprint of iUniverse, Inc.

For information address:
iUniverse, Inc.
2021 Pine Lake Road, Suite 100
Lincoln, NE 68512
www.iuniverse.com

ISBN: 0-595-26590-1

Printed in the United States of America

In memory of my schoolteacher parents,

Cikgu Haji Musa bin Abdullah
(May 24, 1913 to June 15, 2000)

and

Cikgu Hajjah Jauhariah binte Sallam
(June 30, 1917 to May 12, 1997)

Contents

Preface and Acknowledgments

While visiting my parents many years back, our conversation not surprisingly gravitated towards education. Although they had retired from teaching, they maintained an abiding interest in the field. At the time the consuming and acrimonious public debate was on the demand by the Malaysian-Chinese community to set up Merdeka University. This move was generally met with hostile opposition from Malays, and my parents were no exception.

I made the point that it is never a smart idea to stop anyone from expanding opportunities, on the contrary we should be encouraging, not blocking, the building of another university. My parents were surprised by my contrarian viewpoint, and remarked whether I was merely trying to be argumentative or did I really believe in what I said. I quietly explained that we should support the effort to ensure that the university would serve *all* Malaysians and not just a particular community, and that with proper planning and cooperation, the venture could be a win-win situation for all. In the end I made a believer out of them.

My father went further. He encouraged me to pursue my ideas with the authorities so that they too would see my point. I told him that I already had, unfortunately those in power were not so open-minded. Nonetheless he urged me on in the hope that I would change many more minds.

This book is a commitment I made to my late parents those many years ago. That aside, I do hope to win over many, one at a time.

Education in Malaysia is a powerful political and cultural symbol. Being tightly bound up with these extraneous symbolisms takes its toll. As with the discussion on Merdeka University, rational thoughts are quickly replaced with the narrow politics of race and culture. Instead of looking at the potential for mutual benefits, we analyze policies and initiatives in terms of winners and losers. Such discussions and attitudes often result on all sides losing. The very fact that we have framed issues as "us" versus "them" instead of how best to make them work for all is itself destructive.

I do not look at education through the prism of race, politics, or nationalism, rather on how best to make it serve the needs of Malaysians. When that is done right, everything else falls into place. Conversely, when done poorly, the ugly repercussions are borne not only by the unfortunate students and their families but also society.

This book is my effort to make Malaysians look at their education system from a perspective different to what they have been accustomed. Doing this is a necessary prelude to the changing of minds.

These are my personal views and observations. I shy away from philosophical waxing and concentrate instead on the concrete and the mundane. It is said that when you do not know what questions to ask, that is philosophy; when you do know the questions, then you find ways to answer them. That is the realm of science. You seek empirical evidences, try different models (otherwise known as experimenting), and then fashion your own solutions. With Malaysian education, the questions are many and obvious.

There is also an axiom in science to the effect that when you cannot find the solution, chances are you are asking the wrong question. Thus I begin by raising some relevant questions, and once we are agreed upon them, the solutions would be that much less difficult to find.

I have highlighted different models and examples from various countries. It is not my purpose that Malaysia should blindly adopt or copy them rather these are principles to ponder.

I come from a family of teachers; consequently I have tremendous respect and affection for the profession and its practitioners. As a surgeon my work is exciting and very rewarding. But even if I had done my job perfectly, the best that I could achieve is to restore my patients back to their pre-morbid state. (My plastic surgery colleagues claim that they can make their patients better and younger, or at least *feel* and perhaps also *look* that way!) Not so with teachers. When they do their job well, no telling what heights of accomplishment their pupils would reach. Once the intellectual spark is ignited, one never knows where it would lead. I mention this at the very outset because in voicing my criticisms of the system–schools and other institutions–some of them will inevitably rub off on the practitioners. I try to be as narrow and specific as possible when criticizing so as not to tar everyone with a broad brush. The vast majority of our teachers and professors are dedicated professionals doing their best under some very trying circumstances. It is unfortunate that their profession is today increasingly being inundated by the less-than-committed. My purpose is to bring about a better working environment for our teachers and professors so that their new colleagues would be among the brightest and best, and that together they would once again regain their due rewards and respect in our society.

The first half of this book covers general topics on education, its impact and role on society, as well as societal elements that bear on it. I also describe and critique the present system, and review for comparison purposes the system of a few selected countries.

The second half deals specifically with my reform proposals. I begin by critiquing previous and current attempts at reform. This is followed with my specifics on reforming the schools. Not surprisingly this is the longest chapter, as schools are the core of the system. My ideas on revamping higher education and the ministry of education follow in their own separate chapters. The last chapter is essentially a summary.

Portions of this book were written years ago and had appeared in various publications. I apologize for their inclusion here but had to do so for the sake of completeness. My sincere thank you to readers who have kindly written me with their thoughtful viewpoints. Writing would be a futile exercise if not for readers. I value your contributions both when you agree as well as when you disagree with me. Putting my ideas in writing also help elevate them from being mere coffee shop talk.

I am indebted to my late parents for encouraging me to pursue my ideas, and more. They were also my severest critics; as former teachers they brought a much-needed reality check. I also deeply appreciate the editing of my son Zack. His skills honed by years working for his campus newspaper came in handy. Being a teacher, my wife Karen was a careful and critical first reader; she helped sieve the extraneous and lumpy until the final form flowed more smoothly.

M. Bakri Musa
January 2003
Morgan Hill, California
bakrimusa@juno.com

1

A Preemptive Strike

*T*here is considerable anxiety among Malaysians over the state of their schools and universities. This angst is manifested in many ways, from the thousands of children who cross the causeway daily to escape Malaysian schools, to well-to-do parents like the daughter of Prime Minister Mahathir who pack their young to boarding schools abroad.

On a more general level, foreign investments in the county are fast drying up; the ambitious Multimedia Super Corridor and Biotechnology Valley schemes are stalling; and the nation's competitiveness has declined precipitously. There are many other contributing factors for these phenomena, but there is no disagreement that the failure of the education system looms large in all.

To top it, the government is threatening to use the repressive Internal Security Act to browbeat citizens into accepting its brand of education reform. To be sure, education has always been a divisive issue in racially sensitive Malaysia. While it is the aspiration of its leaders right from the very beginning that education should serve to unite the nation, perversely today matters of education remain highly volatile and disruptive.

A look at the current headlines reveals how divisive educational issues are. Today the crisis revolves on the teaching of science and mathematics in English. While the goal is laudatory and agreed upon by most, many strenuously resist or are overtly hostile to the move. The only redeeming aspect to this controversy is that at least it is not along racial lines, meaning many Malays as well as non-Malays oppose the scheme. But this being Malaysia, unless this issue is resolved soon it too will quickly degenerate along the racial divide.

In a plural society, education should mean more than just educating the young. It must be a force for fostering mutual understanding and respect, and thus encouraging greater integration. Failure to do so would result in a society that is highly educated and literate yet remains divided—another Northern Ireland.

The challenge for policy makers is to have an education system that would prepare citizens for the highly competitive world of globalization and simultaneously foster national unity while respecting the cultural and linguistic diversity of our society. The present highly centralized system with its rigid controls and top-down command fails miserably on both counts. Parents are dissatisfied with the quality of education their young are getting, and today's schools and colleges are even more segregated than they were during British rule.

My thesis is that Malaysia can have an education system that would serve her well for the K-(Knowledge) economy and at the same time bring Malaysians together. A diverse curriculum and school system but with a minimal core of commonality would simultaneously meet the needs of the various communities as well as foster greater integration. Such a diverse system would also encourage innovations and competition, to the benefit of all. The commonalities are few and simple; they pertain to the curriculum and enrollment. One, these schools must teach Malay (the national language); English (the language of a globalized world); science; and mathematics. Two, the student body must reflect society at large.

Between these two broad parameters, schools and other educational institutions would be free to chart their own course. If they could attract Malaysians from all communities then they would be doing something right, and thus be deserving of state support. Unity is best achieved not through forcing down uniformity or unanimity, rather through encouraging diversity and flexibility.

Accepting this simple concept requires changing the mindset of our leaders and educators. The present Soviet-style Ministry of Education (MOE), with its tight command and control operations, would have to give way to a more decentralized and democratic system, with decisions shifted to the level closest to the community. The ministry's function would change from a controlling mode to that of monitoring and encouraging innovation. Ministry officials would become enablers and coaches instead of controllers and manipulators. Also implicit in my proposal is that teaching and other educational wisdoms are not the exclusive preserve of ministry bureaucrats and politicians.

The major defect of the current system is that it is trying to force national unity through a rigid common curriculum and school system. The result is that while Malaysians may be learning the same thing, they are not doing it together. When the young do not learn *with* each other, they do not learn *from* one another. Malaysians today remain further apart than ever before because they are not given the chance to come together. After nearly half a century of independence, national unity still eludes the nation.

If the system has a common core and allows for variations at the periphery, we would find that there are common elements among the citizens that transcend race and culture. Academically-inclined Malays would have much in common with similar non-Malays. By building on such natural affinities, Malaysians then would have less reason for self-imposed segregation and instead would more likely develop these common bonds. We can reinforce this unity theme by rewarding those schools and universities that successfully attract students from all races and classes. Such positive reinforcements would bring the nation closer towards its vision of a united *Bangsa Malaysia* better than with punitive and coercive methods.

The present system of national, national-type, and religious schools aggravates and perpetuates existing racial divide. National schools are perceived (rightly) as only Malay schools (that is, schools for Malays), and national-type Chinese schools as Chinese. As for religious schools, well, no infidels need apply. My proposed changes would result in these schools being viewed differently. National schools would be seen more as truly national (that is they attract *all* Malaysians) that happen to use Malay as the language of instruction. Meanwhile national-type Chinese school would also be viewed more as a national school that uses Mandarin as the medium of instruction rather than its present characterization of "Chinese," meaning, catering primarily to Chinese pupils. Religious schools would be integrated into the national stream and their students exposed to those from different faith.

The crux of my proposal is to encourage schools and other institutions attract *all* Malaysians regardless of the medium of instruction, curriculum, or label. Conceivably the nation could have a national-type Swahili school were there to be sufficient demand by a broad spectrum of citizens.

Malaysian Education in Perspective

A measure of the importance of education is reflected by the fact that the ministry has always been regarded as very senior and prestigious. The first minister of education was no less than the deputy prime minister himself, Tun Razak. Every prime minister except the first had been in charge of that portfolio. The ministry consistently gets the largest budget allocation; in the latest (2003) it received a whopping 27 percent of the total outlay.

Despite the generous allotment there is general dissatisfaction with the results and performances. While the statistics are impressive, with more students in schools and universities today than at any other time, nonetheless there is a nagging feeling that while Malaysia has done well quantitatively, the quality remains much to be desired. The inadequacies are made obvious because Malaysia is an open society and citizens can readily compare their system to that of the rest of the world.

The first attempt at rationalizing the system was in 1956, with the release of the Razak Report. It was a comprehensive and daring initiative aimed at creating a uniform system of schools with a common national curriculum. Until then, schools were along racial lines. Malay schools were consumed with religious studies and limited to primary level only. Chinese schools were nothing more than fronts for the Communist Party, obsessed with glorifying the achievements of Mao Zedong and the dubious feats of the Cultural Revolution. Tamil schools might as well have been in Tamil Nadu, India. Only the English schools had a multiracial student body. But they were few, just enough to satisfy the social conscience of the colonial rulers. They were necessarily elitist. Their graduates learned more about old England than their homeland. No surprise then that their products were unabashed anglophiles, complete with their tweed coats and affected English accent. With the latter they consciously tried to distinguish themselves from the local peons who were products of vernacular schools; their tweed coats however, only made them look silly in hot tropical Malaysia.

I am a product of one such English school. While I am no anglophile, nonetheless I remember only too well learning about the English countryside through Wordsworth's beautiful poetry. But I learned very little of my own village and country. Only when I went abroad and actually experienced springtime and saw some daffodils did I appreciate the exquisiteness of his poetry!

The assumption of the Razak initiative was that if young Malaysians read the same books, know the same history facts, and speak the same language, then we would share the same common base and perspective, and national unity would be that much easier to achieve. It was a laudable and not an unreasonable assumption.

Bold and imaginative as the Razak Report was, its subsequent tweaking by lesser lights resulted in the gradual erosion and deterioration of the original core. Today the glaring deficiencies of the system are obvious, and the authorities are finally forced to address them. In October 2001 MOE released a comprehensive report, *Education Development Blueprint 2001-2010*, to address the issues. Just as one finished digesting its contents, the government announced a few months later the formation of a National Brains Trust to examine the whole system again. Not to be outdone, Prime Minster Mahathir announced in late 2002 yet another committee to be chaired by him to review national schools.

The flurries of reviews and studies merely reflect the general anxiety and dissatisfaction over the current system. They also prompted my writing this book because these reports fail to address the fundamental problems. Both say essentially, "We need more of the same" (more English, science, and mathematics), rather than analyzing why the current system fails miserably.

I bring two distinct perspectives. As I no longer live in Malaysia but a frequent visitor, I notice the deterioration much earlier. Also as a consequent of my being away, I can readily compare the Malaysian system with those of other countries.

I first voiced my concerns in private communications to the education establishment as early as the mid 1980s, and when that did not produce any response, I began expressing them in the popular media.

My interest in education however, dates further back to my high school days in Kuala Pilah in the mid 1950s. It was sometime in 1955, shortly after the Alliance Party overwhelmingly won the first general election, when Tun Razak undertook the first massive data gathering exercise aimed at identifying children who would enter school in the following few years. The whole country was mobilized, and I too was involved in trailing the village headman going house to house counting young bodies. Razak wanted an accurate count in order to plan how many schools to be built and teachers trained. He could have taken the easy way out and simply looked at the birth registry, but he was smart enough not to trust the official figures. That massive exercise was appropriately named *Gerakan Lampu Suloh* (Operation Torch). The survey literally touched every hut and every youngster.

Metaphorically, that operation would later bring light to a nation that hitherto been kept in darkness. I was truly impressed with and in awe of the intensive and extensive effort. It was a dramatic and tangible demonstration of the new government's commitment to its citizens. Sadly that was the first and only time I was impressed with the performance of MOE.

A few years later there was a Commission of Inquiry headed by Razak's successor, Rahman Talib. This was over the lack of Malays in science, a problem that still grabs the headlines nearly half a century later. He was to visit our school and the few of us Malay students in science were eagerly anticipating the occasion to present our ideas. On the appointed day the man did show up, but instead of meeting us he was consumed with being feted and led around like a sultan. Up close he was nothing more than the run-off-the-mill pompous politician, his diminutive figure notwithstanding. We were piqued, partly in missing the opportunity to meet a top honcho but more so in not being able to present our ideas. When the commission released its report a few months later, it was full of nonsensical fluffs about worms, culture, and lack of science aptitude among Malays, but addressed none of the practical problems we faced. His report would set the pattern of future policy documents emanating from the ministry–full of blarney and far detached from reality.

To cite one dramatic example of the stupidity of that report, in 1960 in my science class of over 30, there were 20 Malays. Because of the severe shortage of Sixth Form slots, only four were admitted, two were Malays. Six of the Malay students who did not get into Sixth Form eventually managed to get their degree through the circuitous route of technical colleges and other institutions. Among them, one received a master's degree from an Ivy League university (Napsiah Omar), and another, a PhD (Tengku Azmi Ibrahim). Additionally, another six of my Malay classmates were potential university material, but because of the limited space in Sixth Form, their aspirations were thwarted. Had Rahman Talib and his fellow commissioners concentrated on providing enough Sixth Form classes and be less concerned about worms, nutrition, and culture, the number of potential Malay undergraduates then would have been 14 instead of 2, an astounding

700 percent (seven-fold) increase! And this was only from one rural school.

Rahman Talib and all those distinguished commissioners missed this crucial point because they did not listen to those in the trenches. They thought they could solve the problem by just cutting ribbons and being lauded. His present day successors are no different.

A few years later as a medical student in Canada, I spent some time reflecting on the issues that the commission so sorely missed. I put my thoughts into a letter to the Minister of Education (now another person), and mailed a copy to my representative in Parliament. Surely the minister would not toss out a letter from a Malay medical student abroad (at that time a sufficiently rare breed). If he did, then my Member of Parliament would not as he knew me. Imagine my surprise in not getting even an acknowledgment from either!

Soon after I read about a dynamic and up-and-coming young doctor who had been appointed chairman of the Higher Education Commission. On a lark and not having much expectation, I resubmitted my ideas to him. To my utter surprise he wrote back to say that my ideas were "interesting." Then perhaps not meaning to be condescending, he urged me to concentrate on my studies first and wished me the best. That was the end.

Events in Malaysia and in my life then took divergent paths. Malaysia was consumed with the aftermath of the May 1969 trauma, and I was equally absorbed in pursuing my career. Years later the young doctor to whom I had written earlier had by now, after a dramatic detour along the way, been made the Minister of Education, and much later, Prime Minister. But what pleased me even more was that many of the ideas I had mooted earlier were now being implemented. It would be presumptuous of me to claim credit, but at least I knew that there were others who shared my views. It reinforced my conviction that despite being away from Malaysia, my ideas were not on the lunatic fringe.

Here I digress momentarily to reinforce this last point. In 1997 I wrote a series of essays advocating the teaching of science and mathematics in English as a way to attract more Malays into science. This idea came about after my visit to a Malay secondary school. The science textbooks, written in Malay, were deplorable and of inferior quality. Worst was the content; opaque explanations and dense prose. The translations were erratic; where they were not silly, they were simply hilarious. I also watched with the students a videotape in Malay purporting to explain the solar system. The graphics were appalling, and the explanations convoluted. It was a local production, and even with my science background I could not follow it. I was certain the class was lost too.

I had viewed many such educational tapes in America. They were all professionally done and comprehensible, with imaginative and captivating graphics. If those Malay students could understand English, they could have viewed some of these excellent tapes instead of the amateurish local productions. They could also supplement that by reading the numerous excellent texts and reference books available in English.

When the government decided in mid 2002 to teach science and mathematics in English, many of my readers jubilantly wrote me, "See, they are finally accepting your ideas! Keep writing!"

Much as I appreciate the encouragement and presumed credit, I am realistic enough to realize that the government's move has nothing to do with the persuasive powers of my earlier essays. I doubt whether the officials have even read them. It is just that the government is finally forced to see the errors of its ways and now has to adopt my sensible suggestions. Meaning, our officials do come to their senses eventually, it just takes them a bit longer!

Thus it can be said that this book has a long genesis. More practically, it expands on the chapter "Enhancing Bumiputra Competitiveness" in my first book *The Malay Dilemma Revisited*, and the subchapters "Enhancing Human Capital Through Education" and "Islamization of Education" in my second, *Malaysia in the Era of Globalization*.

Basis For Reform

In making my reform proposals, I am guided by the following principles.

In a plural society, education must serve more than just to educate the young. It must also be a force for greater social and racial integration, that is, nation building. This is not a novel idea; I am merely reiterating Tun Razak's vision first enunciated in1956. Also as a consequent of this plurality, there is no "one size fits all;" we should expect and indeed encourage different models. Such diversity must however, have a common underlying theme or core commonality lest young Malaysians would develop along divergent paths. As a corollary to the first two, there must be parental choice. Parents must be free to choose the school that best fits their children. Parents know their children better than any educational expert or ministry official. Parental choice leads to parental involvement; this could only bring positive consequences. The education system must also prepare students for the challenges of the global marketplace. With globalization, good enough for Malaysia isn't. To compete effectively in this K-economy, Malaysians must be fluent in English, science literate, and mathematically competent. Malaysians can no longer be insulated; they have to compete with the outside world. There must also be private sector participation at all levels. This would not only encourage new and innovative models but also lessen the burden on the public purse.

The focus of my reform revolves around three major areas: efficiency, equity, and quality. Efficiency is defined simply as getting better or more with the same resources or input. This efficiency could be viewed technically from the business viewpoint (how many schools can be built for X dollars) as well as the social aspects. That is, the government should help those most deserving and not squander its resources on those who do not need them. This goal ties in with the second theme of equity. Everyone regardless of race, gender, social class, or intellect must be given every opportunity to develop his or her full potential. We should remove all barriers, overt as well as subtle, which prevent a child from getting an education. In Malaysia, the glaring divide between urban and rural schools is a crime, for we are in effect dismissing all those precious minds in the villages. And the last point, quality, speaks for itself.

These issues are very relevant but often ignored. Building a successful school is not the challenge. I can create one where the graduates would qualify for top universities if I choose carefully to admit only the children of the rich and highly educated. Such a school may be considered very successful or "very good" but in effect it has not added much value. The probability of those children achieving superior results would be high anyway regardless of what school they would attend. Their parents would ensure that. The purpose of a good school is to break the vicious cycle where children of those with low socioeconomic status and limited educational achievement would repeat their parents' pattern.

The World Bank describes the three pillars of a good education system: access, quality, and delivery. Access refers to where students are ready to learn in a supportive and healthy environment with adequate supporting elements such as shelter, nutrition, and health. A supportive environment is where the leadership is interested only in education, and where there are clear goals and expectations. Quality means a relevant curriculum that will produce competent products that would thrive in a global economy and contribute to the social development of society. The teaching staff should be well motivated, solidly trained, and have ample avenues for professional growth and enhancement. They should also be adequately compensated. The delivery system should be where the governance has clear responsibility and accountability, and where significant decisions would be made by those most affected by it. Thus there should be appropriate decentralization.

The changes I am proposing follow these themes. My reforms do not question the basic assumptions of nor radically change the present system. The existing structures (number of school years, supremacy of Malay language, national and national-type schools) remain the same.

The emphasis is on strengthening the evident weaknesses, and enhancing and replicating the successes. The changes I am advocating are incremental and evolutionary, not radical and revolutionary.

Integration Through Education

Schools are powerful institutions for acculturating the young. American schools successfully integrate millions of children of immigrants into the mainstream. The elite of America, from government and business to the professions and academia, are inundated with children of first generation immigrants. Every year America garners more than its fair share of Nobel prizewinners, but what is not appreciated is that many of those luminaries are foreign born. What is remarkable is that these naturalized citizens feel and are treated no differently than native-born ones.

Education also serves as a great elevator. As the Commissioner of Education for Massachusetts, Horace Mann, stated in 1848, "Education, beyond all other devices of human origin, is a great equalizer of the conditions of men." With such farsighted individuals in charge of education, no wonder that state in general and Boston in particular are famous for their colleges and intellectuals.

Malaysia has always been conscious of the importance of schools in molding a united Malaysian nation. That was the central aspiration of the Razak Report. Unfortunately, purity and nobility of intentions alone are not enough. Today young Malaysians remain even more segregated. Worse, unlike the segregation of the past that was essentially imposed by the colonial structure, today Malaysians *choose* to remain apart. Malaysian parents deliberately decide that their children attend schools with only their own kind. They express no desire to mix or integrate. You see this not only in schools but also on college campuses.

The British had no grandiose pretensions of trying to unite the various races. On the contrary, the system was designed specifically to perpetuate existing divisions, all part of the colonialists' grand strategy of "divide and conquer." They built just enough schools to produce the necessary functionaries to run the country for the colonial office. Ironically while the British had no desire of bringing the various races together, nonetheless there was far greater social and racial integration among the students during British rule. The English schools with their integrated student body had this unintended consequence.

This integrative role of schools and other educational institutions must be strengthened lest Malaysia becomes a highly educated but divided nation.

The remarkable success of American education is precisely because it is decentralized to the local level. The consequent flexibility allows it to meet the different needs of a diverse nation, while maintaining its core of commonality. There is much that Malaysia can learn from that system.

No One-Size-Fits-All

If I have learned anything about being a parent it is that my three children are all very different. I was fortunate to be sensitive of such individual variations early to be able to help them.

Nowhere are these differences best demonstrated than in their attitude towards school. My two older children managed to go through the large comprehensive public school quite well. My youngest did fine at the small elementary school, but by the time he was ready for middle school, we encountered problems. He made up his mind not to go to the same school his older sister and brother attended. He heard enough horror stories of drugs and bullies. The fact that his older siblings did all right did not impress him. That was before, he said. We did not realize how adamant he was until he absolutely refused to go to school, despite our encouragement, cajoling, and yes, also our anger. He also had a ready and convenient excuse as at that time we had moved out to the country and the school was far away.

Fortunately we were able to put him into a private school in a neighboring town. When we took him for the interview he immediately liked this new school. We did not know what attracted him but months later when we visited him on parents' day, we knew we had made the right choice. My son cheerfully greeted the headmaster who in turn beamed and replied, "Hi Azlan! How's that science project of yours?" You can tell a lot about a school when its principal knows not only the name but also the latest project of some random students who happened to bump into him in the schoolyard.

My son thrived there but when it was time for high school, we had problems. He was accepted to two private schools but they were too far away (there was no private high school in our town). I could not bear to see my wife driving him to and fro every school day. I imagined some horrible road accident on some wet winter day. Thus after much cajoling he agreed to attend the local high school. It was the typical comprehensive American public school with over two thousand students. He managed to stay a year, and what a year it was! He was miserable, had disciplinary problems, and his grades suffered despite our many conferences with his teachers. Fortunately at this time a new public school was being built in a nearby town, and because it was a small district, the school too was small, with less than 200 students, a tenth the size of his present school. We took him there for a week's trial attending classes in converted temporary trailers. Despite the less than ideal surroundings, he liked the school. So we transferred him. He settled in quickly and by the time he was in his last year he was among the top students. What a difference in four years! All we did was listen to him and found a school that met his needs.

I shudder to think had we lived in Malaysia where there are no choices. When I see school-age children loitering and dropping out of schools in Malaysia today, I wonder how many of them could be saved if only we could find a school that would meet their needs. We are more likely to find such schools if we give our children and their parents choices. There is no one school or teaching style that will suit all children. If there are differences in the children from one family, imagine how much dissimilar children would be from different families, races, and cultures. There is no such thing as one national system that would suit all children.

It would be naïve to assume that a system of teaching or schooling that would be suitable for the son of a doctor in Ukay Heights would also be appropriate for the daughter of a rice farmer in Ulu Kelantan. With the former, there is high background intellectual activity and English proficiency at home and in the community, not so with the latter. We ignore such crucial differences at our own peril. More specifically, our children (and so too our nation) will suffer the consequences of such foolish thinking.

America is able to achieve remarkably rapid assimilation of its immigrants' children precisely because there is no central authority governing education for the entire nation. Education is decentralized; with schools under local control and setting their own standards and evaluating their own students. There is no national school-leaving certificate. Similarly for higher education, there is no central bureaucracy controlling the universities. Apart from the public system there are private schools and colleges; they all thrive and meet the needs of various students.

Despite the diversity and bewildering models, the system is able to achieve its primary goals of educating and acculturating young Americans.

What can Malaysia learn from America? Could Malaysia achieve its goals of national integration as well as produce an educated citizenry with such a decentralized system? Absolutely! The whole thesis of my book is to convince readers that this is not only possible indeed it is the only option for Malaysia.

Underlying the diversity of the American system is a core of commonality. All schools use English as the medium of instruction and all students have to take US history and government, science, mathematics, and a foreign language. Although there are no national exit examinations nonetheless there are standardized tests like the Scholastic Achievement Tests (SAT) and Achievement Tests (AT) to enable universities to compare students from various schools and districts. Additionally, students are continuously evaluated throughout their school year by those most competent to do so—their teachers. Many universities now regard this evaluation, the Grade Point Average (GPA), to be more reliable and a better predictor of college performance than standardized test scores.

There is currently a movement to have national or at least statewide school-leaving test, but this has not been widely accepted. Even if it were fully accepted, such testing is designed more to ensure that students achieve minimum competency levels and to make the schools accountable, not to rank the students.

Teachers rightly fear that adopting and emphasizing national tests would cramp their classroom style and freedom. Teachers would then be tempted to "teach to the test" rather than use their imagination and style to fit the individual class and student. It is this freedom that accounts for the unique success of American schools. Students are allowed by their teachers to experiment, explore, and express themselves instead of being bound rigidly to a tight syllabus and examination requirements.

When students in Monterey, California, learn about the environment, they have the vast Pacific Ocean at their doorstep to study, and their teachers plan their lessons to take full advantage of this natural attribute. Students in Colorado have the wonders of the Rocky Mountains. Having a rigid national curriculum would inhibit such local experimentations and variations. Likewise with the study of foreign languages; schools near the Quebec border of Maine would more likely offer French, while those at El Paso, Texas, near the Mexican border, would offer Spanish. The beauty and genius of the American system is precisely this great flexibility to accommodate local and individual variations, a lesson that Malaysia would do well to note.

Education in the Era of Globalization

Globalization is bringing the world closer. With the coming together of the global community, there is an imperative for a common language. By default, English is that language. Why English and not Chinese is an interesting question. In terms of the number of native speakers, more people speak Chinese. Nonetheless the market has spoken, and English is now the most widely spoken. Trying to explain why English and not Chinese is like trying to explain why VHS format is favored over Beta for videotapes, and personal computers over Apple. Undoubtedly had the native English-speaking countries of America and Britain been third-rate economic powers, that language would not have been widely accepted.

The current impetus to improve the English proficiency of Malaysians is because senior civil servants and diplomats are severely handicapped in dealing with international organizations and when negotiating international agreements. Malaysia's interests would not be protected if her negotiators and diplomats do not understand the basic language, much less the nuances.

Malaysia is handicapped because of its British colonial past. Malaysians are rightly leery of anything English. Thus current attempts at improving the English proficiency of students are viewed with deep suspicion as yet another subtle manifestation of the colonial mentality. No amount of rational explanation seems capable of overcoming this deep suspicion. In this regard the Indonesians have an advantage. Although they too had been colonized, it was by the Dutch. Thus the Indonesians do not harbor the same suspicion towards English.

In truth the future does not belong to the English speakers rather those who are fluent in English *and* another language; next would be those who speak only English; and the least advantaged would be those who speak only other than English. The Europeans have known this for along time. In this regard native speakers of English are handicapped because as that language is widely spoken they have little incentive to learn another language. America is awakening to this fact and is now encouraging its students to be bilingual. Being fluently bilingual means more than simply knowing two languages, it offers other cognitive and intellectual advantages.

With globalization the world needs a common standard. This makes sense. We should expect that Chinese pilots be deemed equally competent as American ones so they could land their jet at any airport.

With better and open communications, Malaysians are fully aware of what is going on in the rest of the world. Malaysians would want for themselves and their families the same standard and quality of medical care and education as available elsewhere. When they cannot get that locally or if they deem that the quality of local services is not up to par, they will leave. Every year thousands of Malaysians go abroad for their medical care and education, costing the nation billions in lost foreign exchange. With such matters as health care, education, and personal consumption, nationalism plays a minimal role. Malaysians go to Britain for such matters simply because they perceive they would get better services there, ex-colonialist notwithstanding.

The king flew to Singapore to have his pacemaker inserted, and the wife of the Deputy Prime Minister went to Los Angeles for treatment of her breast cancer. She spoke glowingly of her treatment by American physicians. Despite her husband's Islamic credentials, she had no qualms about being examined by infidel and male doctors. Beyond a certain level you do not care about religious scruples or nationalism, you just want the best for yourself and your loved ones.

When Malaysia built the Petronas TwinTowers, it unhesitatingly employed many skilled foreigners. If Malaysians ever want to participate in such projects not only in Malaysia but also elsewhere, they too must have internationally recognized training and qualifications. Malaysians must now assess themselves by international yardsticks.

Malaysian schools and universities must be cognizant of this. Their graduates must, at a minimum, be bilingual in Malay and English, science literate, and mathematically competent. Anything less would be doing the students, and the nation, a great disservice.

In the modern economy wealth resides less with the natural resources or the strategic location of a country, more with its people. As the UN Human Development Report 2001 states, "People are the real wealth of nations."

Malaysia is proud of its Petronas Twin Towers that grace the skyline of its capital. That monument symbolizes the country's preoccupation with building things physical and material. But the most important infrastructure of the new millennium will be human resources, and the twin pillars to developing that would be education and health. Prime Minister Mahathir never fails to take visitors to see his pride and joy, The Twin Towers. Wouldn't it be nice if our schools and universities too were of such eminence that foreigners would want to visit them?

A Preemptive Strike

Education should concern everyone as it affects us as individuals, parents, employers, and employees.

Many professionals in the field would like us to believe that education is their sole prerogative and that they and they alone have the right to comment on such weighty matters. While I appreciate the professionalism of teachers and educators, nonetheless as education affects us all, we have every right to be involved. My simple rebuttal to such professional parochialism is this: Education is not quantum physics; concepts and issues in education can easily be framed in a fashion understandable to the average citizen. Many of the significant innovations in education in Malaysia and elsewhere have been through the efforts of non-educators.

The first major reform in Malaysian education was undertaken not by a teacher or educator, rather a politician who was a former civil servant–Tun Razak. His professional training was in law. His landmark 1956 Razak Report was responsible for the massive restructuring of the system. Nearly five decades later, the framework of that revolutionary report still underpins the country's education–a testimony to his wisdom and foresight.

Further away in place and time, the greatest innovation in medical education was undertaken not by a medical doctor rather a former school principal, Abraham Flexner. Medical education in America during the early part of the last century was a haphazard affair. Medical schools were less places to train doctors but more moneymaking enterprises. And the results showed: mediocrity. To reform the sorry and dangerous state of affairs, the Carnegie Foundation commissioned Flexner. His searing criticism of the status quo and his bold prescription put American medical education on its firm scientific foundation. In particular, he recommended that medical schools be part of a university rather than freestanding institutions, and that would-be doctors must first have a liberal education and be well versed in the sciences prior to undertaking rigorous medical studies. He further advocated a core of dedicated medical educators, complemented by the clinical faculty, to train these students. Directly as a consequence of Flexner, American medical schools today are unanimously regarded as the best. Like the Razak Report to Malaysian education, the Flexner Report still governs medical education in America and elsewhere.

It would be pretentious of me to consider myself to be in the same league as these two eminent gentlemen. Rather my hope is that this book will be a catalyst for a much-needed wide debate on education in Malaysia. It is only through such broad participation and from hearing the views from the whole spectrum of society will Malaysia discover the system or systems of education that would best fill her needs.

My book is not a compilation of how-to's or a laundry list of what ails the system, rather a discussion of broad concepts and ideas. A recipe book this is not. Absent is the nitty-gritty of the how and what to teach. Nor are details of the curricula or textbooks listed. Those are clearly the prerogative of the professionals. Similarly I will not be citing figures and statistics except in so far as to demonstrate some points.

To better illustrate my approach, I will compare education to my own profession: medicine. How health care is funded, doctors paid, or whether a hospital should be built and where are clearly for society to decide. In making those decisions policymakers must consider the views of health care professionals, but once the priorities are set, then let the professionals free to execute them.

In my practice I actively involve my patients in the decision. The days when doctors were aloof, placed on a pedestal, and practically deified are thankfully gone, and rightly so. When a patient comes to me for a breast lump I do not dictate what she should do, I merely recommend the necessary steps and the consequences of not doing so. Even if the lump proves to be cancerous and the best treatment is surgical, the patient is still intimately involved in the decision. There are still questions as to what type of surgery and whether it should be combined with reconstructive procedures, radiation, and chemotherapy. There is no one right or best solution. Even if there were one best solution that the doctor thinks would suit the patient, she may think otherwise.

I remember a young lady who consulted me for early breast cancer. She would have benefited from conservation breast surgery, removing only a small portion of the organ while maintaining its cosmetic integrity. That too was the consensus of the tumor board reviewing her case. When we presented her with the various options, much to the surprise of all the professionals, she opted to have total removal of her breast. When I inquired why, she replied to the effect that to her that organ no longer defined her beauty and femininity, rather her potential killer. She did not want anything more to do with it. As she aptly put it, "I would prefer it to be in a jar of formalin rather than on my chest!"

Thus even when we professionals think that we have the best solution for a particular patient or client, we can sometimes be very wrong. We have to involve our clients and consumers.

Blindly accepting the doctor's prescription is not good enough. But once the patient has chosen a course of action such as surgery, then let the surgeons operate. Decisions as where to place the incision, types of sutures, and hundreds of other technical details are properly the surgeon's expertise. But even here surgeons have to be mindful of the patient's special needs and wishes. For Jehovah Witness patients whose religious beliefs preclude their accepting blood transfusions, I would be extra meticulous in my dissection. Someone sensitive of the scar, I would make the incision as small and inconspicuous as possible.

Returning to education, in this book there will be no discussion of the details that are properly the purview of the professionals–teachers and educators. How and what they should teach, or how best to motivate and engage the students are clearly their expertise. I would not want to second-guess them. They are the ones who see the children every day, and who have been professionally trained. The choice of textbooks and curriculum too is their prerogative. Nor should I be telling teachers how to test their students. But what we as society should expect of teachers and our schools is that they remain accountable both to the students and their parents, as well as to society.

This accountability can be measured partly by showing that the students are indeed making progress as indicated by their periodic test results. Other measures of accountability could be the dropout rates and the discipline level.

I also shy away from discussing the philosophy of education. This book will deal more with pragmatic issues like ensuring our students are able to read and write, be mathematically competent, and be an asset to the community. All Malaysians deserve the best education regardless of where they live, their parents' political affiliations, or their socioeconomic status.

No Mission Statement

I am not a fan of the modern obsession with mission statements or their equally fashionable "client charters." The more high-sounding and noble they are, the less likely they are to relate to the realities of the organization. MOE has a long mission statement emboldened on its home web page. I can imagine the numerous hours of meetings to compose that. I suggest that those goals and aspirations would be more readily served if only we teach our young well. Once we do that, the values and objectives of that mission statement would fall in place, whether elaborately stated or not.

One of the objectives of the ministry's mission statement is "to inculcate positive values." Whatever that means! The philosophy of education is stated thus: "...developing the potential of individuals in a holistic and integrated manner, so as to produce individuals who are intellectually, spiritually, emotionally and physically balanced and harmonious, based on a firm belief in God." Presumably if you turn out to be an atheist, the system has failed you.

The trouble with such mushy statements and objectives is that they would be difficult to judge when they have been achieved. How would you gauge that someone is "balanced and harmonious?"

If I were to draw up the ministry's objectives, I would state them thus: Our students should be able to read and write in our national language as well as English, do basic computations, understand the physical world around and the living world within them, and have an appreciation of our history and our diversity. With such clear objectives it would be easier to measure whether we are successful or not.

Consequently I have dispensed with discussions of such nebulous issues of building "a society of high moral character, ethical, just," and other highfalutin ideas encompassed in the ministry's mission statement, and concentrated instead only on the pragmatic nuts and bolts issues. How much should we pay teachers so as to attract the talented? Why are our students dropping out in such high numbers? How do we fund adequately school laboratories and libraries? Why are rural schools not provided with generators so they can at least have fans in their classrooms and perhaps later, computers? These are real issues and affect how our young learn, but they are never covered in mission statements or ministerial missives.

I am not an outsider when it comes to education. As a parent I am acutely aware of its importance. I am also born into a family of teachers. My parents were longtime teachers, as are nearly all my siblings. My wife too is a teacher both at high school and college; she taught briefly in Malaysia. I was also a teacher in the early 1960s in the hiatus before entering university, and more than a decade later, I taught medical students in Malaysia.

The one lesson I learned during my teaching tenure in Malaysia was how far detached the policies and statements uttered by top officials were (and still are) from the realities.

When I was teaching at a Malay secondary school, there were no textbooks and the laboratory facilities were rudimentary. Yet that did not stop the leaders from extolling the virtues of such schools. Similarly while the government was pouring funds into building the new medical school, I could not even get such basic supplies as journals and books for my students. Nor I could not get funding for buying papers or paying a secretary to type my surgical seminars for distribution to my trainees. Meanwhile the medical school was paying first class airline tickets for its external examiners and putting them up at luxury hotels. When I complained to the dean, his reply was simply, "We have to maintain our status!" Such misplaced priorities! One does not have to be an educationist to see the idiocy of such viewpoints.

It is also easy to be distracted by discussions on the philosophy of education and other abstract ideas when much more mundane details like lack of textbooks and basic supplies are being ignored.

In this book I avoid listing the deficiencies of the system (that would require a separate volume!) except in so far as to illustrate a particular point. I will be discussing concepts and ideas gleaned from my own experience with the education of my children in America and comparing their experiences with that of their cousins back in Malaysia.

My book is not simply a critique, nor is it the scribbling of a dilettante. I put forth my own proposals for a modern system of education that is worthy of Malaysia. I begin by discussing some general issues on education–its role in development; its political and cultural symbolism; factors in society that bear on education; and the role of technology (Chapter Two). Chapter Three describes the present system, followed by a discussion of its weaknesses and deficiencies. For comparative purposes, I review the education system of a few selected countries, in particular United States, Canada, and Germany (Chapter Five).

There are no shortages of recommendations on reforming the system, and I will critique some of them, in particular MOE's *Education Development 2001-2010*, as well as the recommendations of the National Brains Trust (Chapter Six). My reform proposals are presented in three chapters. Chapter Seven covers the schools, and the chapter following, higher education. Chapter Nine reviews other activities of MOE, in particular *Dewan Bahasa dan Pustaka* (Language and Literary Agency), Accreditation Agency, and the Examination Syndicate. I recommend dispensing or privatizing these ancillary agencies.

My book ends with a summary. I debated whether to put it at the beginning but decided against it. Doing so would have made the book look like a bureaucratic report or Government White Paper. A definite "turn off" for readers! I am after all writing an expository essay, not a policy manual. My aim is to persuade, not to dictate. And if my readers are not persuaded, they can at least begin the debate. That in the end is my objective.

2

It's More Than Just Education

$\mathcal{E}$ducation is more than just schools and colleges. Investment in education benefits the individual, society, and the global community.

For the individual, education is a great leveler. The American patriot John Adams observed that education makes a greater difference between men than nature has made between man and brute. Through education America is able to acculturate and bring into the mainstream its diverse immigrants. A century earlier those immigrants were Jews from Eastern Europe and Catholics from Ireland and Italy. More recently they were Buddhists from Vietnam and Cambodia, and Muslims from Afghanistan and Somalia. Through education they all became Americans and aspired for the American dream. As they better themselves, America too benefits.

In Malay culture an uneducated or unlearned person is likened to a frog underneath a coconut shell (*katak di bawah tempurong*). His or her world is very limited and dark. The idiomatic Sanskrit equivalent is *kupamanduka* (frog in a well). Once outside, the horizon opens up; no telling where the frog would end up. Education and learning are the equivalents of flipping the shell over or lowering a ladder into the well—a way out of the darkness and confining wall.

An indication of the significance of education is that illiteracy is the strongest predictor of poverty. Poverty is a complex issue with many intertwining causes and links, but empirically, providing basic education is the necessary prerequisite in the battle against poverty. Education by itself will not solve Third World poverty, but it is an enabling condition. As the World Bank president James D Wolfensohn observed, "…[T]he single most important key to development and poverty alleviation is education."

At the other end of the spectrum, in a modern economy education is, in the words of Louis Gertsner, chief executive of IBM and head of the foundation that funds the New Century School reform, "the engine of growth and prosperity." This is especially so in this K-economy. The key to Malaysia successfully navigating globalization is through providing high quality education for its citizens.

Another well-documented benefit of education at the individual level is its spillover effect on personal health. The more educated the society is, the more healthy is its members, as indicated by such indices as life expectancy, childhood mortality rates, and general nutritional status.

These effects are more profoundly seen with girls where improved education reduces child mortality and enhances reproductive health, and the subsequent better immunization rates and nutritional status of their babies. Women with formal education also tend to have lower fertility rates, delay marriage and childbearing, and use reliable contraceptives. They have fewer but healthier babies. The World Bank estimates that one year of formal schooling reduces fertility by 10 percent, with the effect most pronounced with secondary schooling.

Malaysia's obscenely high rate of child marriages could be effectively reduced if girls have longer formal education. As most of these child marriages end up in divorce, the fewer such marriages there are, the better it would be for society. "Children having children" is one sure way to entrap the next generation into perpetual poverty. This is true in America as well as in the Third World.

Globally, reduced fertility could only have a positive impact on an already overcrowded planet.

Education is also an essential component of public health. Education is the single most effective preventive weapon in combating diseases like HIV/AIDS, as well as reducing such potentially lethal enteric diseases like cholera and gastroenteritis. HIV/AIDS may be incurable but experiences both in the First World as well as the Third show that effective public health education goes a long way in reducing and preventing the spread of the disease. In San Francisco, the wide dissemination of information on safe sex proved effective; in Uganda the reinforcing through education of traditional Islamic values of abstinence and fidelity had a stunning effect on reducing the incidence of the disease.

The reverse, the impact of health on education, is equally significant. Health, in particular the state of nutrition, has a dramatic influence on learning. America's school lunch programs successfully ameliorate this factor, something that is worthy of Malaysia to emulate. In Africa where AIDS is devastating the bulk of young adults, schools are also terribly impacted through the deaths of teachers as well as their frequent absence through illnesses or having to attend funerals and the sick members of their family.

Education and Development

If we compare countries that are fast developing to those that are stagnating, the glaring difference is the educational attainment of their citizens. This is true not only between but also within nations. In Malaysia much has been said and written on the gaps in development between Malays and non-Malays, and invariably such differences are attributed simplistically to race or culture. But if those researchers and commentators had been more meticulous and looked beyond race, they would find that the better correlate would be educational achievement.

I wrote this once in my column and received a blistering reply from a Malaysian sociologist. How would you explain, he demanded, the lower earnings of Malays with a degree as compared to those of non-Malays? He was intimating that there were other factors, like discrimination. I referred him to some studies that showed the best predictor of success in the workplace is achievement in mathematics, and asked him to review the data to see which was the better correlate, race or scores in mathematics. I predict that a Chinese with a BA in history would earn less than a Malay with an engineering degree. Malay graduates earn less than similarly qualified non-Malays because most Malays have degrees in the liberal arts rather than the sciences. And most schools attended by Malays (national and religious) do not emphasize mathematics. Skills in mathematics have the greatest transferability in the marketplace.

Education benefits society through increases in productivity and earnings of its citizens. This in turn translates directly into superior economic performance and growth of that society.

In my *Malaysia in the Era of Globalization*, I related the dramatic differences in service and productivity between my secretaries in America as compared to the ones I had in Malaysia, and between American limousine drivers as compared to their Malaysian counterparts. This was directly related to the superior education of American workers. I also cited the example of the Japanese factory worker who successfully traced the source of her factory's product defects to the interference from the vibrations of the nearby train. She was able to make the connection because of her superior education. Japanese factory workers are among the most highly educated, very unlike the typical assembly line workers in the Third World.

There are many studies correlating economic development with levels of education of citizens. Of course correlation means just that, it does not imply causation. It may very well be that rich nations could afford to spend more on education and that improved educational achievement is the *result* and not the *cause* of wealth.

Studies show that individual wages increase with years of schooling, with the improvement greatest in poorer countries. In Indonesia the MIT economist Esther Duflo shows that investments in primary education alone resulted in increased economic returns ranging from 6.8 to 10.6 percent. It is estimated that for agricultural workers, four years of education translates into a 10 percent increase in agricultural output. In East Asia, each additional year of education contributes 3 percent in real GDP. An American study on twins showed that every extra year of schooling translated into a 10 percent increase in earnings. These are empirical figures, not guesswork.

American farmers, unlike those in the Third World, are rich because they are highly educated. They typically have a degree from state-supported Agricultural and Mechanical (A & M) universities, very unlike their illiterate counterparts in the developing world. Improving the plight of farmers in Malaysia and other developing countries would take more than just providing better agricultural techniques and supporting infrastructures like irrigation, rather on nourishing and tilling the minds of the farmers in the form of better education. The key to improving agricultural productivity and reducing rural poverty resides not in the rice fields or rubber estates, rather in the classrooms.

Malaysia was fortunate in that its early leaders saw the wisdom of investing in education over everything else, including defense. Tunku Abdul Rahman, the first prime minister, knew that the nation then had limited resources, thus he prudently signed a defense treaty with Britain so he could concentrate on education. Many at that time thought that the country's independence was a sham because of that treaty. But as Tunku wisely observed, he would rather build schools instead of barracks and train teachers instead of soldiers. With defense thus taken care of by the British, Tunku was able to focus on developing his people. Tunku was one of those rare wise leaders who, though not terribly bright, knew exactly his and the nation's limitations. Had Tunku been endowed with Sukarno's megalomaniac ego and grandiose pretensions, and concentrated on buying tanks and battleships instead, Malaysia today would be like Indonesia–stagnant and poverty stricken.

It was the enduring wisdom of Tunku that he was not bothered by being labeled pro-British or a cryptic neocolonialist by signing that treaty; he did what he thought was best for his beloved nation. Malaysia's subsequent trajectory of development owes much to that earlier insight and decision of Tunku's.

Economists have elegant formulas to quantify the benefits (or what they technically refer to as rates of returns on investment–ROI) of education. ROI can be viewed from two perspectives, the individual (Private ROI) and society (Social ROI). The elements considered in calculating Private ROI are the direct costs to the individual of acquiring that education (cost of tuition and books), and the foregone income while attending school or college. Social ROI takes in all the costs in providing that education, the running of the ministry of education, building schools, and training teachers. These are externalities from the perspective of the individual and thus not included in the calculation of Private ROI. The cost factors are necessarily larger with Social ROI, but so too are the returns.

These economic calculations notwithstanding, one can intuitively appreciate that such investments are rewarding and good on their own merit. There is no moral virtue in keeping the citizens ignorant. There is no biblical refrain to the effect that the ignorant shall inherit the earth. The Qur'an exhorts every Muslim to acquire knowledge, and this is reaffirmed by the various *hadith* (sayings of the prophet).

Here, a brief digression. I have always thought this (the value of education and knowledge) to be self-evident and that everyone subscribes to it. Not so. Many years ago I met a senior official (later to become head of education) of Brunei who was on a study tour of America. We got into a discussion on education; he saw no merit in educating the masses, it would only feed their expectations and lead to trouble. The policy of his government, he explicitly told me, was to educate just enough of the citizens to keep the government running. Beyond that he saw no necessity of spending additional precious funds. He also added that Brunei Malays are a very happy lot with this policy. To the likes of him, spending money on royal ponies would yield greater returns.

Lest we think this mentality exists only among medieval Malays of Brunei, consider this recent statement by the Malaysian linguist, Nik Safiah Karim. An extremist nationalist, she vehemently opposes the greater teaching and use of English to the point of calling those advocating such moves traitors to the race and culture. Strong stuff! I respect people with strong convictions, but what troubles me is the basis of her arguments. She exhibits the same medieval mentality as that Brunei official by suggesting that Malaysia needs only about 20 percent of her citizens to be conversant with English, the rest can get by with knowing only Malay. For a supposedly esteemed scholar to say that more knowledge is superfluous is just absurd. Left unstated is that she and her children would be among that 20 percent who should be fluent in English. The rest can languish in their kampongs speaking only Malay.

Poverty and lack of education may seem to be in a vicious cycle, with one feeding the other. This is more apparent than real, for the cycle can be broken through effective strategies and interventions.

Poor Malay fishermen do not invest in their children's education not because they do not value education, rather they could not afford to. While education is the key to eradicating poverty, ironically poverty is also the greatest impediment to getting an education. While to economists the value of the foregone income of the youngster attending school is minimal, to that poor family the son being at school and not being able to help in hauling the net may mean the difference between surviving and not having a meal for that day. The solution to this intractable problem is not simply to lecture the poor fisherman endlessly on the value of education, rather to shift the balance in that family's personal equation to make the child attending school to be worth more than having him out in the high seas. In Chapter Five I discuss the novel Brazilian social experiment of *paying* parents to keep their children in school as one effective way of shifting that balance in the equation.

Investments in education at all levels and across many nations consistently yield double-digit returns. In Venezuela, investments at the primary level yield a private ROI in excess of 25 percent, and a social ROI of 16.9; for secondary education, the returns are respectively 10.6

and 11.5 percent; and for university education, 13.5 and 12.0. The private and social returns are highest for investments at the primary level. This is especially true for developing countries.

Beyond the primary level the picture gets complicated. For the individual, the loss of income while attending school becomes a significant factor. With the child now older and stronger, he or she could earn considerably more, and his help in the field would be greater. Thus the private ROI would be lower. The societal ROI would also be lower as secondary and higher education cost considerably more to provide.

Beyond elementary education, the societal ROI would also be dependent on the nature and kinds of education provided. A system that emphasizes the sciences, mathematics, and foreign language (in particular English) yields the greatest returns. The remarkable economic success of Singapore is attributable in part to the fact that its early leaders intuitively recognized this. Goh Keng Swee, the island's long-time economic minister and the man many regard as the brain behind its remarkable transformation, credited the republic's success to the many parents who encouraged their children to pursue science and mathematics.

It is not enough to simply increase the number of years devoted to science and mathematics. Quality matters more than quantity, as shown by cross-national studies like the Third International Mathematics and Science Studies (TIMSS). Additional studies by California's Public Policy Institute show that the one factor that correlates best with the students' future success in college as well as the workplace is the their achievement in mathematics and language while in school. Skills in both areas have the greatest transferability to other areas.

A system that does not emphasize these key subjects would not yield great returns. India is a striking example, so too are many Muslim countries. Within Malaysia we see this dramatically demonstrated. Malays with degrees earn considerably less than non-Malays both in private and public sectors because Malays tend to have qualifications in other than mathematics or science. They are also markedly deficient in

English proficiency. In many Muslim countries, Malaysia included, literally millions of brains are being wasted in religious schools where the curriculum is singularly devoid of much mathematics and even less science.

In America, differences in economic and social achievements of the various ethnic groups are often attributed to culture (and more sinisterly and unconsciously to race), but had these studies been analyzed more rigorously, education would be the more consistent correlate and accurate predictor. Such thinking also exists in Malaysia. Differences between the achievements of Malays and non-Malays are invariably portrayed as rooted in race and culture when in fact they are more a function of educational attainment. Culture may have a lot to do with Malay attitude towards education, but ultimately the final critical element is still education. Thus to enhance Malay achievements requires exploring ways to improve their education, especially in science and mathematics, and not, as is the present practice, incessantly harping on the inadequacies of culture or race. If this means changing those aspects of Malay culture, social environment, and reward system that impede excellence in education, yes, that would be fruitful. But that is quite a different approach than the wholesale condemnation of Malay culture and mores.

Differences in the economic status of the various regions in Malaysia are also better correlated with educational achievement, not race, culture, or geography. The commonality of poverty among Dayaks in the interior of Sarawak, Tamils on the rubber estates, and Malays in remote kampongs, is due to their poor education.

Our diverse world could only benefit from better education of its inhabitants. Positive exposures to the various cultures would be the first step towards understanding and tolerating the differences among us. Further, transnational issues such as pollution, conservation, and environmental degradation can only be tackled through better education.

Malaysia spends considerable sums on education as compared to many countries, both in absolute terms as well as relative to the economy, population, and overall budget. Yet it has little to show for all the resources expended.

There are many reasons for this. In part the inefficiency is consequent to the ministry's mission being tangled up with extraneous issues like helping Malay contractors. Another, Malaysia does not emphasize mathematics, sciences, and technical fields. This Technical Intellectual Capital (TIC) is a far more powerful predictor of development than just simple education. South Korea emphasizes TIC, catapulting the nation into an economic powerhouse. India by contrast chooses the British route of emphasizing education for its own sake, meaning heavy doses of the non-technical. India is stagnant but has plenty of taxi drivers with degrees and an abundance of petition writers, otherwise known as lawyers.

The remarkable aspect of investments in education is that, properly done, the benefits are both cumulative and synergistic. Stated simply, the more we invest, the more the benefits. Or in the language of the economists, such investments yield high marginal returns. I will illustrate this concept with an example.

My son is an aspiring pilot, but instead of going straight to flight school or joining the air force to get his training, he decided to get his degree in business first and take his pilot training on the side, figuring that his academic qualifications and technical training would enhance his employability. We were watching a television program about a revolutionary jet engine pioneered by NASA and now being incorporated into new model executive jets. They are markedly more efficient, and costing much less to build and operate. My reaction was simply, "Very interesting!" My son however, immediately saw the splendid opportunity for air travel between small towns now not adequately served by major airlines. He saw the potential of an air taxi service using those executive jets at a price comparable to the current coach fares. Additionally passengers would be spared the hassle and delays at major airports especially today with the heightened security checks. As this jet could land at small airports this would reduce congestion of the major ones as well as increase the use of currently underused country airports. He was so excited with the potential that he decided to explore it. The upshot is that he is making that project into his senior thesis and considering running air taxis his career.

My point is that to someone who does not have the necessary background knowledge, the development is simply "interesting." But to him it opens the potential of a new business.

When we embark on seeking new knowledge we will never know where it will lead. At one time many were against spending money on space research contending that the funds were needed more on earth. Today directly as result of those research we see the benefits accruing in medicine, agriculture, and telecommunication. The elemental diet now used widely in clinical medicine was the direct result of space research necessitated by the need to find zero residue diet for astronauts because of the limited lavatory facilities in spaceship. Similarly today's ubiquitous cell phones are the direct spin off of space and satellite research.

The Muslim philosopher Saidina Ali wisely observed on the difference between wealth and knowledge, and the much superior benefits of investing in the latter. Knowledge protects us, but we have to protect our wealth against theft and inflation. Not so with knowledge. My knowledge and skills as a surgeon are always with me, no one can take those away. The world around may crumble but I can still practice my profession. Wealth is reduced and diluted when shared; knowledge on the other hand gets amplified and enhanced when shared, to the benefit of everyone. The remarkable progress of science is precisely because of this open sharing of information, knowledge, and discoveries. Knowledge kept secret would lose its value. Knowledge retains if not increases its value with time, wealth risks being eroded with time and inflation. Investments in knowledge are durable; investments in fancy skyscrapers could be easily destroyed by fire or suicide bombers. Likewise investing in education is durable; nothing could destroy it. The first thing the ancient Mongols did in subjugating and destroying the Muslim civilization was to kill the intellectuals and burn all the books and libraries. They failed; instead they ended up becoming Muslims, a testimony to the power and endurance of knowledge.

Education is no panacea, but a well-educated citizenry is a prerequisite or enabling condition for socioeconomic development. To maximize the returns on investments in education we must also simultaneously provide opportunities. The remarkable transformation of South Korea and Taiwan is because they combined education reforms with increased economic opportunities. Malaysia in contrast invests heavily in its Multimedia Super Corridor and Biovalley, but those programs do not produce the anticipated returns as they are few trained Malaysians able to take advantage of the opportunities. The lack of qualified local personnel is also stalling the projects.

Opportunities are more likely to come to those who are ready with the skills and knowledge; to those who lack such skills and knowledge, the opportunities would simply be missed. And providing quality education is the surest way to make the citizens ready.

If our leaders are worried that Malay culture and race would be lost with globalization, the best and most effective remedy would be to ensure that Malays get the best education.

Malaysia is suddenly realizing that its competitiveness has slipped. This is the final expression of a failed education system. Unless steps are taken to improve the quality, broaden its access, reduce the inequities, and increase its relevance, Malaysia will remain poorly served.

Education As Political and Cultural Symbol

Education is a very powerful political and cultural symbol in Malaysia. This unfortunate association proves to be a major distraction. Major efforts are expended in the name of education not on improving it, rather on scoring political points and furthering the objectives of ambitious politicians.

The consequence of this mindset is that initiatives in education are first analyzed in terms of which race or community "won" and which one "lost." The corollary to this destructive thinking is that what is good for one community must be at the expense of the other–a zero-sum mentality. Chinese parents consider teaching Malay to their children a sop to Malay nationalists rather than as an asset in itself. Fortunately this negative attitude is fast receding. Malays however, are still trapped by the bugaboo of colonialism. Many among the educated and enlightened, as exemplified by Nik Safiah Karim, consider learning English as glorifying the colonialists or worse, of wanting to be a *Mat Salleh* (Malay epithet for the English, an idiomatic equivalent of Uncle Tom). It never occurs to them that English fluency is a highly useful skill.

Because of this powerful political symbolism, ministers of education with rare exceptions have been politicians known best for their ability to "stand up" against non-Malays. Such leaders also have a singularly insular view of the world, in addition to their thin managerial and other talents. The degradation of Malaysian education can be blamed in large part to the appointments in the past of such mediocre personalities as Rahman Talib and Khir Johari as ministers of education. Their more recent successors are not much better.

The sinister aspect to this politicization at the highest level is that it filters down to poison the atmosphere at lower levels. When I was associated with UKM, I had a competent pathologist colleague. He was enthusiastic, hardworking, and very effective; definitely an asset to the university. Imagine my anger and surprise when he approached me one morning with the news that his contract might not be renewed. Only then did I know that he was not a Malaysian. I brought his plight to his departmental head. He assured me (and I believed him) that he was indeed trying very hard to reverse the decision. Unfortunately the hierarchy at UKM was particularly chauvinistic (still is). To them the presence of every foreigner on the faculty is a reflection of the inadequacy of native talent. In the end the man's contract was not renewed. I am sure that those in charge did not even consider the effect of their decision on the students and teaching program.

The challenge for Malaysia is how to de-politicize education. This does not mean that it should operate outside the political realities. Far from it! The successful minister must have the necessary political finesse to balance the conflicting demands of the various constituencies. What he should not do is have his every decision governed by politics.

Aware of the heavy political significance of the portfolio, many ministers have used it to further their personal political agenda. Politicians are inherently ambitious creatures; they cannot fail to note that all of the nation's prime ministers (except of course the first) had been ministers of education. This emboldened those ministers coming later that they too were destined for higher calling.

Anwar Ibrahim, who held the portfolio in the 1980s, was the most obscene example of this crass ambition. His successor Najib Razak also exhibited this tendency, albeit more coyly. But their performance as minister of education was nothing but a running record of ineptitude. The hubris of Anwar was his arrogant attempt to dictate how Malay should be spoken–his famous dictate on the artificial *Bahasa Baku* (original Malay), now thankfully ignored. Najib's legacy was in permitting private colleges and universities. He was very good at it, approving in the space of couple of years hundreds of institutions! He must have had an inflated sense of his (and his subordinates') ability to monitor them all. I have a more suspicious take (pardon the choice of word), for later in 1999 Najib was returned with the highest number of votes as one of UMNO's Vice-Presidents. He ran a very slick and, I might add, a well-financed campaign. The consequence of that flurry of approvals is that today's headlines carry stories of colleges set up by fly-by-night operators and a medical school approved that did not even have a laboratory. Yet this character has the gumption of thinking that he is competent to be a future prime minister!

In a dramatic departure from tradition, in 1999 Prime Minister Mahathir for the first time appointed a non-politician as minister of education. Musa Mohamad was trained as a pharmacist, and was previously the vice-chancellor of Universiti Sains Malaysia (USM), remarkable for someone lacking a terminal qualification in his field and without an iota of scholarly contribution. No surprise then that as minister he has been fumbling from one crisis to another.

The most recent was over the teaching of science and mathematics in English. When the government first announced it, there was considerable opposition. The Chinese objected because their schools were already doing a good job, they saw no reason to change a working formula. Malays viewed such measures as further widening the gulf separating urban from rural (and thus Malay from non-Malay) schools. Online polls conducted by the mainstream media and read mostly by urbanites overwhelmingly favored the proposal. But a similar survey done by *Harakah*, a publication of the opposition Islamic Party PAS, the results were the exact opposite.

The mainstream media (owned by the ruling political party) carried little or no coverage of those opposing the scheme, thus giving readers the false impression that the initiative was universally welcomed.

Had the government concentrated on providing well-trained English teachers to rural schools, the measure would not have generated such hostile responses. Indeed had the government done that, rural (read: Malay) students would have high levels of English fluency and the problem would not have risen in the first place.

This close linking of politics and education means that the ministry's basic mission of providing quality education often gets tangled with and distracted by extraneous considerations. In 2001 as part of the government's economic recovery plan, over RM2 billion were allocated for the building of schools. But because of race politics, these contracts were given only to Bumiputras, thereby effectively ensuring that the costs would be jacked up because of the limited competition. What the government should have done was to open the bids to all, including foreigners, and then accept the best price. In this way it would be spending the scarce resources prudently and would be able to stretch them even further, thus benefiting more students.

I estimate that such restrictive contracts boost the costs in excess of 25-50 percent. In one example, the government spent RM50 million to build a MARA residential school. I visited the site during its construction with a contractor friend who had done many similar projects. We looked at the blue print, talked with the workers, and scouted around for the cost of the land. My contractor friend confidently said that he could have built the same for under RM30 million and still would have made a handsome profit. And by modifying the design to get rid of the extraneous and expensive arches and fancy roofs, he could have brought the price down to under RM25 million, about half price!

Had there been open bids, the government could have built two such schools for the price of one. With the current practice the government may have helped its favorite Bumiputra contractors, with the second it would have helped thousands of young students.

In another instance the ministry embarked on an equally expensive project of building computer labs at schools, a laudatory enterprise. Again the similar restrictions, and as a result less than 10 percent of the projects were completed on time. Appalling! The ministry was saddled with the twin problems of cost overruns and abandoned projects, all because of such favoritism and cronyism. Minister Musa made some seemingly brave statements about penalizing the errant contractors, but in the end nothing was done. The practice continues.

To be fair, such inefficiencies occur regularly in America. In California every school must be designed from scratch. Obviously the architects' lobby inserted that clause! And only unionized workers are to be employed, thus ensuring at least 30 percent hike in labor costs. There are also other rules purportedly for safety. Consequently public schools in California cost nearly twice that of private ones. It can be argued that California is rich and can afford such featherbedding practices. Not so Malaysia.

Another egregious example of prodigious waste was the sending of thousands of Bumiputra students abroad, mostly to mediocre institutions. The 1997 Asian economic crisis thankfully put an end to that profligate practice. While these precious funds were being wasted, local institutions struggled with meager resources. When I queried a senior official about this, his reply was as frank as it was frightening. By sending these students abroad and away from local public scrutiny, the government was hiding the fact it was spending billions on them. I would rather that the government been more prudent and sent only the best students and save the rest of the money to improve rural schools and local universities, thereby helping even more Bumiputras.

The quality of the students sent was such that when a team of officials from USM came to America to recruit potential lecturers among these students, almost all the applicants were rejected for the simple reason that few could communicate well in English. This raised the more fundamental question of why they were sent abroad in the first place.

When I encountered the first few students who had academic difficulties in the early 1980s, I blamed them for being lax and lazy. But when I later discovered that there were many more in the same sad shape, I knew then that it was not individual weaknesses, rather a system failure. I visited the centers that prepared these students and was appalled at both the lack of discipline and sense of purpose among the staff. No wonder few of the students were accepted to good colleges. When I suggested that the selection be more rigorous, the officials replied that none would then qualify. They had such low expectations. I heard every stereotype and caricature of the "lazy and dumb" Malays uttered by these officials who incidentally were also Malays. They further assured me that these students were the best they had.

Note, the remarks were from the principals and senior administrators. Lest I leave a negative impression, I will relate my experience with the teachers. First they apologized for their administrators' dismissive treatment of me. Then they showed me the latest circular from the ministry asking them to further cut their syllabi. In physics they were to completely eliminate the whole section on optics. In chemistry, a number of experiments were now to be demonstrated only, not to be done by the students. When I queried why the ministry was doing this, they could not offer any explanation except to suggest that the ministry was pressuring the centers to pass as many candidates as possible, and to cut down costs.

I met with their biology teacher, and our conversation drifted towards teaching microscope, especially the ones with video and computer attachments so images could be stored on discs and projected onto the screen for the whole class to see. He said that he had been trying to acquire the equipment for the past three years but his request had been consistently deferred. My son's school had just bought similar equipment. The cost? Less than 10 percent of what the Malaysian teachers were quoted! That reason? The school had to buy through the government-approved vendor and thus the consequent horrendous markup.

Multiply such incidents and the aggregate wastage is truly staggering. Politics have corrupted the procurement process, driving up costs.

The more sinister aspect to the intrusion of politics into education is that standards have gone by the wayside. Officials are impatient to get "good" results to prove a political point, thus they lower the standards. Had they raised the standard, Malay students would have responded. There may be a year or two of bad results until the message gets through, but in the end they will respond.

Further, had such poor results persisted they would have elicited howling protests from the public and would have forced the ministry to rectify the inadequacies of the system. But by lowering the standards, more Malays appeared to be qualified and everyone was happy– until the day of reckoning.

Malaysian schools are also fast becoming the favorite hobbyhorse for ambitious politicians. In his zeal to prove his presumed piety and religiosity, Anwar Ibrahim instituted more teaching of Islamic Studies.

Later another politician, not to be outdone, pushed for teaching entre-preneurial studies, no doubt to boost his credentials among Malay business types. And a third was advocating his pet subject–tourism! The latest is the Deputy Prime Minister pushing for IT. These politi-cians forget that there are only so many hours in the school day.

The current appalling standards of education at all levels are the consequence of having ignored the problems and letting them fester. A good start at reform would be to divorce as far as possible politics, espe-cially the race and party variety, from education. Doing so would enable those involved in our schools and universities to focus on their basic mission of providing quality education to all.

Socioeconomic Factors Affecting Education

While it is important that we focus on schools to make sure that they are adequately funded, well equipped, and have trained teachers, we should not be blind to the social factors that can have a major impact on students' performance. Access to schools, even when they are made free and readily available, can be blocked by seemingly innocuous fac-tors like the need for school uniforms and transportation. We should also be mindful that what many would regard as opportunities, to the disadvantaged they may well be looked upon as obstacles.

There are many factors outside of education, in particular the social environment and culture, which affect educational attainment. We ignore them at our own peril.

In a landmark 1966 study, the American sociologist James S. Cole-man showed that the most important factor influencing school perfor-mance is the family, not the type of school or the amount of funding it receives. Parental involvement in the school is the best predictor of aca-demic performance. Or as an old English saying would have it, one father is more effective than a hundred schoolmasters.

California publishes an annual evaluation of its schools, the Aca-demic Performance Index (API), based on such indicators as test scores and graduation rates. What is remarkable is that the API correlates very well with the socio-economic status of the parents, leading many to dub it as the Affluent Parents Index.

US News publishes an annual report on the best American high schools. Invariably the top ones are the elite private prep schools. But I am not impressed with them; with their high fees and rigorous selection process they would pick only the best. Those students would have done well even if they had attended the local high school. Occasionally the list comes up with some regular public schools, those are the ones that truly impress me because they and their teachers have truly added value to their students.

One such school was Garfield High, a public inner city school in East Los Angeles with predominantly poor minority students. Their teacher, Jaime Escalante, successfully challenged them to take rigorous mathematic classes including advanced calculus. His students did so well on the College Board examinations that it thought that they had cheated, and under some pretext so as not to arouse suspicion, asked them to re-sit the test. Again they scored well. When word spread about the truth for the re-examination, the students were at first furious and then on reflection, they felt truly proud of their achievement. Their teacher became a celebrity, later portrayed in the 1988 movie *Stand and Deliver*. His was not an easy task; he had to spend years upgrading the math classes at the lower levels first.

Singapore, with its obsession of aping everything American, has a similar ranking exercise of its schools, except that the paternal government does it. The same schools come on top every year. Again that does not impress me. Had the rankings been based on the educational achievements and socio-economic status of the parents, the list would be identical. Sorry, no kudos for the teachers at its top schools.

This is true of schools as well as universities. It is well known that graduates of elite universities consistently earn more than those of less selective ones, leading many to credit those august institutions. This makes intuitive sense too. But a recent study by the National Bureau of Economic Research put things in their proper perspective. Instead of simplistically comparing the earnings of graduates of top universities to those attending other institutions, they studied the subgroup of students who were admitted to elite institutions but instead chose for a variety of reasons to attend less well-known universities. It turns out both groups do equally well. Essentially if you are smart and hardworking it does not matter whether you attend Harvard or Podunk State University, you will do well.

American prep schools actively diversify their student body by granting scholarships to talented minority students. These schools also have special coaching classes to scout for promising candidates. The ABC (A Better Choice) is one such successful program. The socioeconomic trap can be broken with imaginative policies. Even here there are pitfalls and failures. To a few, being selected for Groton and Exeter is not an opportunity rather a severe culture shock.

The importance of parental involvement in education may be self-evident, but we need to look further and ask the even more basic question: Why are poor parents not involved in their children's education? While we seek answers to that, we must also explore the exceptions, that is, where poor parents are deeply involved with their children's education to the point of willingly sacrificing everything.

In America private Catholic schools in the inner cities do a much better job than public schools despite being less generously funded. One reason is that when parents send their children to these schools, they believe in the system. The schools reinforce the parents' traditional values; that in turn encourages even more parental involvement. This does not happen only with Catholic schools. Later I will describe the experience of Deborah Meier with her small school in East Harlem where over 90 percent of her students go on to college, a rate nearly twice the national average and certainly way ahead of other inner city public schools. Her secret? Getting the parents involved by respecting them, and by having high expectations of their children.

The same phenomenon is also seen among Malays. Malay children attending religious schools have low rates of absenteeism and dropouts.

The schools reinforce the parents' traditional values, and the parents in turn feel involved with and are connected to the schools. Parents do not fear that the school is imparting an alien value system. Their teachers too are committed, believing that they are doing Allah's work. We should capitalize on this affinity and use Islam as a powerful motivator to keep children in school, and their parents involved. As Malays are attracted to Islamic schools, all the more that we must make sure that these schools provide the education these children need to face the modern age.

The success of Catholic schools in America and Islamic schools in Malaysia may be attributed to what is called the Rosenthal effect. Robert Rosenthal is a Distinguished Professor of Psychology at UCLA who discovered that experimenters' expectations and teachers' biases often influence the results of an experiment or class. That is, expectations are self-fulfilling. This is also termed the Pygmalion effect, after George Bernard Shaw's play made famous by the Broadway show *My Fair Lady*. The sheer confidence of the lead character, Professor Higgins, in transforming a lowly Cockney lass into a refined lady made it happen.

A major portion of my reform addresses specifically this important issue of the Rosenthal phenomenon. The frequent harping on the poor performance of Malays in science and mathematics may have the perverse effect of perpetuating it. When this assumption gets ingrained, it affects everyone: teachers, students, and policy makers. The teacher would, through his or her manner of speech, voice, body language, and facial expressions, communicate this message to the students. The students in turn would quickly pick up on them. And policy makers would purposely dumb down the standards. Thus expectations become reality.

The Stanford psychologist Claude Steele describes the phenomenon of "stereotype threat" felt by those long stigmatized. When Malay students fail in science and mathematics, it is not simply that they have not studied hard enough or have not been taught well rather they are fulfilling the stereotype expectations of their race. Extra tutoring and better teachers could remedy the first two, but the last premise is more difficult to eradicate.

We should assume that Malays are just as capable in science and mathematics; they must take these subjects. Make them mandatory even in religious schools. Because religious schools are popular and successful with Malays, we must make these schools like their Catholic counterpart in America. Religion should only be one subject, not the consuming curriculum. These schools must produce their share of the nation's scientists, engineers, and executives.

During my school days under the British, my parents were not involved with my school although they did keep a close eye on my report card. The reason was simple; they physically could not do so as the school was far away. Even if they could, the language used was alien to them. This was typical of most Malay parents at the time; no surprise then the dropout rate for Malays was atrocious.

Today many schools in California have newsletters in Spanish as well as English in order to reach out to Hispanic parents. Additionally many schools have after-hours adult programs involving the parents. One school, recognizing that many of the parents do not speak English, has evening classes to teach English, as well as other subjects specifically tailored to their needs such as how to become citizens. In this way parents would be made to feel involved with and connected to the school. These gestures go a long way to make parents (especially those from minority groups) feel welcome and be part of the school community.

Gender is also a formidable barrier to education especially in traditional societies. Many Malaysian parents actively discourage schooling for girls believing that such investments would be wasted. In Malay society specifically, this was a prevalent practice until a few years ago. Today the achievements of Malay girls are much superior to that of boys, indicating that such cultural barriers can indeed be changed for the better.

Even mundane details like textbooks and uniforms affect school performance. Studies in Kenya show that when children are provided with free textbooks and uniforms (often substantial cost factors for rural families) these pupils tend to stay in school.

Research shows that among Malaysians, family size is inversely related to educational attainment. That is, the bigger the family the lower the educational attainment of its members. Schools entail costs, thus poor families conserve their scant resources by limiting schooling only to their more promising progenies. In the past it was quite common for other siblings to sacrifice so one could finish his (usually a son) schooling. Such socioeconomic barriers can be effectively overcome by imaginative policies. It is interesting that for Malay children born after 1970, that correlation no longer holds. That year is significant in that the NEP was introduced giving Malays substantial aids in education. It was effective in breaking down that barrier for Malays.

For Muslims yet a major impediment to excellence is their attitude towards education, in particular, secular education. This barrier arises from the traditional interpretations of and differentiation between worldly and religious knowledge. Present day Muslim scholars disparage the pursuit of the former lest it would contaminate their piety and religiosity. Much of the attempts at educational reforms in the Muslim world are geared towards the "Islamization" of the curriculum, that is, trying to put an Islamic spin to secular knowledge. This is a retrograde step as it merely reinforces this artificial separation and further demotes the value of secular education.

This fad is already entrenched among Muslim intellectuals in the social sciences. Unfortunately those in the natural sciences too are not spared. Inevitably this results in their producing adulterated "scientific findings" that will never see the pages of reputable journals. Worse, now we have Islamic "scientists" who have never seen, let alone used, a test tube. Consider the absurd comments of Muslim "scientists" attributing computer viruses to the works of *jinn* (devil)!

Science is science. Hydrogen mixes with oxygen under the right conditions to produce water, Islamic science or not. Science and religion is complementary, not adversarial. Science explores the world around and within us while religion answers our spiritual needs. Advancements in science benefit all mankind; we should not belittle these discoveries. In trying to discern differences where none exists, these intellectuals and scientists are wasting their energy. They would be better off trying to elucidate the secrets of Allah. Such "Islamizing" activities simply mask their lack of intellectual ingenuity and curiosity. They cannot discover or contribute anything original so they seek refuge in concocting such puerile intellectual pursuits as Islamizing established principles.

A more sinister aspect to these pseudo-intellectual activities is that their practitioners are hiding behind their Islamic cloak to advance their career. Religion has always been the refuge of scoundrels including academic ones. Nobody dares call them to the carpet for fear of being labeled anti-religious. These Islamic intellectuals remind me of third-rate Soviet scientists and scholars who, unable to advance on their own talent, hide behind their communist party credentials. In truth those who truly uplift the image of Islam are the scientists who diligently pursue their curiosity. Scientists like Abdus Salam (1979 Nobel laureate in physics) and Ahmad Zeweil (Chemistry 1999), like thousands of others quietly toiling in their laboratories discovering the secrets of Allah, do more for Islam than third-rate scientists cloaking themselves in the veneer of the faith.

It is interesting that both Salam and Zewail found the fullest expression and appreciation of their vast talent in the West. More poignantly for Salam, his native Pakistan's parliament passed a special resolution condemning him as an infidel. So much for the Islamic respect for knowledge!

A more fruitful approach, and the one that I am advocating, is to remove this artificial barrier. All knowledge–secular and religious–originates from God and thus is worthy of our quest.

Education and Technology

My discussion revolves around two central issues. One, how well the education system prepares young Malaysians for this age of IT, and two, the role of IT in education. I will tackle the much easier second topic first.

Technology has long been used in education. During my school days there were the radio programs, usually broadcasts of some classic plays enacted on air. What I remember most of those sessions was staring at a lifeless box and having a tough time keeping awake.

The brilliant economist Ungku Aziz extended the medium into adult education with his wildly popular and very successful *Kursus Ekonomi Radio* (Economic Course via Radio). This was decades before the concept of distant learning. I had no difficulty keeping awake listening to his animated explanations!

At about this time in America, Thomas Skinner and his brand of behavioral psychology were the rage. There was much hype about his "teaching machines," where students could be taught pretty much like pigeons, through "operant conditioning," that is, by rewarding every time they make a correct response—a form of positive reinforcement. Thankfully Malaysia and the rest of the world were spared the fad simply because those machines were prohibitively expensive.

Later with the introduction of television, there was Educational TV, crafted along the old school radio broadcasts but with pictures. And with video recorders there was a quantum leap in effectiveness. Teachers could stop and rewind the tape for replay and emphasis.

Living in Silicon Valley, California, the nexus of IT, I am very much aware of the impact of high technology. With the introduction of personal computers in the 1980s and the Internet a decade after that, IT has been democratized. It has reached the masses.

IT enhances the reach and capability of television broadcasts and videotapes. Through web casting I can watch in the comfort of my home a master surgeon operate in real time just as if I were standing with him in the operating room. This is a considerable improvement over the old "wet clinic" where visiting surgeons would watch from the visitors' gallery and all they could see was the surgeon's back. Through web casting I can listen to a university lecture given thousands of miles away, or to a *khutba* (sermon) delivered by Tok Guru Nik Aziz, leader of the Islamic Party PAS. It is disorienting to hear this medieval-minded *ulama* using a high-tech medium to convey his ancient messages!

Computers are like automobiles in their ubiquity, utility, and impact on the economy. I can extend the analogy further to illustrate the point I wish to explore here.

We readily appreciate the usefulness of cars; many would be paralyzed without them. We take the automobile in all its shapes and forms for granted. Everyone knows what a truck is for as compared to a limousine. One does not have to be a car buff to appreciate the difference between a Porshe and a Proton Saga. Yet despite our familiarity, few really understand (or need to) how the machine works. Car owners do not have to understand the complexity of the laws of thermodynamics—the essence of internal combustion engine—to drive their car. Nor do most drivers know the significance of gear differentials. All they know is that when they are starting the car or going uphill, shift into lower gear, and when they want to go fast, shift to high gear. No need to know the complicated calculations of mechanical advantage or velocity ratio.

So it is with computers. One does not have to know the difference between bytes and bits to use and benefit from computers. I need not know the details to know that my new computer can download some jazzy graphics faster than my old one; or that with my old software I could not do the fancy editing and neat fonts that I now readily do with the upgraded version.

I cannot understand the present hullabaloo and obsession with making our students computer literate. My father-in-law was 72 years old when he first learned the computer. The only reason he did it was that the computer was in the guest room where he was staying when visiting us. Seeing my children pounding on the keyboard intrigued him and twigged his curiosity. He was determined to learn, and learned it he did, in a few days. Today he e-mails me about how to font his electronic newsletter and how to crop his "jpg" (picture graphic) files. He learned by doing and asking.

Yet today's headlines carry the concerns of educators and politicians about how to make our students computer literate. The answer is simple: provide them with computers and let them loose. They will learn from each other and by trial and error, or if you want them to learn faster, organize a few classes in the afternoon or weekends. There is no need to take away valuable classroom time to teach these simple practical subjects.

The Indian computer scientist Sugata Mitra had a novel experiment of bringing IT to poor children. He placed in the slums and villages of India Internet-connected computers in a hole in the wall covered with a touch screen, and then monitored the activities around them via remote video camera. Within hours curious children were already learning how to use the machine and surfing the Web, visiting Disneyland websites, playing games, using paint world, and downloading Napster music files. They did not know what computers or Internet meant but they were able to use the device by fiddling with it. The adults in the village meanwhile were demanding why the government (whom they assumed put the computers up) did not send someone to train them how to use the machines. They obviously did not learn from their children. This experiment, appropriately called "Hole in the Wall," has now spread to over 52 villages.

Clifford Stoll, the Berkeley astronomer and a severe critique of modern technology, goes so far as to say that computers do not belong in the classroom. I disagree with that extreme position but his point is well taken. Computers are expensive and they become obsolete very quickly. I still cannot read some of my old letters and essays that were written using PFS as the new software is unable to read those old versions. And I do not want to waste my time rebooting my old jalopy to retrieve those ancient files. So my articles and notes of only a decade ago exist only in bits and bytes encrypted on some old floppy discs that no present-day computer could access.

Stoll's basic argument (and I agree completely) is that we should not be mesmerized with computers and technology generally to the point that we neglect the basics. Schools must first have good teachers, adequate libraries, and well-equipped laboratories before we waste valuable funds on fancy computer labs. IT enhances the reach and effectiveness of the teacher but is not a substitute for one. Similarly IT complements but does not replace the basic school facilities.

A well-trained teacher who can capture the imagination of students is still the most important element in learning. We should not be distracted from this cardinal point. If I were to create a priority list, it would be thus: good teachers, single session, music lessons, library, laboratory, air-conditioned classrooms, and then computers. I would venture that our students would learn more if classrooms were air-conditioned. That would not only make the environment more conducive to intellectual activities but also cut out the extraneous noise. Teachers know how difficult it is to get the children's attention in the heat of the day.

Singapore's Senior Minister Lee Kuan Yew observes that air-conditioning is the most important invention of the millennium. It enables those in the tropics to compete intellectually with those in the temperate zones. Seeing how advanced that island republic is, he may be on to something profound.

Numerous studies show the benefit of early musical education. I would thus provide musical instruments and music classes ahead of computers. Music lessons are also much cheaper. Music would teach these youngsters the concept of symbols and abstractions, and also teamwork. Very few Malaysian schools now have music programs.

While we have been bludgeoned with the mantra that information is power, in truth it isn't. As Stoll so rightly points out in his book *High Tech Heretic*, librarians are famous for having the most information, yet they lack power. Politicians on the other hand have no or very little information yet they are very powerful. Having the information is only the first step, the more important issue is how to evaluate that information and put it in the proper perspective. That requires a faculty for critical thinking, rational reasoning, and a high degree of skepticism.

Again comparing with the car, the skills or level of understanding needed to use one is very simple. Start the engine (two seconds instructions: insert and turn key) and then practice steering and braking. With those simple instructions you could drive the car safely on a deserted road. But if you want to take the car on the freeway, then you will need more skills lest you become a menace to yourself and others. You would need to improve your steering and braking, and learn defensive driving and rules of the road. If you want to fix the engine then you would need to learn to be a mechanic. Going further, if you want to design cars or build a better suspension system, then you would need to go to design or engineering school.

Likewise with computers; if you want to write software, then you would need to learn one of the programming languages. But for the vast majority of users, all you have to know is which key to punch to get a certain result on the screen. That is all. The most frequent question asked when I was learning the computer was, "How do I do…?"

You do not need special classes in the school curriculum to teach how to use word processor and e-mail, connect to the Internet, or access data from the Web. A visitor from Malaysia learned all these in one evening, and by the time my wife was ready with dinner, he had already sent his first e-mail. Yet this gentleman and his colleagues back home had been clamoring for the government to set up special computer classes for senior civil servants!

If you want to get fancy you could learn other slightly involved software like spreadsheet (good for accounting), PowerPoint (for slide presentations), and web authoring. Once you have the basics and are comfortable with computers, then you wonder how on earth you coped in the days before word processing! Today I rarely compose an essay on paper anymore, I do it straight on the keyboard, editing as I go along.

While learning how to use word processor is easy enough, writing is not. That requires a patient teacher, frequent exercises, and the availability of good books. If your prose is of the variety, "It was a dark and stormy night...," no amount of fancy fonts and jazzing up on the word processor will improve it. Had you written, "I could barely make out his wet face amidst the rough rustling of the reeds..." then regardless whether you have fancy fonts or merely scribble it on a yellowing piece of paper, your readers would know that it was a dark and stormy night. More importantly, they would more likely to continue reading.

It is more important to teach students how to write using the word processor rather than simply teaching them how to use the software. Likewise it is better to teach them how to collect, present, and interpret data using the database and spreadsheet rather than simply teaching them about the software.

The government has a high-level committee looking into bringing IT to the schools. I agree that schools should have computers, but before spending billions in wiring our schools, I would first attend to the basics. Having done that then I would introduce IT, starting at the upper levels, the universities. I would provide every faculty member with a free computer and unlimited Internet access. I would also ensure that the campus is "wired" and encourage the faculty to post their class assignments and reading lists online. Students too should be encouraged to submit their assignments electronically. All incoming students must be computer literate. I do not mean that the university should run word processing classes rather students would have to spend the months while waiting to enter the university acquiring those skills. There are plenty of proprietary classes where they can do this. Even the mosque in Section 14, Petaling Jaya, has such classes. There is no need to waste expensive university personnel or resources for students to acquire these basic computer skills.

Having computers in schools would be useless if there are no changes with the present Internet hook up fee structure. In America there is a fixed fee for unlimited access; in Malaysia it is hourly rates. Thus users are inhibited from reaping the vast potential of the Internet because of the additional costs incurred.

Deputy Prime Minister Badawi in a fit of enthusiasm recently proposed that IT be taught in schools. The curriculum is already crowded. Besides, I do not know exactly what he meant by it. Teach programming, software writing, and website designing? Surely our students have plenty of time acquiring those skills after they have mastered the basics and developed critical thinking. But if he means that students should be able to use computers and be comfortable with them, then you do not need to have a separate subject for that; it can be done in computer clubs and as extracurricular activities. Frankly I do not think Badawi himself knows what he is talking about. To him IT is only the latest buzzword to sprinkle his speeches.

The government demonstrated its commitment to IT by funding it massively, nearly a billion ringgit for 2003. In contrast only RM 850million for implementing single session schools. The amount allocated for teacher training was considerably less and did not merit a separate line item. The prime minister is deluded into thinking that teachers could be mere facilitators, their job reduced to turning on the computers and letting the students learn via electronic modules. Nothing could be further from the truth.

We have to differentiate *computer literacy* from *computational literacy*. The former as it is commonly understood means the ability to use the computer; it is a tool. In a way this is a misuse of the word literacy. A better term would be computer familiarity or facility. *Computational literacy* on the other hand is the ability to use programming language and to think, visualize, and extrapolate concepts in that medium. An illustration and comparison with text literacy would clarify my point.

Text literacy means more than just being able to read and write. It is a basic instrument to understand and communicate with the written word. Text literacy produces the works of Shakespeare and Steinbeck, and also the countless memos, letters, and little notes we write each other. It is a basic tool: an intellectual infrastructure. Through it we can communicate our deepest thoughts and emotions, a significant advancement over communication via cave wall drawings and oral traditions. The discovery of the printing press brought a quantum leap forward in enhancing the utility of and democratizing text literacy. It brought literacy to the masses.

Computational literacy is also an infrastructure, and computers enhance it in much the same way that printing presses do to text literacy. With our understanding of the language of computers we would be able to think and project our messages and thoughts or otherwise communicate in this new medium.

Andrea di Sessa (the man who coined the term computational literacy) in his book *Changing Minds* describe an experiment with computational literacy using his Boxer programming language to teach the physics of motion and other abstract mathematical concepts to Grade 6 students. The students were asked to picture someone on a roller blade sliding down the street with a tennis ball in his hand. He then dropped the ball from his chest while skating. The class was asked to visualize the motion of the ball from three perspectives: the skater, a miniature man looking up from the skateboard, and an observer standing by the roadside. This was an exercise on relative velocity, a difficult concept to teach.

The student who was asked to present the view from the skateboard explained his very simply. He pressed a function key and a small dot appeared in the middle of the computer screen. This then rapidly enlarged to fill the entire screen. He had to write only a line of codes in the program to effect this, and it captured accurately in a visual and concrete manner the image of a ball dropping and landing directly on the eye of the miniature observer on the skateboard. It would be tough to explain the motion of the ball using conventional text literacy or even standard mathematical formula. With computers, the message and the concept are readily grasped–very graphic representation and easily understood.

It is this ability to look at concepts differently that is so promising about computational literacy. At its most optimistic level, computational literacy would have the potential to do what text literacy and mathematical literacy do to our present understanding and level of communication. Galileo's theory of motion took pages to explain in texts but only a few crisp lines of formulas to explain fully using modern algebra. He took that long because algebra was not yet invented in his time. Similarly with calculus; we could not begin to describe such concepts as acceleration without it. But with calculus, acceleration is merely a differential of velocity (dv/dt), or in words, the rate of change of velocity. Today calculus is taught at high school and is widely used to describe relationships and phenomena in the social as well as natural sciences.

Computational literacy is still rather primitive, or to use the ubiquitous phrase of the web, "under construction." Past attempts at teaching programming in schools using first BASIC and later, LOGO, have floundered. But with better programs like Boxer, developed at the University of California Berkeley and tailored specifically for learning purposes and not to write applications, computational literacy may yet prove to be as infrastructural as text literacy. Malaysia must participate in these leading edge trials at selected schools but only under strict research protocol. But this is a totally different idea than the current mindless agitation for teaching IT in schools.

I am cynical of the current move to bring IT to the classrooms and provide teachers with laptops. This has less to do with enhancing the quality of education and everything to do with business. If it were the former I would expect the ministry to provide computers to university lecturers and teacher trainees first; they need them more. Think of the billions worth of contracts, enough to make any executive drool at the prospects. Not to mention interested politicians who would gain by being the lucrative intermediaries. The whole scheme is business driven and corrupt, the pupils' interest is only incidental. This program will end up like the computer ownership scheme sponsored by the Employees Provident Fund. It failed because EPF did not get substantial discounts or wholesale prices. Instead there were significant markups because of the "commissions" paid to politician middlemen. Likewise the schools and teachers will end up paying highly inflated prices.

The literature on the effectiveness of computers in classrooms is mixed and contradictory. Where they are successful it is because the authorities have clear and definable goals, and the efforts initially focused on few demonstration projects where the kinks could be ironed out. Once the project is running smoothly then it can be replicated and expanded. In choosing the software, teachers must have clear goals: computer assisted learning (CAL) as with self-directed drills in mathematics and language learning; for simulation and exploration; as computational tools as with word processing, spreadsheet, and Power-Point; part of a communication network; or merely as pedagogical administrative tool to keep track of students' achievements.

Once the objectives are clear and agreed upon, key personnel can then be trained. It is better to concentrate the effort initially, once we can have a nucleus of competently trained experts, they can then spread their skills. The most logical place to start would be the teachers' colleges and with teacher trainees. Once these are done only then could we consider selecting the hardware. With the goals and objectives clear, the hardware and specifications would be that much easier to define.

In 1999 Malaysia embarked on an ambitious "Smart School" project of bringing IT to selected schools. This program had yet to be digested and its lessons learned when the government embarked in its current and more massive project of providing laptops and LCD projectors to all schools. This is exactly the wrong approach. First, the teachers have yet to be trained and two, the objectives are not yet clearly delineated. By next year all those expensive gadgets would be stored untouched or more likely be reported "stolen". The students would be no further ahead.

There is one place where computers would be useful, and that is to help with the administrative chores like monitoring student attendance, payroll, accounting, and keeping tabs on supplies and budgeting. Not only would this be very efficient and accurate but it would also force the headmasters to be familiar with computers.

While it is easy to teach students how to use computers and surf the Net, the more difficult part would be to teach them the limitations and dangers lurking in cyberspace. The Internet is not filtered or censored; Einstein would have the same prominence in cyberspace as the simple villager. Those using the 'Net must have the ability to think critically and be skeptical of the materials they get. The age of IT calls for even more emphasis on such traditional higher order intellectual activities like critical thinking, abstract reasoning, and information processing. These can only be learned with the help of a good teacher.

This point was illustrated to me recently when my readers asked me which websites they should look up on some questions about Islam I had discussed in one of my essays. How could they be sure that the information is genuine and the site authentic, and not the work of some anti-Muslim groups masquerading as believers? The answer is, you cannot be sure. Thus you must be able to evaluate critically the information as to its veracity and validity. There is nobody out there in cyberspace who will put a stamp of approval or to check the facts. The web is uncensored; that is its beauty.

This fact is extremely pertinent especially with medically related web sites. If someone suggests taking arsenic as a cure for baldness, you take that advice at your own risk. One needs to use one's judgment. There is a lot of what is called "noise," that is, irrelevant and nonsensical if not downright dangerous materials on the web.

There is also much hype on using IT for distance or e(electronic)-learning. I am in favor of this to a point. The Internet is much better and more efficient than the old correspondence schools. It is immediate; you do not have to wait for the mail and you can post your questions and have them answered immediately. It is also cheaper (after you invest in the computer) as there are no postages and papers. But this does not mean that e-learning could replace traditional classrooms. There is much more to learning than the mere transfer of information from teacher to student. The class discussions and the social interactions are also very important. In a classroom you learn to relate with those you like and tolerate those you don't–very important lessons in life. You cannot get that sitting alone before a computer screen. We must appreciate what can be achieved through e-learning as well as the limitations. I use e-learning for my continuing medical education (CME) but only as a supplement. It does not replace the live conferences and seminars.

The best e-learning programs are precisely those that combine distance learning with in-depth and intensive face-to-face class and residential experiences. One of the best executive e-learning programs is that of Duke's Fuqua School of Business. Students gather every two months at various locations around the world for concentrated "live" sessions with their fellow students and instructors. In between they communicate and receive lessons via the 'Net. Such programs are ideal for working executives who would have difficulty taking long stretches of time away from their jobs.

My small hospital has an electronic hookup with a tertiary medical center where we could participate in live CME conferences. Through a two-way cable hookup we can see the speaker and he could see us, and we could communicate in real time as if we are in the same room. This is entirely different from e-learning via the computer. Such hookups via satellite would be ideal to connect a Third World university with an elite institution in the West. MIT has a similar program with the two public universities in Singapore to conduct joint "real-time" seminars. Malaysian universities should have similar links. With the 12-hour time difference, an early morning lecture would be an early evening one in Malaysia.

There is a great potential for IT in enhancing the learning experience, but in our enthusiasm we should not forget that the basics remain the first priority.

The second more important issue of how well the education system prepares Malaysians for the age of IT can be turned around by asking the more fundamental question: What are the skills required to thrive in this age of IT? The specific and basic skills required are English fluency, high mathematical competency, and science literacy. Our students must also be adept at critical thinking and higher-level reasoning. They must have flexible and transferable skills. We should also inculcate early the need and importance of life-long learning.

It is in all these areas that our education system has failed miserably. The good news is that the government is finally waking up to this fact, forced by the overwhelming evidence that it can no longer ignore. The entire premise of my reform is to prepare Malaysians for the competitive era of IT and globalization.

Education, The Economy, and Demographics

The two most important factors that bear on the quality of education lie outside its sphere: the economy and demographics. Stated differently, Malaysia cannot have a strong education system with a weak economy, nor a First World standard of education with a Third World demographics. If we look at countries that have superior education systems, the remarkable correlates are that they all have healthy economies and low birth rates.

A strong economy does not guarantee a superior education system. Indonesia had an impressive economy under Suharto, but it squandered that golden opportunity by diverting it away from improving its schools. The Indian state of Kerala has a much superior education system and other social services despite an economy one hundredth that of Canada and a population of comparable size. Kerala's literacy rates and educational attainment are the highest in India and near that of the First World. Similarly Cuba, despite a crawling if not stagnant economy, has universal literacy and high caliber education. Because of that it is a major force for biogenetic engineering, producing such sophisticated products like Hepatitis B vaccine.

A robust economy enables the nation to devote the necessary resources to improving its education system. Superior schools and universities in turn help buffer and sustain the economy. Much has been written on the rapid recovery of South Korea, Taiwan, and to a certain extent Malaysia following the 1997 economic crisis, but I venture that a major contributing factor is their superior education system. Indonesia and Thailand did not bounce back fast because their education system is that much more inferior.

The other important correlate of a superior education system is low population growth. Cuba and Kerala may have moribund economy, but their slow population growth enables them to devote their resources towards improving their social services instead of just trying to keep up with the population growth. China will leapfrog into the First World simply because it has tackled the most important factor, that of reducing its previously horrendous birth rates. This together with a rapidly expanding economy ensures that China would be a major power soon. Indonesia and India on the other hand are still struggling merely to keep up, whatever gains they have in their economy are quickly absorbed and diluted by a rapidly expanding population.

Malaysia has the typical Third World demographics, with a pyramidal age distribution, in contrast to the more cylindrical First World pattern. Meaning, Malaysia has the greatest proportion of its citizens in the lower age groups. Additionally it is also at a dangerous transition with a rapidly increasing aging population to boot, thanks to its improving health care. Graphically the apex of the pyramid is broader, meaning more resources would have to be diverted to serve the needs of the elderly and consequently less for schools.

Assume an inflation and population growth rates of 3 percent each. This means the government would have to spend 6 percent more every year just to maintain the status quo, with none going towards improvement in quality. Every year Malaysia spends millions more on education, but these additional funds are simply consumed with building new classrooms and training new teachers just to keep up with the number of additional new school children.

I estimate that the number of births in Malaysia last year was around 600,000, and increasing at 3 percent annually. That means that country will have to build classrooms and find new teachers for 18,000 new children every year until those children finish their schooling 11 years later. The following year we will have to repeat the same process all over again. The cumulative costs are astronomical. But if we have an effective family planning program and manage to keep the number of new births constant, we do not need to build those extra classrooms and train those new teachers. Or if we do, then we could use the extra resources to reduce class overcrowding and pupil/teacher ratio. This would inevitably lead to improvement in quality. If we go beyond and reduce the number of births by only 1 percent, then we could use the resources currently used by the 6,000 fewer children to further benefit the rest. Note these savings would recur every year and be cumulative and additive.

Seventeen years later we would see even greater savings when we do not have to provide the additional spaces at the colleges and universities.

It is not enough to merely stabilize the fertility rates as you would then still have a steady increase in the number of births because the present cohort of childbearing women would continue to increase for at least the next 30 to 40 years. Thus Malaysia must go beyond and actually reduce the number of new births. To do this it has to markedly reduce the fertility rates to compensate for the increasing number of childbearing women now already in the pipeline.

Countries like Singapore and Ireland have improved their education system immensely not so much because their leaders are particularly smart or astute but because their nation's birth rate has plummeted.

Thus they can devote their resources to improving the quality instead of merely trying to cope up.

It is beyond the scope of my book to discuss ways to curb population growth; suffice to say that that is an important strategy to improving the quality of education and other social services. Malaysia can significantly reduce its population growth by making family planning readily available. It does not have to resort to the crude and intrusive ways of the Communist Chinese. Unfortunately Malaysia has the perverse policy of pursuing increased population growth rate with its misguided 70 Million Population program. This will make attaining the goal of a quality education that much more difficult to achieve.

3

The Present System

T he present system of education is based on the Razak Report of 1956. There had only been minimal modifications at the periphery since then. The core assumption of that report is that Malaysians should have a uniform system of schooling with a common curriculum so as to foster national unity.

Prior to the Razak Report, Malaysian schools were based along the British model. There were essentially two systems: English and vernacular schools. English schools were mainly in the major towns and catered mostly to urban dwellers. These happened to be mostly non-Malays at the time. Some were missionary schools, and with such names as The Convent of the Holy Infant Jesus they not surprisingly did not attract many Malays. The curriculum was entirely British, right down to the choice of textbooks, with no attempt at modifying to suit local conditions.

These schools were not free; in addition to tuition fees there were other incidental expenses for sports and library for example that added up quickly. Then there were the textbooks and uniforms. Even students' exercise books were imported, making them very expensive. Students were not allowed to use the cheap local variety. For rural children, an additional significant cost was for transportation. Not surprisingly many dropped out; their families unable to afford to keep them in school.

The British tried to accommodate rural children by having hostels attached to these schools. It also gave scholarships to promising Malay students based on need.

Malay schools were state supported and free. They were also conveniently located in the villages. There were no additional assorted fees and expenses; the pupils need not even have uniforms. Many were barefooted. Such schools were referred to as *sekolah kaki ayam*, schools for the chicken-footed (barefooted). The school years did not extend beyond six, most only for four–very elementary. The pupils learned only the minimum of arithmetic, reading, and writing, all in Malay. The brighter graduates would have a chance to undergo two years of teacher training and then they were let loose to teach. My parents were two such teachers. Teaching was the only avenue of employment for the lucky few. A few more could find employment as police constables, the armed services, or as petty clerks in the civil service. The vast majority would continue with their village life as before; nothing would have changed for them. As Roff noted, from the point of view of utility alone, many Malays saw little advantage in vernacular education. In 1903, of the 2,900 boys who passed Malay schools in Perak, 24 became domestic or office servants, ten schoolteachers, one a clerk, and another a policeman. That pattern persisted throughout the entire British rule.

Tamil schools were just as sorry. Chinese schools were much better as they were better funded by their community. They also provided education up to the upper secondary levels. They essentially used the textbooks available in China. Because these schools emphasized mathematics, their students were able to transfer their skills readily to the marketplace.

These vernacular schools were left entirely to their own devices, the colonial version of benign neglect. Consequently they developed along divergent paths. Students in Chinese schools learned more about China and Mao Zedong than about Malaysia and Malaysian heroes. Students in Tamil schools were more concerned with events in India and knew more about the Indian independence movement than Malaysia's own history.

The country's first Minister of Education, Tun Razak, quickly grasped the potential danger to the new nation with the young being educated separately. His bold plan called for the setting up of national schools, a fully integrated system with a common curriculum and language, Malay.

Chinese educationists strenuously opposed Razak's plan. During the first few years following the adoption of the plan, Chinese schools were hotbeds of protests and student radicalism. These groups appeared at times to hold the government and the nation hostage. Only the resolve and firm handling by Razak prevented the issue from tearing the young nation apart. Today nearly five decades later, all acknowledge the wisdom of Razak's premise and approach.

Malaysian Schools Today

Education in Malaysia is federal responsibility. It is highly centralized with MOE controlling every detail of the system, from the curriculum and syllabus right down to the choosing, printing, and distributing of textbooks. At one time the ministry also had its own architectural and public works department responsible for designing and building schools. State governments do not partake in education except for some religious schools in PAS-controlled Kelantan and Trengganu. This may change soon, as there are other states like Selangor and Negri Sembilan that are planning to have their own universities.

Malaysia provides for 11 years of free but not compulsory schooling; 6 primary, and 5 secondary. As of 2003 primary schooling would be compulsory. There are preschools for 4-5 years old, mostly run by private entities and as expected, located mainly in urban areas. There are some public ones run by MOE as well as the Ministries of Rural Development and of Unity and Community Development.

The term "free schooling" requires clarification. It means only that there are no tuition fees, but parents still incur other expenses for sports and other extra curricular activities, in addition to books, transportation, uniforms, and lunches. These are substantial. For rural students transportation can be a major cost although now with many schools built in villages, this is becoming less a significant factor.

After preschool, children enter primary school at age six, and after six years move on to five years of secondary schooling. This is the national stream where the medium of instruction is Malay. English is taught only as a subject, and although it is taught at all levels it is not a compulsory subject in the sense that students need not pass it.

To cater for the needs and sensitivities of the vernacular groups, there are the "national-type" schools at the primary level where pupils are taught in their mother tongue (Chinese or Tamil), and Malay only as a subject. After Primary 6 the pupils would spend a year in Malay immersion class (Remove Class) prior to entering the regular "national" stream for their secondary education. The old Chinese secondary schools still exist physically but they now use the national curriculum with Malay as the medium of instruction.

Students sit for standardized national tests at the end of Primary 6; Form 3 (Year 9); and Form 5 (Year 11).

There is a separate parallel Islamic stream, starting at preschool and going all the way up to Year 13 and the university. Here as expected, the emphasis is exclusively on Islamic Studies. These schools claim that they also teach other subjects like mathematics and science; in reality those are being taught at the most elementary level. Their laboratories (only in the most generous way can they be called as such) would be lucky to have a few test tubes–for demonstration purposes only! The Islamic stream has its own matriculation examination where only Islamic Studies subjects are tested.

This education dualism of two separate and mutually exclusive streams operating independently is the dilemma facing Malaysia today, especially when the philosophies and goals of the two streams contradict each other. One is essentially secular, the other religious. One tries to be inclusive and integrative, the other is exclusive and prides on its insularity. The divisive potential of this dualism is finally dawning on policymakers, but because of the powerful symbolism of Islam, the challenge of reconciling the two would be immense. Worse, there has been little or no attempt at doing that.

There are also special education schools, few in numbers, to take care of those with special needs. In addition some of the regular schools also have limited facilities to handle these students.

For Bumiputra students, the Year 6 examination is critical as the top scorers are offered the opportunity to continue their secondary education at residential schools where tuition and boarding are free.

The Form 3 examination is also critical, as students would be streamed to enter the academic, technical, or vocational stream at the upper secondary level. Students chosen for the academic pathway are further streamed into Arts or Science.

Beyond Form 5 the system gets messy. Students either leave to enter the workforce, enter two years of pre-university class (Form 6–Upper and Lower), or seek further training at teachers', technical, and other colleges. As expected, those chosen for Form 6 would be the top scorers.

Within the last two decades Form Six has been emasculated, with students now increasingly choosing the faster path of matriculation classes (*matrikulasi*) run by local universities. *Matrikulasi*, designed specifically for Bumiputras, is popular as it cuts the pre-university years to one. Non-Bumiputras too are shying away from Sixth Form; instead they enroll in the many private colleges and sit for foreign matriculation examinations. Of the 350,000 candidates who sat for the Form V examination in 2001, less than 30,000 continued on into Sixth Form.

Most schools are day schools, with some providing limited hostel facilities for students staying far away from campus. The government also operates a number of fully residential secondary schools both under MOE as well as the Ministry of Entrepreneur Development (through MARA). There is also one under the Defense Ministry (The Royal Military College). The oldest is the all-boys Malay College Kuala Kangsar (MCKK), established in 1905 by the British to educate children of royal families and nobility to prepare them for junior positions in the colonial civil service. Such modest goals notwithstanding, to Malays that school is revered as *Babut Darjat* (Gate to Heaven). Evidently Malays then (and perhaps now too) did not have high aspirations; they were easily satisfied with the crumbs handed to them by the British.

After independence the college began admitting those from the peasant class. This was not an attempt at meritocracy or democratization, rather a reflection of the dwindling numbers from the upper class who could benefit from the college or could fill the classes.

Despite the moniker college, MCKK is merely a residential school. During the 1960s and 70s with the influx of talent beyond the royalty class, the college did produce some luminaries. Its top students routinely matriculated into elite universities. Come the1980s with the general emasculation of Sixth Form, MCKK also dispensed with its Sixth Form. Its graduates now have to spend an additional year or two elsewhere for finishing school prior to entering university; a definite step down in mission.

A comparable institution for girls, The Malay Girls (now Tunku Kurshiah) College (TKC) was set up in 1949. Like their counterpart at MCKK, TKC graduates too now have to go elsewhere for matriculation.

Following the successes of these two schools in the 60s and 70s,the government expanded the program and set up dozens more. This substantially increased the number of Malay undergraduates. One of my recommendations back in the mid 1960s was precisely to expand these residential schools, but to limit them to children of disadvantaged Bumiputras. Today these schools are a mere shadow of their former glory. Few prepare their students for matriculation, the rest like MCKK and TKC goes only to Form 5. The few exceptions include the MARA Junior College in Banting that prepares students for the rigorous International Baccalaureate (IB) program.

The government is committed to expanding these very expensive schools. The Eighth Malaysia Plan calls for building at least a dozen more such schools. These schools cater exclusively for Bumiputras, but in March 2002 the government announced as part of a general plan to introduce meritocracy and greater competition, that 10 percent of the slots be allocated to non-Bumiputras, at least for MARA residential schools. The residential schools emphasize the sciences, all part of the national effort to increase the number of Malays in the sciences.

The figure that is most interesting is that less than 5 percent of Chinese students choose the national schools, and that number is fast declining. The figures for Indians are only slightly higher. Thus national schools are essentially schools for Malays. In contrast, in the last few years there is an increasing tendency for Malays to choose Chinese schools. Additionally many more Malays are opting out of the national stream into religious schools.

The much-vaunted national schools are now losing students from both Malays and non-Malays. The Razak Plan, tinkered once too many, is finally unraveling.

Other relevant statistics to ponder are these. Out of a population of over 23 million, there are about 2.9 million students in primary and 2 million in secondary schools. There are over 6,000 national primary schools and 1,700 secondary ones. The Chinese and Tamil schools number 1,300 and 530 respectively. The pupil to teacher ratio at the primary level is 19:1; at secondary, 17:1. These ratios look impressive but I have yet to see a class with less than 40 pupils. These figures, like others emanating from MOE, are suspect.

Public Universities and Other Post Secondary Institutions

Until recently all universities in Malaysia are public institutions. There has been a proliferation of new universities built to cater for the increased demand brought on by the expansion of the schools.

University of Malaya (UM) was the first. It began in Singapore in1949 with the merging of Raffles College (a liberal arts institution) and the King Edward Medical College. In 1959 it established an autonomous branch in Kuala Lumpur, and in 1962 it severed its link with Singapore, taking with it the original name. The University of Malaya that was in Singapore then became the National University of Singapore. Being a colonial institution UM used English as the medium of instruction. With the introduction of Malay as the sole medium of instruction in Malaysian schools, UM later switched to Malay. As it has a strong tradition and foundation of English, that language is still widely used especially in the professional faculties.

The first university established to use exclusively Malay was the Universiti Kebangsaan Malaysia (UKM–National University of Malaysia). It took its first students in1970, a year following the race riot. The institution represented the pinnacle of achievement of the Malay language nationalists. Up to this day the university remains the hotbed of these extremists.

All public universities except one are under MOE, and it keeps a very close tab on them. The minister appoints not only the governing board but also senior academic officers. No surprise then these institutions ended up as pale clones of one another. The mistakes of one are quickly replicated at other institutions.

The one university not under MOE is the International Islamic University (IIU). It was started and thus partly financed by the International Islamic Secretariat, and set up under the Companies Act, and thus came under the purview of, of all things, the Ministry of Trade and Industry! It uses English as the medium of instruction. This was the only way to circumvent the then national policy of using only Malay in all institutions under MOE. On paper at least IIU is an economic enterprise, not an academic institution. How ingenious! Because of their superior English proficiency, IIU graduates are highly sought after by private industry. Its student body is also the most diverse in Malaysia or even Asia. It has the largest percentage of foreign students, attracting many from all over, including America.

Interestingly there were no howling protests from Malay language nationalists with IIU using English. For one, the Islamic cachet caught them at bay; they did not have the courage to criticize something with an Islamic label even if that institution grossly violated the stated national education policy. In Malaysia, Islam is a much more powerful symbol among Malays, much more than that of language or culture. IIU also proves that when there is the political will, even the most stringent regulations and insurmountable bureaucratic obstacles can easily be bypassed!

Today Malaysia has over a dozen (15 to be exact, and counting) public universities enrolling a total of over 320,000 students (2000 figures). Hardly a day goes by without some officials announcing the planning of yet another campus to keep up with the growing demand. Obviously to them, the setting up of a university is a trivial affair, perhaps akin to building another kampong hut. The results show. Most of these new universities have the academic atmosphere of a junior college, at best. Because officials do not pause and learn from each experience, the same mistakes get repeated and amplified. It reminds me of the wise observation of the legendary American surgeon William Mayo to the effect that some surgeons make the same mistake a hundred times and call that experience. Malaysian officials unabashedly boast of their vast experience setting up new universities. In contrast, California, a state with considerably greater financial and academic resources, managed to build only a couple of new campuses in the last decade. The mediocre quality of these new institutions led former Deputy Prime Minister Musa Hitam, himself a former education minister, to call them *kampong kampus*. Kampong is the Malay word for village, but idiomatically it refers to an insular state of mind.

As part of the general plan to allow greater autonomy, the government embarked on legally incorporating public universities. This began with UM, and thus far it remains the only one to be "corporatized." The premise of the exercise is to allow these institutions to operate more as private entities rather than as government agencies. They would be able to raise funds independently and be given more room to innovate after being let loose from the tight strictures of the civil service code.

Sadly like everything else associated with MOE, the reality is far different. The plan was enmeshed with controversy right from the very beginning. Even though it was ultimately concluded and UM is now a corporation, in reality and ambience, nothing has changed. The key personnel remain the same and senior appointments are still made by the minister with no input from the faculty. The transformation happened only on paper; on the ground nothing changed.

Public universities in Malaysia are essentially, in the words of a foreign academic familiar with the situation, "teaching factories." Their commitment to research is minimal. There are no special funds set aside to support such activities. Worse, those few productive scholars and researchers are not even appreciated. Professors in the sciences are rarely provided with funds for research and laboratory assistants. Senior academic appointments are given more to political types. Perusing the resume of senior university officials, one is hard pressed to discern their significant (or any) academic achievements.

In the last few years the older public universities are beginning to emphasize research and setting up their own graduate schools. Except for Universiti Putra Malaysia (UPM), most of the graduate degrees are in liberal arts and social sciences rather than the natural sciences.

Apart from universities there are numerous other public institutions of higher education like teachers' and technical colleges, polytechnics, and specialized training institutes. Most, like teachers' and technical colleges, come under the purview of MOE, others under Health (nursing schools), Human Resources (various training institutes), Entrepreneur Development (various MARA training centers), Defense (Military College), Agriculture (Cooperative Colleges), and the various state governments.

The entry requirement for these non-degree granting institutions is usually SPM (*Sijil Perseketuan Malaysia*–Malaysian Certificate of Education, given at Year 11). There is minimal transferability between these institutions and universities; no formal mechanism for students to continue on to universities.

Malaysia has not succumbed to the Western habit of puffing up its other tertiary institutions into universities. In America what was once teachers' colleges are now full-fledged universities. Britain too is doing the same thing with its technical colleges and polytechnics. Whether such moves enhance these institutions or merely debase the status of universities is debatable.

Public universities and other tertiary institutions are heavily subsidized. Tuition covers less than 10 percent of their operating costs. For teachers' colleges and nursing schools, students are paid in return for their services on graduation.

In 2000, about 25 percent of the 17-23 age cohorts are in higher education. The government hopes to boost this to 25 percent by 2005, and 40 percent by 2010. By 2020 that figure should exceed 50 percent, and will place the nation in the same league as the developed countries, thus fulfilling the aspirations of Vision 2020.

Private Sector Involvement

Until recently private sector involvement is permitted only at the polar ends of the education spectrum: at preschool and tertiary levels. The government monopolizes education from Years 1 to 11. This was not always the case. In the 1950s it was common to have private English schools to complement the few government ones. But with independence and the aggressiveness of Tun Razak in building many more government schools, these private schools fell by the wayside. Even my own village in Sri Menanti had a private English school started by the parents with no governmental support. The students were either flunkies from or those unable to secure a slot in government schools. The point I wish to highlight here (and I will revisit later when discussing private universities) is that when there are good public institutions, private institutions do not thrive. The corollary is that when private institutions proliferate, that usually means the failure of public institutions.

The government does not presently control preschools but that too is set to change. By 2003 all preschools must follow MOE's guidelines as to the curriculum. There is no shortage of preschools in urban areas provided mostly by private entrepreneurs and "mom and pop" operators. The government does not regulate them either with regards to quality or for compliance with health and safety regulations. This is strictly a situation of buyer beware or more correctly, parents beware.

This prohibition against private sector involvement has one glaring exception–religious schools. Typically these are nothing more than the one-teacher huts or *pondoks* and *madrasahs* that are scattered all over the villages in heavily Malay populated states. Not much is expected of such schools and not much is delivered. In the past such schools were meant primarily to provide religious instructions to students from the regular schools. Today as all national schools are mandated to provide religious classes, these *madrasahs* have become redundant. Nonetheless they are still active to cater for those who believe that the Islam propagated in the secular schools is less than pristine. In light of the 9-11 terrorists' attacks on America, these *madarasahs* are getting greater scrutiny from the government. They preach a particularly suffocating brand of Islam, more along the Taliban variety.

These *madarasahs* and other private religious schools are in technical violation of the education code. The government does not credential their teachers nor approve the curriculum. Despite such glaring breaches the government does not dare close them for fear of being tarred as anti-Islamic–politically a very damaging accusation in a religiously obsessed nation.

There are also subsidized religious schools, *Sekolah Agama Rakyat* (People's Religious Schools). These too preach a narrow brand of Islam. Recently (October 2002) the government, piqued with the alleged anti-government propaganda preached at these schools, suspended their grants.

Apart from the *madrasahs*, there are private international schools to cater for children of expatriates. Malaysians are barred from enrolling except in rare instances, and only with the special dispensation from the minister himself. This stricture against private schools is slowly relaxing; there are now emerging private schools that are extensions of private colleges. There is no proper policy governing these institutions and their permits are being issued on an ad hoc basis.

Malaysia, like East Asian nations, has many private "tuition centers" to give extra help for those able to afford their fees. Thankfully the Malaysian system has not yet degenerated into the brute competitive atmosphere that gives rise to the torture chambers that are the Japanese "cram schools." The government recently introduced a voucher system enabling children of the poor to partake in these extra hours tuition. It would have been smarter to incorporate these sessions into the regular school day.

Moving on to higher education, until recently only public institutions can grant degrees. But with the increased demand the government finally relented and allowed private universities. The situation was made acute following the 1997 Asian economic crisis when the cost of an overseas education became prohibitive with the ringgit devaluation.

Since the passage of the Higher Education Act of 1996, and with it the removal of the prohibition against private universities, there has been a mushrooming of private colleges and universities. No less than 700 at last count, with the overwhelming majority set up within the last few years. This reflects either extraordinary vigor of the private sector or more likely, trivialization of higher education.

Even before the Act was amended, there were private colleges but they were not allowed to grant degrees. They offered instead their own diplomas or prepared their students for foreign (usually British) professional qualifications in accountancy, law, secretarial, and engineering. Many easily circumvented the stricture against degree granting by offering courses for external degrees of British universities. Others had linked academic programs, popularly known as "twinning," where students would complete their first few years in Malaysia and then spend the finishing years at the host university abroad.

Private universities are set up primarily by four entities. First are the established colleges like Taylor and Stamford. With the liberalization of the rules, they are able to expand significantly their academic offerings to include not only twinning programs but also their own degrees, usually in conjunction with foreign universities. Next are the large public corporations like Petronas (the national oil company), Telekom (phone company) and Tenaga Nasional (utility). These companies are only nominally private as they are owned and controlled principally by The Ministry of Finance, Inc. and statutory bodies. In ambiance and character, their universities operate no differently from the public ones. The overwhelming majority of their students are Bumiputras, just like the public universities. The third entity comprises institutions sponsored or owned by the governing political parties. The Malaysian Chinese Association (MCA) has Universiti Tunku Abdual Rahman (UTAR), and the Malaysian Indian Congress (MIC) has TAFE College and the Asian Institute of Medical Science. The fourth group consists of branch campuses of established foreign universities like Monash and the University of Nottingham.

In 2002 there are 16 private universities with an enrollment of nearly 25,000, including four branches of major foreign universities with fewer than 2,500 students total. As can be seen by the average number of students per campus, these institutions are still very much work in progress.

These private institutions use English as their medium of instruction (except for the few operated by Bumiputras that use Malay). Thus their graduates enjoy a premium in the marketplace. Their tuition and other fees are, as expected, considerably higher. While tuition at public universities runs at about RM1,400 per year, the private ones charge in excess of RM20,000. Despite that they are still very popular simply because expensive as they are, they are still cheap as compared to going abroad.

Many of the private universities including the local branch of reputable foreign institutions have a long way to go before they can be regarded as anything close to a traditional campus with dormitories, athletic facilities, and cultural amenities. The University of Nottingham for example, is located in a shopping complex, although it is planning a brand new traditional campus outside of Kuala Lumpur. Universities like Uniten that are associated with large government-owned corporations have traditional campuses.

Some of the private universities also offer graduate degrees. Like the public institutions, the disciplines offered are mostly in the soft sciences and management. The one exception is MUST (Malaysian University of Science and Technology) set up in conjunction with Boston's MIT. This arrangement was a short circuit attempt to ride on MIT's prestige, but in matters academic, close association means nothing. MUST will have to develop its own reputation. Thus far the practical effect of the association has simply been for MUST to pay exorbitant consulting fees to MIT. Unlike other universities in Malaysia, MUST is exclusively a graduate school.

There is one other institution that is exclusively a graduate school, The International Institute of Islamic Thought and Civilization (ISTAC), started by Syed Naquib Al-Attas and sponsored by the International Islamic Secretariat. It boasts an impressive faculty of PhDs from leading Western universities like Princeton and McGill. Its enrolment of 55 doctoral and 66 masters' students easily makes it the largest graduate academic unit in the country. Though ISTAC gets rave reviews from Islamic scholars, a number of its features disturb me. First is its physical location, away from other academic institutions. Its scholars and students thus do not get to mix with those from other disciplines, a situation that can easily lead to both social and intellectual isolation. Second, it accepts only Muslims as students and staff. ISTAC has the ambience of a monastery rather than an academic institution. It perpetuates the intellectual and social insularity typical of many present-day Islamic institutions.

There are other private specialized training institutions like the nursing school run by a private hospital in association with an Australian institution, as well as numerous technical institutes. Their aggregate contributions are still minimal.

There are still many teething problems with private sector involvement in education. The government has yet to unleash the maximal potential of this sector to contribute to the training of its citizens.

My next chapter will review the weaknesses and strengths of the current system.

4

Deficiencies Of The System

Were Malaysians to be polled today on whether their education system serves the nation well, the overwhelming answer would be a resounding, "No!"

This is not an arrogant presumption on my part, rather the evidences, both anecdotal and statistical, are glaring. Whereas before the deficiencies were noticed only by parents, teachers, and those closely involved, today they are obvious and have reached the top leadership. The problems can no longer be ignored as they are adversely impacting the nation's competitiveness and threatening to derail the nation's ambitious Vision 2020 aspirations. Willing or not, the leaders have to confront them. Everyday conversations as well as the daily headlines attest to the angst felt by all.

As of late 2002 these concerns have been expressed in a series of reform proposals. Nothing concrete has been done or implemented. In the colloquial, it is all talk.

As a parent I became aware of the shortcomings of the system way back in the late 1970s when my oldest child was about to enter school in Johor Baru. I had enrolled her at a private preschool and could not help but notice the difference in her attitude towards school as compared to that of the neighbor's daughter. Whereas my daughter was keen and eager every morning to put on her uniform and knapsack raring to go, the neighbor's child was screaming and had to be literally dragged into the car. This prompted me to investigate the school where my neighbor's daughter was attending and where mine would be going the following year.

I was not impressed, to put it mildly. Hot, noisy, and overcrowded classrooms; playground with uncut grass blasted by the blistering sun, as the principal had earlier cut down the shade-giving trees for reasons only he knew best. There were nearly 50 pupils in the classroom, as compared to 18 in my daughter's preschool class. As the school was on the main bus line, the diesel fumes were nauseating. The children in turn were uncomfortable and listless, their teachers haggard. The last hour of the day was completely wasted with the noise and hassle outside of pupils coming in for the afternoon session.

I shuddered to think what my daughter would have to endure. No wonder the neighbor's girl was screaming every morning. She was trying to say something important, but nobody was listening.

In conversations with fellow parents of my daughter's classmates, to a person they have all decided to send their children to schools in Singapore. They were already discussing car pool arrangements. This was in 1978. The trickle of carloads then is today a steady stream of family cars and *bas sekolah* (school buses).

A year earlier at the opposite end of the scale, I had an equally jarring experience teaching medical students from UKM. I related this in my first book *The Malay Dilemma Revisited.* The university was an all-Malay language institution, but there were no textbooks. As a result the lecturers were haphazardly translating as they went along, making their lectures sound like Pidgin English. I did not see the wisdom of such an approach; it would simply confuse the students. So I decided to lecture in English.

It was slow and tough in the beginning, but gradually the students caught on. What was most gratifying was their increasing confidence as their English improved. This transferred to their ward performances; they were much more confident and eager to participate in the clinical discussions. By the end of the year I could not tell them apart from the students I had from UM where English was used.

Looking back, this should not have been a surprise. These students had been exposed to English throughout their school years. It was just that everyone–teachers, lecturers, and leaders–had not impressed upon them the value and importance of knowing a second language well. Somehow they had been brainwashed into thinking that English fluency is tantamount to being colonized.

Actually my misgivings of our education system began much earlier. In 1963 I was a temporary science teacher at a Malay secondary school. The first class was started six years earlier, so it was not something new or novel. After all those years I would have expected that they would have ironed out the problems with textbooks and terminologies. Yet there I was, struggling with inadequate and technically poor textbooks. As if that was not bad enough, early in August and a month prior to my leaving, my principal called me in and asked me to speed up my teaching and finish the year's syllabus. He informed me that there was no replacement for me for at least the next few years as no science teachers were being trained. Those poor Malay students would be stranded.

Imagine starting an important program without careful planning. I felt terrible for those young minds that were being sacrificed not just at that one school but also throughout the nation. There must have been thousands.

Those in authority knew then that they did not have the system ready. Why did they aggressively push it? Why didn't they start small or with some pilot projects, iron out the problems, and then once running smoothly, expand the system? Did they think that those precious young minds were expendable, so much cannon fodder in the politicians' battle for supremacy of the Malay language? What was most disgusting was that while these leaders were exhorting parents to send their children to these new schools, the ministers and top politicians were sneakily sending their own children into English schools. Some including Minister of Education Tun Razak was sending theirs to Britain. These leaders expected the best for their children. Malay schools were good enough for children of the rest of us. Such hypocrisy!

Today I still see some of those students. A few are successful because they had the initiative to learn English on their own and thus enhanced their employability. The rest are stuck in the village, their education system had failed them. They have every right to be angry.

I have one other episode to relate on my experience teaching medical students. During my first few lectures my students were all very quiet. Tried as I would, I could not ignite any spark. So one day I spent the first fifteen minutes of my lecture telling them the right material, but then in the second fifteen I went ahead and purposely contradicted what I had said earlier. Of course I saw many perplexed faces, but I pretended as if nothing had happened. Then as was my practice, I paused and asked them if they had any questions, and waited patiently. As usual, there was dead silence; only glum confused looks. Finally one brave soul put her hands up and said I had uttered something different in the early part of my lecture. I feigned surprise and asked which part I had contradicted, and she rightly pointed it out. Scratching my head while pretending serious contemplation, I admitted that I had indeed made a mistake and thanked her profusely for bringing it to my attention. I complimented her for saving the class and me. She beamed. Soon there were other brave souls eagerly pointing out my errors. I thanked each one of them, and concocted some lame excuse for my errors.

At last the ice was broken. The obstructing iceberg began to break and the class discussions began to flow. I had disabused these students that professors are not infallible and all knowing, and that they are quite capable of, and indeed frequently do, utter something erroneous if not downright stupid. Earlier I had done the same trick with my house officers in a seminar, and that too worked wonderfully. As a result my students and house officers soon became a lively bunch. They did not hesitate in challenging me, and I enjoyed the banter immensely. For one it kept everybody awake, for another it gave them a chance to practice their spoken English.

All went well until a new colleague returned fresh from his postgraduate studies abroad. He should be "red hot." I suggested that he give a seminar to my students and medical officers, and he readily agreed. On the appointed day I warmly introduced him and then as was my custom, left him to carry on.

Following the seminar my students and junior doctors joined me on the ward. They all had glum faces. I inquired how the seminar went, and no one was keen to volunteer a response. Finally one sputtered, "He is a strange guy!" It turned out that this lecturer, as was (perhaps still is) typical of local professors, did not take kindly to being asked many questions. Later at lunch that new lecturer pounced into me, and his first comment was how rude and impudent my students and junior doctors were. "No respect for professors and elders!" was how he put it.

More than 25 years later I still get a tickle in relating this incident. The undue reverence students have of their teachers and professors still exists today. This is common in Asia, a reflection of the culture of reverence towards elders generally. Reverence and respect yes; blind obedience and uncritically accepting what is being uttered, no!

On another front, I often get letters from readers who disagree with me, but instead of rebutting my arguments they would challenge my competence or right to put forth such views. When I write about Islam they would argue that since I am not an *ulama*, I should not comment on religious matters. When I write on Malaysian affairs, their immediate rebuttal seems to be that since I live abroad, my views are no longer valid. Not once do they consider the merits of my arguments. Worse, they would say that some professors or *ulama* somewhere with better qualifications have said something different, and since they are professors ipso facto, their views must automatically be *sahih* (correct). These readers suspend their critical judgment, and spend more time evaluating the credentials of the writer than on the merits of the arguments. I am not surprised that Malaysian students have these views as their professors too exhibit similar insularity.

Such anecdotes and incidents, hilarious as they are, do not indict the system. For that I need more solid empirical evidences. I will do this by systemically dissecting the system and critiquing each segment.

The P-13 Years

I will examine the system from three perspectives: access, equity, and quality. Stated differently, how easy it is for citizens to get an education; do all have the same opportunity; and lastly, the overall standard and quality. Malaysia has done reasonably well with the first, moderately successful with the second, and poorly with the third.

Although Malaysia has near universal primary education, with participation rate in excess of 94 percent, at the preschool the rate is much lower (64 percent). At this level much work remains to be done, especially in rural areas.

Of the pupils who entered Primary 1 in 1995, about 3.1 percent dropped out by Primary 6. And of the students entering Form One that same year, about 20 percent did not complete their Form Five. The government estimates that the participation rate at the secondary level is 85 percent. This is overly optimistic. If every student in the age group had enrolled in Form 1, the participation rate would have been only about 80 percent, but since the participation rate at the primary level is only 94 percent, the participation rate for the secondary level should be even lower, in the low 70s by my estimation. Nonetheless this is a marked improvement over the 1990 figure of 52 percent.

The difficulties I have in checking government figures is that they simply do not add up. I do not believe that these officials are purposely misleading the public rather they do not understand the meaning and relationship of these figures to one another. They do not crosscheck one set of figures against others for reliability and accuracy.

These are national averages; the rates for rural and estate schools are much worse. In one rural primary school the dropout rate was in excess of 20 percent, that is, one in five students did not complete their schooling at the primary level. The figures for rural secondary schools are also appalling. The government does not release this subset of figures (perhaps it does not have them) but one can get a sense of this by visiting rural areas on any school day. There are kids loitering all over. When I was vacationing in east coast Malaysia recently, the one jarring sight was seeing so many school-age boys working at major resorts doing odd jobs. They cannot do much more as few could speak English. If you ask them why they quit school, invariably their answer is, "It's boring!" One fisherman who had his son helping him said the he could teach his son better by having the boy work with him than being at school. Before you dismiss the fisherman's attitude, you should first visit the local school.

I was donating some books to my village school. The gift was very modest nonetheless I was taken aback by how genuinely pleased and appreciative the headmaster and teachers were. When I checked their library I understood why. Their books were old and in poor shape. They had no recent acquisitions, as there was no funding. The laboratories too were equally pathetic. There were very few test tubes, and experiments were often demonstrated rather than done by students because the teachers had to conserve those precious test tubes. Thus all the joys of experimenting–the very essence of science–were taken away. No wonder these pupils did not enjoy the subject. My village is on the west coast, much more developed than those in the east coast. Imagine the condition at a comparable school in Ulu Kelantan.

This brings to my second point of equity. Contrary to most people's understanding, equity does not mean treating everybody the same or giving every school the same amount of funds or delivering the same package of services. The greatest inequity, as the great America jurist Felix Frankfurter observed, is to treat the unequal equally. Giving the same amount of funds and services for a school in Ulu Kelantan as that in Ukay Heights may seem as if we would be treating the two equally, in reality we would not. That Ukay Heights' school would be able to supplement its programs with generous contributions from affluent parents. Further, those pupils would get much intellectual and educational support at home. There would also be a high level of intellectual stimulation in the community, with good libraries and other amenities. Rural schools on the other hand, have students who would not have regular breakfast and whose parents would not have high levels of educational attainment or aspirations. Further, that school in Ulu Kelantan would less likely to attract capable and talented teachers. Thus to treat both schools equally, we would have to give more to the rural school to adequately compensate for its many disadvantages. We also would have to pay its teachers more to attract them and to offset the less-than-alluring lifestyle. Its library too would have to be doubly well endowed to make up for the lack of intellectual stimulation at home and in the community.

The greatest inequity is the urban and rural divide. By whatever measure we choose, the divide is obvious and widening, from absenteeism and dropout rates to performances at national examinations. Unfortunately this divide also parallels racial lines, with rural schools having mostly Malay pupils. Thus the poisonous atmosphere of racism is unnecessarily injected into the discussion of rural and urban schools. The equally dismal performance of small estate schools attended by Tamil pupils is a ready rebuttal to that race argument.

A large part of my reform addresses the issue of how to improve rural schools so they would be *better* than urban ones. They have to be in order to compensate for their disadvantaged environment.

The third issue, quality, is most important. I have the vantage point of having my children schooled in America and thus can readily compare their experience with that of their cousins in Malaysia. Jarring differences emerged quickly. First is the quality of teachers. All my children's teachers, even in the lower grades, had a degree. My son's grade school teacher even had a master's, but instead of taking an administrative position she returned to her first love—the classroom—and did not suffer any career loss. I disagree that primary level teachers be graduates; my point here is that American teachers are generally better trained. In Malaysia, the path for advancement is through administration, not by remaining in the classroom.

Then there are the textbooks. My children all have attractive and well-designed textbooks, with colorful pictures, thick papers, and large print for ease of reading. And they are free even for children of doctors. The school also provides free bus service.

The mathematics texts have real life problems. In geometry there was an assignment for estimating the height of a flagpole by measuring the angle of the sun and the length of the pole's shadow. Similarly the biology lesson in middle school involved examining the pellets of owl droppings and inferring from that the bird's diet. They went further and were able to reconstruct the skeleton of the rodent the owl had swallowed. All involved direct observation and collection of data and their interpretation, which is what science is all about.

The most striking difference is the curriculum. In America it is flexible, with room for electives. Even though my children were academically oriented nonetheless they all took fine arts and crafts. The requirements for entry into the prestigious University of California system include a year of fine arts or crafts at high school.

Students in America are taught early how to do independent research. In my son's social studies class in high school, he did a report on Afghanistan. He even wrote to its embassy in Washington, DC, to obtain some materials, and discussed by phone with one of its officials. He did such a credible report that five years later when he was in college and the Afghan war broke out, we had to ask him about the background information. He knew more about the recent history of that country than anyone else in the family or even the media commentators.

The school library is also excellent, and this is supplemented by an equally well-stocked public library.

Lest readers think that I am uncritically glorifying the American system, let me cite other opinions. I meet a number of older Malaysians either studying at graduate level or working in America for Malaysian agencies. They usually have their children with them. The uppermost anxiety they have when they finish their tour of duty is how their children will cope with Malaysian schools after they have enjoyed the freedom and free-spirited inquiry in an American classroom. They worry about their children surviving the strict regimentation back in Malaysia. One parent went so far as to leave his son behind to finish his schooling.

These anecdotes give a personal flavor to the assessment, but for a more rigorous and objective take we must look elsewhere.

In 1999 Malaysia took part in the Third International Mathematics and Science Studies (TIMSS). The original studies were done in1995 and assessed students at the Years 4, 8, and 11, but Malaysia did not take part in that. The 1999 studies were a repeat (TIMSS-R), involving only Year 8 students. Malaysia scored somewhere in the middle for both mathematics and science (18 and 22). We are no doubt ahead of the Philippines, Thailand, and Indonesia, but way behind Singapore, South Korea, Japan, or Taiwan.

That study was extensive, generating mountains of data. While others were busy poring over them and trying to discern the weaknesses and strength of their system, in Malaysia no mention was made of that study. My enquiries to the lead official at MOE and some researchers at the universities drew a blank. Malaysia spent considerable resources and efforts in taking part in that study, yet its officials show scant interest in analyzing the results.

Singapore, which scored at or near the top on both surveys, has done a credible job in reviewing its data. Not surprisingly it found that the scores were correlated with the students' socioeconomic status and home educational activities, reaffirming the points I raised earlier. One interesting observation is that 96 percent of Singapore Chinese students scored above the 50th percentile internationally for mathematics, while 83 percent of Malays did the same. For science, the figures are 86 and 61 percent respectively. Note this is a crude and simplistic analysis based on race. There was no attempt to factor in the all-important socioeconomic status. How do Chinese and Malays of the same socio-economic status and comparable parents' educational background fare, for example?

That criticism aside, the Singapore figures reveal something important for Malaysia. That is, Singapore Malays do better both in mathematics and science as compared to their international counterparts, and certainly way ahead of Malays from Malaysia.

Equally remarkable were the responses of the various officials. In America there was hue and cry that triggered massive movements for reform. Meanwhile Singapore's Minister of Education was busy visiting top American schools. When asked that perhaps American officials should visit Singapore instead, he replied modestly that while his students had done well in the tests, he felt that they lacked the more important qualities like independent and critical thinking, innovation, and creativity.

Meanwhile Malaysia's Minister of Education hardly commented on TIMSS. He was not interested in the results or the details; he was busy bragging about Malaysia being a center of educational excellence and far ahead of Zambia.

Amazing the differences in reaction!

Concomitant with the deteriorating quality of education is the deplorable physical facilities. Double sessions are now common and take a severe toll on facilities and personnel. The initial rationale for double sessions was reasonable–to provide education to as many pupils as possible. As these schools are not air-conditioned, the productivity of both students and teachers in the oppressive heat is severely tested. Imagine trying to teach mathematics or English in the hot afternoon! Teachers have a tough time keeping the children awake. When I was in school the headmaster purposely planned the timetable so that subjects requiring intense mental activities like mathematics are taught in the morning. Students are sharpest at that time because of the coolness.

More significantly, studies show that the promised hours of teaching in the afternoon are always interfered with or cut short for a variety of reasons. In one World Bank study, about 20 percent of the instructional hours are lost. Long before the afternoon session begins, the commotion and crowd outside would effectively disturb the last hour of the morning's session. Leaders have made repeated pledges to eliminate double sessions. Thus far those have been nothing more than the typical politician's pre-election promises.

Visit a class in the second session. The first half hour would be wasted, waiting for the children to settle down from the heat, sweat, and noise. The government implicitly recognizes the limitations of afternoon sessions by limiting them to classes that do not have to sit for important national examinations.

The greatest failure of the system impacts two particular groups of students: those who are not academically inclined, and students in the religious stream.

Vocational education is a haphazard affair. There are not enough vocational schools and they offer courses of little relevance. No surprise as ministry bureaucrats who are ignorant of market realities draft the curriculum. For example, while the construction industry is desperately looking for plumbers, plasterers, and electricians, few schools produce them. In the east coast states with their fishing industry, one would expect the schools there to have programs in marine repairs and refrigeration. Not so. And homeowners know the difficulty in getting skilled craftsmen. Often the only training these workers have is simply on the job, and done erratically. Few vocational schools offer woodworking and other useful crafts.

While American schools have Future Farmers of America clubs and active agricultural and horticultural programs, few in Malaysia have comparable curriculum. The school in my town has an active agricultural club that sells flowers at Christmas. Similarly students in the animal husbandry class raise farm animals that are exhibited at county fairs and later auctioned off. I fail to see why rural schools in Malaysia do not have comparable programs. There could be rice or banana planting clubs, raising various varieties of fruits and doing simple experiments on cross pollinating and grafting. Why cannot rural schools have experimental farms and gardens for the students to grow vegetables and raise small animals? In this way if these students do end up staying in their villages, at least they would have enhanced farming skills. More importantly, by teaching such agricultural and vocational subjects, we legitimize those vocations. During British rule, it was quite common for rural Malay schools to teach these skills. But with independence these activities are disparaged, not befitting for a school to partake.

The avenues and opportunities for learning in these vocational subjects are limitless. We should use all the natural resources and attributes available to benefit the students. Besides, there is a lot of science and mathematics that can be fitted into these subjects. In primary school I remember the enchantment of watching and measuring germinating seeds and the metamorphoses of pupa wrapped in banana leaves. A lot of biology can be taught in incubating eggs. For good measure we can throw in some mathematics and statistics too! Those are not demeaning pursuits, in fact the very same research is being done at universities all over.

The important objective in vocational schools should be to relate knowledge with its applications. There is a lot of geometry that can be taught in woodworking. Watch a carpenter build a door frame, and see how he "squares" it by ensuring that the distances between the opposite corners (hypotenuses) are equal. It is wrong to assume that those who are vocationally and mechanically inclined cannot think, rather they think more with their hands. Anyone watching a skilled craftsman or mechanic at work can attest to this.

If we have attractive and meaningful vocational and technical programs to cater for those not academically inclined, we give them an opportunity to shine in their own special areas. The remarkable insight in education is that if students are allowed to succeed in one area, it will open the doors to learning in other areas. Hence the importance of having not only these technical and vocational programs but also such activities as sports, music, and drama in the overall school experience.

Apart from neglecting those not in the academic stream, the system also fails the thousands now in religious schools. The whole philosophy of these schools is misguided. They are not concerned with education rather with indoctrination. These *madrasahs* and religious schools are not so much schools as seminaries. Their obsession is with preparing children for the hereafter, forgetting that these children would first have to live the present life.

The Malaysian model of religious education is patterned after those of backward Muslim countries. There is no Muslim country with superior education system that is worthy of our emulation. The obsession of these religious schools focuses on aping the Arabs rather than propagating the message of Islam. On the one hand Malays have a phobia about being colonized by the West, but they have no compulsion of being mentally and culturally colonized by the Bedouins. Malay students go out of their way to blindly ape the Arabs, never mind that those thick flowing robes and huge turbans are totally inappropriate for tropical Malaysia. Male teachers sport unshaven face and collect multiple wives, as if piety resides in those external manifestations. It is pathetic that of the many sterling qualities of our holy prophet (peace be upon him), these are the only attributes modern Muslims feel compelled to emulate. Pity them! It is the students who suffer from their particularly myopic interpretation of Islam. Students are not taught to think, rather how to memorize and parrot what had been said before.

Students in the religious stream are exclusively Malays, and those who are not academically inclined are also mostly Malays. Thus we have the supreme irony of an education system designed and controlled by and purportedly to help Malays failing to meet the needs of a significant number of them.

Malaysian schools remain dangerously segregated racially. The goal that national schools are for all is but a dream; today they are essentially for Malays, having failed to attract non-Malays. Increasingly

Malays too are abandoning the national stream for the religious one. Apart from their other failures, our schools have also utterly failed in their basic mission of uniting the young. This is not just my opinion, it is also shared by no less than Prime Minister Mahathir.

Our schools are nothing but cookie-cutter versions of one another not only physically but also in their academic offerings. They all use the same textbooks and offer the same subjects. There is little attempt at differentiation. There are no schools that emphasize foreign languages or the performing arts. About the only specialized ones are the science residential schools. I venture that the school bells are also timed to ring at the same time throughout the country.

Teachers are allowed little room to display their initiative and creativity. Every school minute has been planned for or programmed by the bureaucrats. Just follow the script. Headmasters have little power; they do not get to choose the teachers, the ministry does that. When it assigns a science teacher when the school needs an English teacher, well, that is just too bad. That teacher will just have to teach English rather than science. No surprise then that many are unhappy and quit early in their career.

I asked one headmaster his annual budget to run his school and he could not even venture a guess. He had no clue; the teachers were paid directly by ministry, and the books and supplies were shipped from headquarters. The headmaster is merely an administrative functionary, and not surprisingly, the post attracts not superior teachers rather administrative types. They look upon the promotion as an escape from the classroom. Headmasterships are rarely terminal appointments; headmasters are transferred as part of their promotion exercise. When you ask these headmasters their legacy at their former school, they would be dumbfounded. They have none.

Visit any school and chances are the headmaster is away off campus. One study by the teachers' union showed that headmasters spend less than 20 percent their time on campus! At one school, despite my making a prior appointment, I still could not meet the headmaster. On the morning we were supposed to meet, he was off to a district meeting concerning, of all things, rural development. I met him briefly at noon on campus while he was on his way out again to another meeting, this time for an upcoming Qur'an reading contest. He was busy with every-thing except his primary responsibility–running his school.

While the government is supposedly emphasizing the sciences, very few headmasters have that background, which is a curious way to encourage the subject. It is the unstated policy of MOE that only Malays be appointed to senior positions like headmasterships. And since most Malays have degrees in soft subjects like Malay Studies and rarely in the sciences, not surprisingly they do not understand the tech-nical needs of science teachers and therefore rarely support the science program.

The weaknesses of our schools extend from their physical structures and management to the curriculum and teachers. All these elements will have to be reformed.

Residential Schools and *Matrikulasi*

The track record of the system in meeting the needs of the more aca-demically inclined is not much better either. Bright Bumiputra stu-dents are selected to continue their secondary studies at residential schools. These schools are free; in addition students from poor families receive a stipend.

These schools are also very expensive to operate with the bulk of the funds going merely to feed and house the students. With such diver-sion of resources, little is left for academic activities. Thus even though these schools get the best students, their aggregate academic perfor-mance is wanting.

In the past students who passed the special entrance examination would continue right away into the two-year pre-university (Sixth Form) in January. They had 24 months of continuous academic study that prepared them well for university. Stories abound of students who failed Sixth Form and were not accepted to local universities only to shine when they went abroad, a reflection of the rigor of the program. Unfortunately nobody thought of expanding the program and before long it became a chokehold on the supply of undergraduates, especially Bumiputras.

In an effort to boost the number of Bumiputra undergraduates, UM embarked on an imaginative outreach program where selected students would be brought on campus after completing their Form 5. The argument was that if they were exposed early to the campus environment and taught by qualified personnel, they would do well. The experiment was a resounding success and these students indeed did indeed excel. *Matrikulasi* was designed specifically for Bumiputras as few of them successfully came through Sixth Form. Most schools where they attended were in small towns and did not have Sixth Form. Thus the overall quality of teaching suffered, with the students poorly prepared for the entrance examination. Further, undoubtedly related, Bumiputra students who did manage to enter Sixth Form did not perform well, reflecting the poor teaching of science and mathematics at the lower levels. *Matrikulasi* was thus to augment and complement Sixth Form. The success of *matrikulasi* emboldened the government to expand it. Today *matrikulasi* has effectively supplanted Sixth Form.

I have not visited the *matrikulasi* run directly by the universities. Looking at the facilities and qualifications of the instructors (many with doctoral degrees), I have no doubt that these programs are far superior to the old Sixth Form. But it is the freestanding programs and those "franchised" to private institutions that concern me. I have visited some of them, talked to the instructors, and examined the students' handbooks. Their courses are definitely watered down. This is not a surprise. For one, *matrikulasi* runs for one year (actually two semesters, which are shorter than one school year) while Sixth Form is two full *school* years. In terms of actual instructional hours, *matrikulasi* is less than half of Sixth Form. Additionally Sixth Form begins immediately in January while *matrikulasi* starts typically in June. During that long hiatus considerable attrition of knowledge occurs. The first few weeks or even months of *matrikulasi* involve reviewing old material.

The most damning criticism of *matrikulasi* is that despite having been in place for over three decades, there is little research comparing its efficacy to that of Sixth Form or other matriculating examinations. One study done by UUM's researchers showed that students who went through Sixth Form performed better than those from *matrikulasi*. This was presented at an academic forum and was widely reported in the national press under the banner, "Malay students perform poorly as compared to non-Malays." The basis for that conclusion was that students in Sixth Form were non-Malays while *matrikulasi*, Malays. Looking at the data, an equally valid conclusion would be that *matrikulasi* prepares students poorly for university and that race has nothing to do with the results. Indeed had the researchers drawn this conclusion, the next logical question to ask is, "Why?" One clue would be to look at the number of instructional hours.

I am appalled that such half-baked studies, poorly designed, and the data erroneously interpreted were even accepted for presentation and then widely and uncritically reported in the media. Even more surprising was that no professional educators challenged the obviously silly findings. I e-mailed the coauthors of the paper with my criticism; none bothered to reply.

This lack of solid research is even more revealing when one considers that many of the programs are being run by the universities. This lack of intellectual curiosity on the part of the academic community is truly shocking.

A more damning criticism of both residential schools and *matrikulasi* is the insularity and homogeneity of their students, thus diminishing the overall quality of the education itself. These students compete in a limited environment.

These residential schools take away bright students from regular schools, depleting the overall caliber of those remaining. This demoralizes the teachers, as there is no nucleus or core of bright students to stimulate and motivate the class. When I visit rural schools, the frequent excuse I get from the teachers is that their bright students have been siphoned off to residential schools.

Our schools have not served the non-academically inclined as well as those aspiring for universities. Who exactly have they served?

The Universities

The recent widely publicized plight of over 40,000 graduates unable to find jobs is emblematic of the failure of Malaysian higher education. The overwhelming majority (over 94 percent) were Malay graduates of local institutions.

The public was stunned by the revelation, the sudden realization that the blight had infected the cream. The whole edifice might crumble. There was no shortage of commentaries and finger pointing, with some blaming the students for being choosy, and others the universities for being out of touch with reality.

In all those discussions the basic question was not asked, let alone answered. Were these graduates unemployed or simply unemployable? With the former, the answer would rest with the greater economy; with the latter it would be with the education system.

It is hard to imagine with the current near full employment and with the country having to import thousands of workers that these graduates would have difficulty finding jobs. It is my contention that the universities have done a lousy job to ensure that their products are employable.

Mustapa Mohamad, chairman of the National Economic Action Council, identified this as essentially a Bumiputra problem. Again, this reflects the tendency of officials to view problems through the prism of race; it permeates their thinking. As graduates of local public universities are mostly Malays, the poor Malay race again gets blamed when in actuality it is the universities' fault in doing a lousy job of preparing their graduates for the realities of the marketplace.

Sadly, the government again reverted to pat pattern in solving the problem, by pouring more money on these graduates. The results will be no better than other similar programs to help Bumiputras, and will be just as expensive and wasteful. The government has done enough already by giving them the opportunity to get a university education. If they cannot go on their own after that, then there is no hope that they ever will. Spending more money only heightens their already inflated sense of entitlement and ingrains their dependency mentality. These graduates are getting RM500 monthly allowance; a hawker can easily earn much more. If an illegal and illiterate Bangladesh immigrant can earn a living in Malaysia, I see no reason why these graduates could not do the same. It is not ordained that our graduates cannot be construction workers, taxi drivers, farmers, or hawkers. Indeed with their university education they would become better and more productive at those jobs.

The government's various attachment schemes for graduates are nothing more than camouflaged public works programs. They are meant more to provide an income to the graduates rather than equipping them with the necessary salable skills. I would scrap the entire program and use the funds to retrain them with marketable skills. Enhance their English fluency, mathematical competency, and IT training, and they will find ready employers.

The only avenue of employment for arts graduates from local universities is with the government. They have no useable skills needed in the private sector. Blame our pubic universities for this. Had our universities followed the example of leading American colleges and made a year of English, mathematics, and laboratory science mandatory, then our graduates would have greater flexibility not only in the marketplace but also in their further studies. In America, because of its broad-based liberal education, it is quite common for a religious studies or history major to go into medical, law or business school, or to change their field of study at the graduate level.

There have been tepid attempts at broadening the undergraduate program. Deputy Prime Minister Badawi suggested that Islamic Studies students take one elective outside their major. UUM students now have to take at least three courses conducted entirely in English. This will go a long way to stem the decline of English fluency of its graduates. To date this sensible idea has not spilled over to the other campuses.

Despite the glut of jobless graduates, the government continues to provide scholarships and loans for students to pursue the liberal arts. It should be sending a very strong signal to would-be undergraduates by sharply curtailing financial support for those pursuing these unneeded disciplines. Additionally, again through the funding mechanism, I would send the appropriate message to the universities to cut their intake for such disciplines. These academics are being irresponsible in churning out products that are not needed in the marketplace.

Concomitant with the reduction in intake for the arts stream, the government should also broaden the curriculum by making these students take English, science, and mathematics to enhance their employability.

There is a sinister but hidden aspect to the government's help for these jobless graduates. There is no incentive for would-be undergraduates to choose carefully their majors, as no matter what, the government would be there to bail them out in the end.

The problem with our public universities is that with Malay being the medium of instruction, students have low English proficiency. There are limited number of books and reference materials in Malay, meaning that the students' intellectual horizon is necessarily limited. Their reading list is extremely short, and students rarely venture beyond the few prescribed texts.

The typical Third World professor is also aloof, all knowing, and imperious, a demeanor not likely to encourage or tolerate vigorous class discussions or intellectual debates. Consequently Malaysian students are passive listeners; their classroom involvement is merely to show up. A senior history professor from UM lamented that his students were reduced to being silent stenographers dutifully transcribing everything he uttered, and regurgitating them at examination time. The professor was as much at fault. If he was worried about his students becoming stenographers, why, simply publish and distribute his lecture notes. To encourage class discussion, try assigned seating and have class participation factored in the final grades. Or he could use some of my tricks mentioned earlier in teaching medical students where I simply uttered something ridiculous and see the students' reactions. Similarly he could have "open book" examinations and design his questions to minimize rote memory and mindless regurgitation.

What goes on in the lecture halls and seminar rooms on Malaysian campuses is essentially a one-way communication, a monologue from the lecturer. Students are treated simply as empty dustbins to be filled with data and dogma rather than curious minds to be stimulated. Students in turn treat everything emanating from the professor as gospel truth.

While student evaluation of professors is standard on American campuses, it is unthinkable at a Malaysian university. While Malaysian academics endlessly exhort their students to be original and creative, these professors hardly contribute anything creative or original.

This lifelessness did not develop overnight. The government is directly responsible and indeed actively promotes this sorry state of affair. Such an atmosphere is not conducive for excellence or innovation.

If one were to look for the turning point that led to the current state of mediocrity, it would be the introduction of the Universities and Colleges Act of 1971. The original intent of the Act was benign enough, to prevent a recurrence of the nightmare of the race riot of 1969. But the Act has been "strengthened," that is, made more repressive with subsequent amendments, in particular the one in 1975. The Act not only did away with what little academic freedom the professors and universities had, but more menacingly created a palpable atmosphere of repression on campus. The university was put on a very tight leash; those who dared stray would be jerked right back, or worse.

Those who dare express independent viewpoints, meaning not what the government or ruling party wants to hear, would suffer the consequences, and many have. A professor of sociology active in the opposition party had his teaching contract not renewed; actually he was fired, just in case the message did not register with his colleagues. Justice finally prevailed with the professor winning his case in court. The verdict itself was a surprise. No, he was not reinstated, merely awarded monetary damages.

Academics quickly learn that if you want to progress you have to ingratiate yourself if not overtly suck up to the powerful. No surprise then that the universities have failed the nation; they are led by the meek and the toady rather than the brilliant and innovative.

Malaysian universities are not autonomous; they are divisions within MOE. Faculty members are treated (and they in turn behave) more as civil servants rather than as scholars and scientists. Discussions in the faculty club often revolve around one's position on the salary scheme rather than papers published or patents applied. Senior academic positions are chosen not by the university community rather appointed by the minister. Often they are civil servants seconded from the Tourism Ministry while on their way to be undersecretary at the Sports Ministry.

This civil service milieu is purposely created. And like the civil service, brilliance, creativity, and innovations give way to precedent, seniority, and general orders.

For the past few years the regional publication *Asiaweek* (now defunct) conducted regular surveys of Asian universities. Already in that short space of time we see the steady decline in the ranking of local institutions. In its first survey in 1997, Malaysia' leading and oldest university, UM, was ranked 11th, two years later it slipped to 27th, and in the last survey (2000) it dropped to 47th. Meanwhile UKM made the list once at the very beginning and then dropped out of sight. Only

UPM improved its standing from 69th in 1999 to 52nd in 2000. One may argue with the criteria used, but there is no mistaking the trend. Of course the typical ministerial response is, well, we are still ahead of Papua New Guinea!

Those attempting reform must be prepared to address not only the institutional issues but equally important, the cultural impediments to change. Before presenting my proposals, I will examine the system of education of a few select countries that is worthy of Malaysia to note. This would be followed by a chapter reviewing attempts at reforming the system, in particular the two current proposals, MOE's *Education Development 2001-2010*, and the more recent report of the National Brains Trust.

5

A Look At Other Models

In this chapter I will examine the education system of three countries: United States, Canada, and Germany. American universities are the best; many countries are now adopting its system of broadbased liberal education with emphasis on languages, the sciences, and mathematics. Canada's biculturalism and bilingualism are of special relevance to Malaysia. For Germany, the superiority of its vocational education is widely acknowledged.

There are many other countries with superior systems of education, but I choose not to include them. Britain is one. Its public schools and rigorous matriculating examination–the GCE Advanced level–are universally highly regarded, recent scandals on markings notwithstanding. Students with A level pass are routinely granted first year college credits at American campuses. I have not included the British system simply because Malaysians are already very familiar with it.

Nor will I discuss except in passing the excellent schools of some Asian countries like Japan, South Korea, and Singapore. Their schools are widely lauded and their students consistently score at the top in international tests. The world may sing praises for their system, but their own students and parents think differently. To them their school is nothing but a relentless and uncompromising system of rote learning, regularly punctuated by grueling examinations. Their young hardly had time to enjoy their childhood as their waking hours are spent cramming for tests after tests. And when they are not doing that they are busy at private tuition or attending "cram schools." Their leaders and educators erroneously equate test scores as the be-all and end-all of education.

A measure of the inadequacy of their system can be gauged by the fact that South Korean parents would do anything to have their young escape the torture that is their school system. Many are sending their young to Canada and America, accompanied by their mothers while the rest of the family are stuck back home, with the father busy working hard to pay for that expensive education abroad. A more recent phenomenon would have pregnant Korean mothers flying to America for delivery so as to obtain an automatic American passport for the baby. After delivery both mother and baby would fly back home. When it is time for high school, that baby—now a young teenager— would be back in America as an American. All these elaborate schemes are designed simply so Korean parents could spare their young from attending the torture system that is their high school. If Korean parents go to such extremes, I do not think their schools are worthy models for Malaysia.

Singapore, despite its excellent schools, has little to offer Malaysia. Like Japan and South Korea, Singapore does not have problems of cultural and linguistic diversities. Sure it has small minority groups but Singapore does not exactly demonstrate much sensitivity to them. Singapore's treatment of its minorities is not exactly the one that Malaysia should emulate. In terms of size, Singapore's schools would be the equivalent of a midsize American school district. There is not much that Malaysia can learn from Singapore or any of the other two Asian countries.

Singapore does have something going for it. Its schools have high standards of English, science, and mathematics. Its teachers are well paid and highly regarded. Teaching still attracts top talent, a far cry from the situation in Malaysia.

In addition to reviewing the education system of the different countries, I will also review two exemplary programs at opposite ends of the spectrum. First is the International Baccalaureate (IB), widely recognized as a superior matriculating examination, and second, Brazil's *Bolsa Escola* program which deals with problems in the polar opposite–of how to keep children in school.

The American System

America, like Malaysia, is a diverse nation and faces the same problems of integrating her various ethnic groups. Like Malaysia, the educational achievements of its various groups are closely related to ethnicity. Both countries have the same problem of increasing the English proficiency of a large segment of its student population who are not native English speakers.

Even though American students do not score at the top in TIMSS, nonetheless they turn out to be very productive, innovative, and creative. Many attribute the remarkable strength and buoyancy of the American economy to its highly talented workers. Ministers of Education from Singapore to Hungary trot to America to learn the secrets of its system.

The prominent feature of the American system is its decentralization. Up until recently there was no equivalent of a federal Ministry of Education. Education is state responsibility, and that authority is further delegated to the local districts with elected trustees. Teachers in each district are paid by and are accountable to the local school board, not the state superintendent or the federal Secretary of Education in Washington, DC.

These districts vary in size from a few hundred students to one with literally millions as in Los Angeles and New York. They are also incredibly diverse. A school in downtown Los Angeles can have pupils speaking a hundred different languages! And that school will be very different from the one in Minnesota or even close by in affluent Santa Monica. The differences between a school in Ulu Kelantan and Ukay Heights are nothing compared to the varieties in America. Despite such diversity the system is remarkably successful in integrating and acculturating the students into the American mainstream, a point that should interest Malaysians.

Because of the tremendous diversity it is difficult to describe the typical American system. For purposes of discussion, I will use California as an example. Even within a single state there are considerable variations.

The American system consists of Kindergarten to Year 12 (K-12). Children enter at age 5. Some districts offer preschool beginning as early as age 3 or 4, especially in poorer areas. After kindergarten they move on to six years of elementary school, followed by two years of middle school and four years of high school. American schools are all single session, typically ending in mid afternoon; preschools are half days.

In elementary school the pupils learn to read and write, do basic arithmetic, and explore the world around them. Creative arts like singing and drawing are emphasized. Pupils stay with the same teacher, except for subjects like music and special education. Some schools are experimenting with having the same teacher for the entire six years, to maintain continuity. You can be certain that the teachers know their students very well at such schools.

In middle school the variety of subjects offered broadens, and students move from class to class, each taught by a different teacher. Students take a core curriculum of English, science, mathematics, and social studies. The rest of the school day is taken up by electives, which include such subjects as woodworking and creative arts. There may be a home teacher who will teach two or three of the core subjects in the homeroom. He or she also serves as a center point for the students, a stabilizing focus for them. Some schools have the same home teacher for both years.

High school is similar in that students move from class to class, with different teachers for the various subjects. Apart from the core curriculum, the students again have electives to meet their special needs and interests. Students also have to take a foreign language, although in many districts that exposure could begin earlier in middle or even elementary school.

Most American high schools are the typical large comprehensive variety offering wide range of subjects from agriculture and woodworking to auto shop and welding, as well as highly academic subjects like calculus, economics, and statistics. The more academic schools offer Advanced Placement (AP) classes, the equivalent of first year college courses.

The student's interests and future goals dictate the courses chosen, with guidance from the counselors. Those aspiring for highly selective colleges take four years of English, science, mathematics, and a foreign language, plus suitable electives in the social studies and fine arts. The transcripts would be greatly enhanced by taking these courses right up to the AP level. Those planning to enter the workforce upon graduation or whose academic goals are less lofty, would still have to take these core subjects except that instead of taking calculus for example, they would opt for "consumer math;" and instead of physics, a less demanding physical science.

The present large comprehensive schools were started in the 1950s and early 60s through the influence of James B. Conant, the former president of Harvard. Prior to that American schools were akin to cottage industries–small and scattered, and thought to be inefficient. The impetus for change was precipitated by the Soviet launching of the Sputnik satellite in 1957. That shocked Americans into realizing how far behind they were in science and mathematics.

Merging these small schools into a single large campus was thought to be the most efficient (meaning, cheapest) way to educate as many students as possible. With a sufficiently large pool of students the number of subjects offered could be expanded. It was also a reflection of the era when assembly line and "scientific" production championed by the likes of Charles Taylor were the rage. Implicit in that model is the lumping of all students together with no streaming. The assumption is that students learn from each other, the slower ones from their brighter classmates. The system works up to a point. To Conant, these comprehensive public schools also serve as a melting pot not only racially but also socially.

Increasingly today these giant educational factories are exacting their toll. Students feel alienated, disciplinary problems abound, and crowd control becomes a major issue. On many campuses there are metal detectors and armed policemen. And an irony that cannot be dismissed, these policemen earn more than the teachers! Columbine High School, Colorado, the scene of the deadly shootout a few years ago, is typical of such campuses with over 3,000 students.

This lack of streaming is more apparent than real. Many districts now have magnet schools and special GATE (gifted and talented) programs. Further, parents do their own streaming. Increasingly when people buy homes, the first question asked is, "How is the neighborhood school?" The high school at Palo Alto, California, regularly sends its top students to elite universities; meanwhile a stone's throw away across the freeway in East Palo Alto, the story is very different.

The preceding describes the public system. America also has vigorous and extensive private schools run by churches and other organizations. For the most part they are academically oriented "prep" schools, meaning they "prepare" students for top colleges. Some like Groton and Exeter count among their graduates, luminaries in government, business, and the professions. They are also increasingly attracting many foreign students.

There are many recent attempts at reforming the schools, but Conant's comprehensive schools remain the staple to this day. In 1983 a committee chaired by David Gardner, later to become president of the prestigious University of California System, produced its landmark report, *A Nation At Risk. The Imperative for Educational Reform*, in which it laments the declining academic rigor of American high schools that fill their curriculum with soft subjects like consumer math and driver ed. "The educational foundations of our society," the report notes, "are presently being eroded by a rising tide of mediocrity that threatens our very future as a nation and a people."

Gardner's report was commissioned in response to the challenge coming from what was then widely accepted as the rising East, in particular Japan. Gardner's committee lacked enforcing power; it was merely advisory. As a result nothing much happened.

Since then there have been many other reform movements. Though they have not caught on nationally, nonetheless in their aggregate, they produce far greater changes. These include the voucher system, charter schools, and the movement of returning to the basics, in particular the Coalition of Essential Schools (CES). Vouchers are meant to empower poor children trapped in lousy school districts. With vouchers these students would be free to enroll in any school, public or private. Presently the system works well in some districts (Milwaukee) where the vouchers are restricted to poor families. Elsewhere the voucher system is entangled in protracted lawsuits. California voters rejected the system because they believed it would simply subsidize those currently enrolled in private schools. The California initiative would more likely be palatable if it had been restricted to the poor, as in Milwaukee. My concern with unrestricted vouchers is that they would perpetuate if not promote self-segregation, with Jewish parents sending their children to Jewish schools, Arab parents to Arabic schools, Serbians to Serb's. A generation hence and America would be like the Middle East and the Balkans.

CES, unlike the other reform movements, was started by educators and teachers rather than citizen activists or politicians. Theodore Sizer, a longtime teacher and former headmaster of Phillips Academy, a prestigious New England prep school, started the movement to revamp the way schools teach. Instead of the present factory and assembly-like module system, students would be divided into groups and taught by a team of teachers. The idea is to dismantle the artificial boundaries separating the different academic disciplines and have the teachers communicate with each other more. Thus instead of one teacher teaching chemistry and being oblivious of what the others are doing in physics or history, with team teaching every teacher is made aware of each other's lesson plans, and their teaching would be interrelated and integrated. A major feature of CES is that for graduation, students must present an exhibition on a topic of their choice for each subject. This is comparable to the student's portfolio in a fine arts academy.

I am familiar with CES as one of my sons attended such a school and I was on the governing board. One of his exhibitions (for chemistry) was on the internal combustion engine in history, which neatly combined elements of mathematics (laws of thermodynamics), history, and social science in addition to chemistry. The unique feature of CES is that it works within the system; there is no need for special legislation or increased funding. CES involves rearranging the present elements. To join CES, the teachers would have to petition for it and then agree to the guidelines. Unlike other reforms that are often forced upon the working professionals, CES is teacher-driven, which explains its remarkable success and acceptance.

Many American high schools work closely with nearby colleges so ambitious students could simultaneously take college courses for credits. Bard College goes further with an innovative program of fully integrating the last two years of school with the first two years of college for highly talented and motivated students.

There is no national or standard exit examination in America. Each teacher assesses the students on his or her own terms. The school district lays down the graduation requirements. Students are continuously assessed throughout the school year rather than in one final examination. Even their homework and other assignments are graded and contribute to this final score. The student's Grade Point Average (GPA) represents the yearlong assessment and not a snapshot as one would get with a single Malaysian type end-of-year examination.

There are standardized national tests like the Scholastic Achievement Test (SAT), Achievement Test (AT), and AP. Many universities use both standardized test scores and GPAs in evaluating students.

There is a trend among top-ranked colleges of doing away with SAT. This sentiment has professional backing. The American Psychological Association in its guidelines for test use specifically prohibits basing any consequential judgment about individuals on a single test score. The reason is the significant margin for error. The solution is to use multiple measures, including test scores, GPAs, teachers' recommendations as well as reviewing the portfolio. For admission to select music, drama, and design schools, the student's portfolio is the determining factor.

SAT does serve a purpose; it allows comparisons between schools. It does not say much about the academic rigor (or at least the rigor of its testing) of a school if collectively it's "A" students score poorly at SAT. SAT and similar tests serve to assess the schools as much as the students. For the individual student however, the predictive value of such standardized tests is more problematic. There are few students who excel in class but perform poorly in these "filling-in-the-blanks" tests. Texas and California now accept the top 5 percent of graduates from each school into their elite universities regardless of their SAT scores.

Doing away with standardized tests creates its own problems because of the variability of school quality. The less selective California State University (CSU) System does not require SAT; it relies exclusively on GPAs. Consequently half of its freshmen have to take remedial classes in English and mathematics.

American universities are just as varied. They vary in their requirements for admission and graduation, academic and social ambience, and also most importantly, in academic reputation. The crowd attracted to and accepted by Harvard is very different from those of Podunk State. But what is important is that both institutions serve the nation well.

American universities are either public or private. As education is state responsibility, the federal government does not operate any university except for service academies like West Point and Annapolis. Public universities are mostly state institutions although there are a few operated by municipalities (Pittsburgh and Cincinnati). The private ones are typically set up as not-for-profit bodies (Harvard and Stanford), or by religious organizations (Georgetown and Notre Dame). There are some for profit (proprietary) institutions (University of Phoenix); few are of superior quality. This is worth mentioning because in Malaysia all private colleges and universities are profit-making entities. There is no exemplary model for Malaysia to follow.

In terms of funding, there is little difference between public and private universities as both receive substantial public funds. The private Caltech gets nearly half its revenue from government sources in the form of research grants and consultancy fees, while public UCLA gets only 27 percent of its funding from the state government. This is important for Malaysia to note.

The fees for public institutions are as expected highly subsidized and affordable. The junior colleges are practically free. The fee differential between private and public universities can be as high as ten fold. Students attending private institutions are treated no differently from those attending public ones with regards to government study loans and scholarships.

There is a definite class system in American higher education. This fact is not well appreciated by foreigners especially those from the Third World who think that a degree is a degree. In the marketplace, those parchment papers command different premiums depending on the institution issuing them.

Of the over 3,000 degree-granting institutions, only about 300 (less than 10 percent) can be considered competitive. That is, they do not admit everyone who applies. The rest will admit anyone with a high school diploma, and who can afford the fees. The Carnegie Foundation for the Advancement of Teaching classifies American universities as follows: doctoral universities (offering up to doctoral degrees); Masters' institutions; baccalaureate colleges; junior colleges (offering only Associate degree); and specialized institutions (Julliard School of Music and California Institute of Technology). By this classification, Harvard is lumped together with Idaho State University (ISU). While people at ISU may be flattered by this categorization, consumers (that is, would-be students) are not much helped. Under the old Carnegie classification, Harvard is classified as Research University I (offering more than 50 doctorates per year) and ISU, Research University II.

This class system is best demonstrated in California where the top 12.5 percent of high school students are eligible for the elite University of California (UC) System with its nine campuses, while the top third qualify for the CSU System with its 22 campuses. The junior colleges admit everyone including those over 18 who do not have high school diploma.

An outstanding feature of American undergraduate education is its broad-based liberal curriculum. Regardless of their ultimate career goals, students have to take a year of English, mathematics, laboratory science, foreign language, and the humanities. The first two years (freshman and sophomore) are spent fulfilling these "general ed" requirements. Only in the last two years (junior and senior) do the students concentrate on their majors.

American universities, especially the top ones, also have incredibly diverse student body. This is by design. Harvard has no difficulty filling its slots with Americans, yet it actively seeks bright young students worldwide. It is this diversity that gives American campuses their intellectual spark.

Top American colleges in addition have freshman seminars, where first year students gather in small groups under a professor, with the emphasis on oral communication and class participation. Students also have to enroll in writing classes. At a quality school a student typically writes dozens of term papers in addition to the senior thesis.

It usually takes four years to complete the baccalaureate program, although students who enter with advanced standing and who take summer courses could accelerate their studies. Conversely, students could take a more leisurely pace or skip a year or two. Many, especially the talented, are doing exactly that–for travel, preparing for the Olympics, writing a novel, or even starting a business. Some like Bill Gates and Tiger Woods became so successful that they never returned to complete their degree.

Another innovation at many American universities is the year off campus where students can study at an approved foreign university and have the academic credits transferred back to his home campus.

It is this liberal and flexible education that gives American graduates an edge in the marketplace. It is also the reason why the best and brightest from around the globe compete vigorously to enter the system.

The Canadian System

The Canadian system is similar to the American in being highly decentralized. Education falls under provincial jurisdiction, thus variations between the provinces. While most have K-12, Ontario and British Columbia have K-13. Like America, schools are under the local control of elected trustees. Unlike America, there are two school boards, the Public and Separate (or Catholic). Traditionally the Catholics are mainly French-Canadians; their own school board allows them to maintain their religious, cultural, and linguistic heritage.

The curricular pattern is similar to America. Unlike America, Canadian high schools have common exit examinations ("departmental") that serve as the matriculation qualification. There is no national examination equivalent to the American SAT. Interestingly America too is toying with similar exit examinations but for a different purpose—to ensure minimal competency, not to rank the students.

Most Canadian universities are public, operated by the provinces. Their fees are low and highly subsidized. There are few private universities modeled after the American non-for-profit ones like Simon Fraser and George Williams.

Canadian universities too offer broad based liberal education but generally it is less liberal and broad than the American. Electives are often prescribed, you choose among a given group rather than a free wide choice.

Canada is of particular interest in that it has to deal with two languages and cultures (English and French), and has done so successfully. While in the past there was resistance to learning a second language, today all young Canadians are functionally bilingual. Previously it was considered surrendering or giving in for a French-Canadian to learn English (or an English-Canadian to learn French), an attitude not dissimilar to that held by many Malaysians. Fortunately Canadians are much more enlightened today; now it is an asset to be bilingual.

The main lesson from Canada is how it handles the bilingual and bicultural issue, in particular how it successfully integrates the two groups despite having dual school systems. The difference between the Public and Catholic systems is much greater than that of national and religious schools in Malaysia. With the former there are differences of religion and ethnicity (Protestant English and Catholic French), while in Malaysia the clientele of the dual system share the same race and religion (Malay-Muslims). Despite the lesser difference Malaysia still has difficulty integrating the religious with the national stream. In Canada both streams contribute their share of educating future citizens. In marked contrast, religious schools in Malaysia are fast turning into seminaries; they do not contribute to the education of the nation's future professionals and executives.

Although both Public and Catholic schools have different curriculum, nonetheless there is a core of commonality such that students could switch from one to the other without much disruption. Further, all fields of studies in higher education are available for graduates from both streams. In comparison, products of Malaysian religious schools could continue their higher education only in Islamic Studies.

In my reform I propose that Islamic schools become more like Catholic schools in Canada.

Germany's Dual System

German education is also highly decentralized, with each state having its own separate rules. German children are not required to enroll in kindergarten but many do, and they can start as early as age three. They enter elementary school (*Grundschule*) at age six, and after Year 4 they are streamed. There is the general school (*Hauptschule*), Intermediate (*Realschule*), and the academic *Gymnasium* where they will spend the next six years. There is a fourth comprehensive school (*Gesamtschule*) that combines elements of all three so students could switch between streams without changing campus.

After Year 10 students would continue for another two or three years in vocational and technical training or academic stream. German universities charge very low fees; additionally, students get a state subsidy, the amount dependent on the parents' income.

There are private schools and universities, but they play a minor role.

I choose Germany to highlight its much-vaunted vocational training, the Dual System. So called because students undertake vocational and occupational training while at the same time attend school. They spend part of their day or certain days of the week in school, and the rest working in industry. Thus students are exposed simultaneously to educators (teachers) as well as master craftsmen and skilled technicians. Students combine the fundamentals of a general education and learning the theories of the trade both by the book as well as hands-on.

The important feature of the dual system is that it is a joint government and industry endeavor. The local government finances the schools, while the state pays for personnel. Industry provides the cost of the vocational training, including paying wages to the students. The role of the federal government is mainly that of a facilitator and regulator.

As employers pay for the direct costs of the vocational training, they (through a committee) control the curriculum and type of skills the students should learn. The committee also determines the suitability of firms providing the training, monitors the quality, and sets the necessary standards and examinations.

Many Third World countries including Malaysia are eagerly importing the German Dual System with varying success. As the World Bank noted, there are many salient features of the German system that must be appreciated.

First, Germany has a large manufacturing and service industry providing 90 percent of the jobs. The figures for most developing countries are considerably lower. In Malaysia, government, agriculture, and the "informal sector" are still major sources of employment. These sectors are unlikely to partake or be competent to contribute to the dual system. If Malaysia were to adopt the dual system it would have to be modified to prepare workers for those areas (especially agriculture) and of employing practitioners in the field as instructors. In Germany, vocational education was introduced long after there had been a formal apprenticeship program. Thus it was easy to graft the two together. Malaysia does not as yet have such widespread skill-training programs. The German system must be modified to cater for these local deficiencies.

Second, the German workplace is highly regulated and the workforce heavily unionized. There is greater compliance with safety and other rules that do not normally exist in the Third World. Student safety must be a top priority for the program to succeed.

Third, industry controls the vocational component. It sets the curriculum, standards, rules, and examinations. Third World countries trying to copy the system usually have bureaucrats in the distant ministry controlling the program. The government often meddles by insisting on minimum wages and other work conditions that are not tolerated by industry. MARA's many apprenticeship programs suffer from this grave error, in particular, lack of industry input. As a result their products are not readily employable. In Germany participation by industry is voluntary. Companies would not loose their government contracts if they do not partake in the program.

Fourth, and most important, vocational training is not regarded as a dead end stream or a pathway for those not qualified to enter university. The system provides increasing levels of technical training so motivated students could continue on right up to the highest level of technical colleges and universities. Equally important, the educational and vocational components complement each other.

Vocational training is expensive and should come only after the basic education needs of the citizens are taken care. Countries like Indonesia that attempt to graft the dual system fail miserably because scarce resources are diverted away from basic education. Malaysia however has solved the problem of providing primary and lower secondary education and thus is in a better position to benefit from the dual system. Malaysia's many vocational schools would benefit greatly from close industry collaboration. Future schools could also be built near industrial estates or major plants. The important element is that there must be major input from industry.

International Baccalaureate

The International Baccalaureate (IB) is a Geneva-based non-profit organization established in1968 to cater initially for the needs of children of internationally mobile families. In the short space of time it has already acquired a deservedly high reputation among universities worldwide for its rigorous matriculating examination. Schools in over 112 countries subscribe to the IB program, including many American magnet schools. In Malaysia apart from the few international schools, only MARA College, Banting, offers IB diploma. The college has done exceptionally well, including producing the best results worldwide for the last two consecutive years.

The IB school years resemble the Malaysian pattern, with six years of primary, five of secondary, and two years of matriculation (pre-university or Sixth Form).

The curriculum is both broad and deep, integrated, and emphasizes critical thinking. There is also a strong component of community service. The matriculation program revolves around six core areas: primary language, second language, social sciences and history, mathematics, natural sciences, and an elective. Students choose three or four subjects at the higher level (HL) for more in depth studies and instructional hours. HL would be equivalent to Sixth Form's principal level. The rest of the subjects are taken at the standard level (SL), equivalent to the Sixth Form's subsidiary level. This combination of SL and HL neatly tackles both breadth as well as depth. Students with an "artsy" bend need not take mathematics and science at the same intense level as would-be engineers.

This integrative approach is reflected in that all students have to take three common core elements. First is the Theory of Knowledge that emphasizes critical thinking and relates knowledge in the overall grand scheme of things. Second, students choose a topic for an in depth study, culminating in the writing of an extended essay, similar to the portfolio exhibition of the American CES schools. Third, students participate in a community project (CAS) that involves the three elements of creativity (C), action (A), and service (S).

IB's HL pass is so highly regarded that even elite American universities give college credits for it. The American National Research Council praises IB, considering it one of the two best programs to prepare students to pursue science and mathematics in college, the other being AP.

The secret for IB's success is its strict adherence to standards. Participating schools not only have to pay the equivalent of a franchise fee, but they also have to be regularly accredited. There are regular professional development programs for teachers as well as continuing curricular support for them available on-line. The emphasis on class participation and group projects means that IB, unlike other matriculating examinations, cannot be obtained through home schooling or correspondence courses. But like SAT, IB is both broad and comprehensive. All matriculating examinations have the same disadvantage of being a single end-of-year assessment, instead of regular and ongoing as with GPA. In this regard IB has a slight advantage in that with its science subjects, 26% of the final marks are based on teachers' internal evaluation of the students' laboratory work.

IB is sufficiently flexible to meet the national needs of various countries. I suggest modifying Sixth Form towards the IB model.

Brazil's *Bolsa Escola*

Brazil, like many developing countries, has appalling rural poverty, child labor, and dropout rates. *Bolsa Escola* (School Bursary Program) was started in 1995 to overcome these problems by *paying* poor families to keep their children in school. The theoretical and intellectual underpinning of this bold social engineering program was provided by the American Nobel laureate in economics, Gary Becker, who advocated that investments in human capital is just as valid and can be as productive as investments in physical infrastructures.

Poor parents of pupils of ages 7-14 are paid if they keep their children in school. These parents are given a monthly income equivalent to the prevailing wage for one year. This would continue monthly thereafter only if all their children attend school for over 90 percent of the time in the previous month. Most of the beneficiaries are families headed by single mothers.

The immediate results were impressive and went beyond merely improved school attendance. In one study there was a remarkable drop (by 36 percent) in child employment rate and a significant drop in street children. But most spectacular was the reduction in school dropout rates. Control districts (that is, comparable areas not under the program) had dropout rates of about 7.4 percent; in subsidized areas, a stunning under 0.4 percent–a near 20-fold difference.

The program has since been refined with payments dependent on the number of school-age children, and reduced proportionately when only one child is missing school rather than the previous all-or-none rule. Some programs also incorporate nutrition and health care. Further, the minimum number of years of support is now two instead of one, and the period extended to a maximum of eight years. These families are further encouraged to be involved in the school.

The World Bank studied this program and offers some useful lessons. One is the careful selection of candidates so as not to miss those most deserving. Two, the selection criteria must be objective and transparent, and understood by all, especially the local bureaucrats and citizens. Most importantly, the program should not be tied to any political party or be used as a tool to curry citizens' political favors or votes. Brazil's program is also highly decentralized, as only the government entity closest to the people can best know who are the most needy.

The Bank is sufficiently impressed with the program to fund its expansion. The Bank also notes other equally significant accompanying benefits besides increased educational achievements, like reduction of poverty and child labor. It suggests further refinements, for example to base payments on the number of children and not just school-age children. The Bank reiterates the importance of decentralization and local control to avoid leakage, that is, missing those deserving. At the same time the Bank cautions that these programs should not be at the expense of basic investments in schools. There is no point in giving grants to families and then have no money left over for improving schools or providing for teachers.

The program is currently being replicated elsewhere in Latin America with equally impressive results. Mexico has the comparable and equally successful *Progressa* program.

Another innovation of *Bolsa Escola* is that recipients are now given ATM cards so they can collect their money without having to face the local petty bureaucrats, thus eliminating a potential source of corruption. This also introduces the recipients to the modern concepts of banks and ATM cards.

I recommend a Malaysian variation of *Bolsa Escola* for the poorest areas. The decision as to who would qualify should rest with those who know the students and their parents well–the teachers. Further, I would restrict the payments only to children attending secular and not religious schools. I would also expand the social experiment by introducing other subsidy models and then evaluate to see which ones work best. In some districts I would improve the physical facilities by providing air-conditioned classrooms, single session, and extended school day, in others by providing nutritious meals. One of these interventions might well be just the right ticket to keep our poor children in school.

◆   ◆   ◆

The examples cited here all offer some relevant lessons for Malaysia. My reform proposals incorporate some elements from each of these, modifying them to suit Malaysian conditions. Before I get to the specifics I will first critique past and present attempts at reform. The next chapter will also review recent reforms in other countries for lessons that would be of relevance to Malaysia.

6

Attempts At Reform

*T*here have been many amendments to the Education Act since the landmark Razak Report of 1956. Most involved mere tinkering at the edges. Interestingly the legislation that had the greatest impact on education–the New Economic Policy (NEP) of 1970–was not directed specifically at education. That bold social engineering experiment changed not only the nature of Malaysian society but also the structure of education. NEP institutionalized quotas especially in higher education, and radically expanded the access to education for Bumiputras.

The second watermark period was when Malay replaced English as the medium of instruction in schools (except vernacular primary schools). The first batch of students to enter university under this new system of all-Malay instruction was in 1982. To some, that represented the pinnacle of achievement; to others, the beginning of the decline.

I belong to the second group, and was roundly chastised for my supposedly anti-nationalist sentiments. While I agreed that Malay should have wider usage as befitting a national language and that the then existing English schools were doing a poor job in teaching the language, my proposed remedy was very different. Instead of converting the then existing English schools into Malay, I suggested instead that more subjects be taught in Malay in these schools. History and geography would have been the ideal candidates, but keep science and mathematics in English. My reason then was practical, we did not have enough textbooks or Malays qualified to translate or write them. Nor did we have enough qualified teachers. My proposal would have achieved the same end results as what we are trying to reach today: for

Malaysians to be fluently bilingual and at the same time have a good command of science and mathematics.

I made my views known to the political establishment as well as to the Director of DBP in the form of an article submission. I was severely berated by the director for being ungrateful and having no pride in my own heritage. Something about a pea forgetting its pod (*kacang lupakan kulit*). I would have been satisfied with a simple, "No thank you!" rejection letter.

The agency then was headed by one Syed Nasir Ismail, a vigorous advocate of Malay language and a top UMNO functionary. At the time he was tipped to be the next education minister, which was the reason I wrote him. If Syed Nasir had his way, he would have wiped out all signs in the country other than those in Malay.

With clear hindsight the significance of that change into an all-Malay instruction can now be more objectively assessed. The man who claimed so much of the credit for introducing that change more than two decades ago is today spearheading a movement in the opposite direction. Then, Mahathir Mohamad as Education Minister was basking in the glory of having "restored" the honor of Malay language and of championing the cause of the race. Today as Prime Minister, Mahathir is advocating reintroducing English schools. Perversely, he is again being regarded as the nation's savior!

At the risk of appearing to gloat, had the government then been more cautious and proceeded along the lines I suggested, the nation today would not have the mess it has. By aggressively promoting Malay, the government sacrificed the greatest asset of its people, their English fluency. As we are now finding out, once we lost something, it is mighty difficult to reclaim it.

While the language nationalists may have their victory parade celebrating their "success" in extinguishing English and substituting Malay instead, the economic costs for this loss has yet to be estimated. Apart from the direct added costs of having translators, think of the immense potential loss through businesses and investments going elsewhere because our workers cannot communicate in English.

Another pivotal point was in 1996, with the amendment to permit the setting up of private universities. Within a few years literally hundreds of private institutions were established. For the first time the monopoly of the government in providing education, at least at the tertiary level, was broken. This was significant as it created the momentum for further change.

The nation had barely digested that innovation when the new millennium brought in more radical changes. One was *Education Blueprint 2001-2010*, the grand design envisioned by ministry bureaucrats; and soon right after, the National Brains Trust Report of 2002. It is highly significant that these two major proposals, with their far ranging implications, were made without wide public discussions or input. They were not even presented to Parliament.

In addition to these two major reform efforts, there were other significant decisions made during this time that had great impact on schools specifically and education generally. What is significant and frightening was the cavalier way in which these weighty matters were decided. The use of English to teach mathematics and science was made in response to a resolution passed at an UMNO divisional meeting. Of course the division that made the resolution was the prime minister's own; hence its extraordinary holding power. In Malaysia nothing happens spontaneously.

The other equally significant initiative–to admit non-Malays into MARA residential schools–was also made extemporaneously by the prime minister. Purportedly this was part of his overall attempt at injecting merit into the system. The only revealing aspect to that decision is that he now finally acknowledges that there is no consideration of merit in the current system.

I agree with both initiatives and made similar recommendations in my *The Malay Dilemma Revisited*. I advocated non-Bumiputras be admitted to all residential schools both to increase the competitiveness as well as reduce the insularity. But I went further. These non-Bumiputras as well as those Bumiputras who could afford it, should bear the full costs. These schools should revert to their original mission of being an outreach program for the poor who do not have ready access to quality schools.

My other recommendation was to teach science and mathematics in English at these schools. It would be a way to attract more Bumiputras to pursue those subjects, and as the students are smarter, the plan would more likely succeed and the kinks more easily ironed out. Once the system was running smoothly, then it could be expanded onto regular schools.

Like others, I too have deep reservations on the workability of the government's current proposals. It would not surprise me that there would be few non-Bumiputras eager for the MARA slots. This was confirmed by the headlines in November 2002. Non-Bumiputras are not the only ones who are unimpressed with MARA. To many Malays especially those in the private sector and the professions, MARA is synonymous with mediocrity. Few send their children to MARA institutions. Likewise with the teaching of science and mathematics in English; I anticipate problems not only with textbooks but also the teachers.

Education Development 2001-2010

In October 2001, MOE released a 250-page document, *Pembangunan Pendidikan 20001-2010: Rancangan Bersepadu Penjana Cemerlangan Pendidikan* (Education Development 2010-2010: Plan for Unity Through Educational Excellence–my translation). It was a comprehensive look at the system, from preschool to tertiary institutions. The ministry described it with such words as "sweeping," "radical," and "revolutionary." For a document that is supposed to be the basis for wide public discussion on such an important issue, it was strangely not widely distributed.

My attempts at getting a copy were unsuccessful. Supposedly it was out of print, only a few months after its release. No bookstore carries it. Nor is the document available on the ministry's website, which is not surprising as that website is more show than a meaningful mechanism for the dissemination of information. An opposition politician too claimed that he was unable to secure a copy. The minister himself was strangely uninterested to discuss the report publicly or give it wide coverage. More perplexing was the media; none covered the report extensively. The exception is the monthly publication *Education Quarterly* which did an excellent job summarizing it.

Regardless, that document was soon made irrelevant by subsequent developments, in particular the decision to teach mathematics and science in English, and the National Brains Trust Report. Still, as *Education Development* represents the thinking of ministry officials, it is worthwhile to review it if for nothing else than to get a glimpse of their mindset.

As is typical of many official documents and policy statements, *Education Development* is full of lofty ideas and the prerequisite current buzzwords like "globalization," "knowledge workers," and "IT." But it offers precious few details. Nor does it address, despite its promising subtitle, how to stem the rapidly declining standards and increasing segregation of our schools and universities. The report is prominent for its lack of innovative ideas to tackle such glaring issues as the lack of IT workers, and the low English fluency, scientific literacy, and mathematical competency of our students. It bravely puts a target of 60 percent of secondary school students to be in the science and technical streams, but offers precious little guidance on how to get there. These goals have been stated many times before; no special insight is needed to recognize the problem, the genius lies with providing the solution. The document offers none.

One of its ambitious goals is to build a community college in every parliamentary district. That is as ambitious as it is expensive. There is no clear definition of the mission of such colleges. Are they meant, as in America, to provide a channel for adult and re-entry students, to cater for those unable to make it into the universities the first time around, or to produce workers with marketable skills and specialized training? What I fear is that these colleges will issue yet another set of diplomas that would be worthless in the marketplace. That would be a disaster, especially after expectations have been raised so high. We already have a glut of unemployed graduates.

Again, as is typical of the ministry's pronouncements, there are repeated assertions of the nation's aspiration of being the center of educational excellence. Fantasy would be more appropriate than aspiration.

The document has one radical suggestion, reducing the school years from 13 to 12, with the format of K-6/2/2/2, and eliminating the current Form 3 examination. This is purportedly to make the system conform to international, in particular American, pattern. As usual, Malaysia is learning the wrong lesson.

While it is true that in America it is K-12, what Malaysian officials fail to note is that the vast majority of Americans go on to postsecondary institutions. With the wide availability of junior colleges, two years of college is now the norm. There is a movement to make that the new standard, in recognition of the need for a highly educated workforce to face the global competition. Thus in reality America has a K-14, not K-12 system.

American schools are also making their curriculum more rigorous. Many offer Advanced Placement classes. Mentioned earlier was the experiment by Bard College in collaboration with New York Public School Board that combines the last two years of high school with the first two years of college. In striking contrast, Malaysian schools are "dumbing down" their curriculum. Even leading residential schools like MCKK and TKC do not prepare their students for entry into universities.

Those ministry bureaucrats obviously did not think through their proposal. Presently the plan is bogged down, with the implementation delayed, because officials have not anticipated the obvious problem of the double cohorts of students entering university with the conversion from 13 to 12 years.

The basic message the ministry is sending through its *Education Development* is wrong. It is saying that Malaysians need fewer years of schooling while in the rest of the world it is just the opposite.

Meritokrasi and The Teaching of Science and Mathematics in English

The year 2002 was a tumultuous one for Malaysian education. Two major decisions–the introduction of *meritokrasi* (meritocracy) and the teaching of science and mathematics in English–were made almost casually, through executive mandate rather than after wide public discussions and parliamentary debates.

Meritokrasi was meant to improve the quality of education by relying more on academic criteria rather than quotas and special set-aside programs in the selection of students. It is widely acknowledged that many Bumiputra undergraduates would not be there but for special privileges.

Prime Minister Mahathir and other UMNO leaders were becoming increasingly piqued by the behavior of these undergraduates. They expressed their contempt for the government generally and UMNO specifically by actively campaigning for the opposition parties during recent elections.

The pivotal moment came when the landmark Chancellor's Hall on UM was burnt down. There was immediate speculation of arson as the prime minister was scheduled to speak in that auditorium the very next day. To date there has been no satisfactory or official explanation of the fire. The fire department intimated faulty wirings. Few believe that, least of all UMNO leaders who by now could hardly contain their displeasure and anger at the undergraduates. The new head of Puteri (Young Women) UMNO, Azalina Othman, eager to show her stripes, angrily called for the firing of the university's vice-chancellor, Dr. Annuar Zaini, for failing to "control" the students. This is surprising as Annuar Zaini is a highly qualified and respected academic physician. He is among the few who rose through the academic ranks instead of the usual path of politics and the civil service.

The decision to use merit as the basis for admission was not to enhance the academic standards as widely proclaimed, rather to give those "ungrateful" Bumiputra students their just comeuppance. Thus chastened they would then concentrate more on their studies and would be less interested in politics. Or if they were, they would be more supportive of the government lest they risk losing their cherished special privileges and quotas. At least that was the expectations of the UMNO hierarchy.

Consequently there was much anticipation of the effect of this new policy on the incoming class of 2002. Judging from the statements of UMNO leaders, they were eagerly expecting the shocking news of fewer Bumiputras admitted to universities so UMNO leaders could browbeat those students. "See, if not for us guarding your special privileges, you Bumiputras would not stand a chance!"

Come June when the figures were released, there were gasps of astonishment. The number of Bumiputras admitted under the new merit-based criteria increased, not dropped. To those who think that Malays are dumb (this includes many among UMNO leaders), that shocking news was not expected. One would have thought that there would be hearty messages of congratulations to these students for having done well. Instead there were snide remarks that the process was rigged. How else to explain the success of Malays?

Although I expected such remarks from non-Malays–after all they too needed some rationalization for their less than expected outcome– what stunned me was the disbelief among Malays leaders. The Prime Minster who long championed the cause of Malays went so far as to claim that it was a statistical quirk and that it would not happen again. Not once did he applaud the students for having done well. Instead he and many others went out of their way to deride and belittle the students' achievements. Some suggested that because most Malay students entered through *matrikulasi* while non-Malays through Sixth Form, the former must be of lower standard. Their presumption is that Malays are dumb; so *matrikulasi* must be easier.

As stated earlier, I believe *matrikulasi* is a watered-down program. But don't blame the students; blame those who run the program and the bureaucrats who juggled the scores. Meanwhile I heartily congratulate those hard working Malay students who have done well and thus surprised their leaders. May you have continued success, even though your leaders may lack faith in you. Prove them wrong again!

For now *meritokrasi* stays, the government's weapon to bludgeon the students effectively neutralized. Those "ungrateful" Malay students have yet to be punished.

The second decision, to use English to teach science and mathematics, had a similar seat-of-the-pants quality to the decision making process.

One would have thought that such a radical change would have been undertaken only after meticulous and exhaustive study. We are dealing with the future of our young, something not to be taken lightly. Instead the decision was rushed. The matter was discussed at UMNO Supreme Council meetings, and only minimally in the cabinet. There was no parliamentary debate. Despite howling protests from various groups, the decision stayed. Instead of engaging its many critics, the government threatened to use the Internal Security Act to silence them.

Yet legitimate questions remain, like the availability of competent teachers and suitable textbooks. These are simply brushed aside. The leaders have spoken and it shall be so. The magic wand has been waved, and all problems will miraculously vanish.

The plan is to be implemented in January 2003, but as late as November 2002 the final form and manner has yet to be finalized. Initially it is to begin at Primary 1 and at selected secondary levels, but with protests from Chinese-based political parties, that timetable is now under review.

The authorities had numerous meetings to iron out the kinks. It is instructive that none of these meetings involved teachers or educators. The issue had been discussed entirely in the political arena, indicating that the decision had less to do with education and everything to do with politics.

The rationale of the policy is valid: to enhance the scientific knowledge and mathematical competency of students and at the same encourage the wider use of English. But as presently implemented, and without much prior planning and preparation, the policy will, like the decision to introduce *meritokrasi*, back fire.

These two initiatives prove that momentous decisions can be made within the constraints of the present framework; there is no need to amend the constitution or have Royal Commissions of Inquiry. Whether these essentially wise decisions will achieve their intended results remain to be seen. I await their implementation.

National Brains Trust Report 2002

Less than a year after the release of *Education Development 2001-2010*, a high-level committee, dubbed the National Brains Trust, released its report, *Master Plan for the Knowledge-Based Economy*. It contains 136 recommendations, of which 64 relate to human resources, and half of that (32) concern education. I will discuss those 32 recommendations, but first some comments on the committee.

It was led by one Nordin Sopiee, a London School of Economics PhD and head of a government think tank. He is more widely remembered as the man who took a full-page newspaper ad supporting Prime Minister Mahathir following US Vice President Al Gore's intemperate remarks during a state dinner supporting the *refomasi* movement. Prudent thing to do as his organization is dependent on the government for funding. More importantly, at that infamous dinner Nordin Sopiee was seen to applaud the vice president. Thus to local cynics, Nordin's widely publicized action in taking out the ad was seen more as a crass display of *bodek* (sucking up to the powerful). His committee of 68 luminaries (some reports claimed 95; a committee member could not tell me the exact number) was widely lauded in the media.

The report is like other official papers–dry, more like a recipe book. There is little discussion of background information or references to primary sources and experiences of other countries. It correctly highlights the recent steady decline in the nation's competitiveness. It stood at 17 in 1997, but slipped to 41 in the latest ranking (2001). While other factors certainly contribute to this precipitous slide, the report makes no references to them. Instead it focuses primarily on the inadequacies of the education system. In this the report is hardly comprehensive. It makes scant reference to the evident decline of Malaysian universities. I am told that there would be a recommendation for yet another committee to look specifically at higher education. The only suggestion it has for universities is that they should review the salary scheme of its junior lecturers. Even here the committee is missing the mark. Our universities need to improve the pay of its academic staff at all levels.

One recommendation beyond education that caught my eye is for allowing local companies to import top talent, that is, foreigners earning in excess of RM20,000 per month should be given automatic work visa. I would go further; I would grant them permanent status. For these highly talented individuals, the demand for their skills is truly global. Malaysia must be willing to pay competitive salaries to attract them. While I applaud the committee for making this sensible recommendation, the committee then undermines this by putting a limit to the number of such individuals a company could hire. Surely if we value them, then more is better. Why the restrictions? The committee could not escape its parochialism in protecting Malaysians in these high-paying jobs. Malaysians with that kind of talent do not need such protection. The challenge is to entice them to remain at home.

The report rightly highlights the mediocre pay for teachers. Although Malaysian teachers earn as much as their American counterpart relative to the per capita GDP, the more important indicator is how well they are paid relative to other professions. When a tour guide or a fish hawker earns considerably more, then we have a problem. In Malaysia (and also in America) this is manifested by the fact that the profession no longer attracts the best and talented. With low pay comes low status.

In my *The Malay Dilemma Revisited*, I referred to Lat's cartoons to illustrate this point. One sketch of a 1950s' scene showed a schoolteacher in his sleek car, with a father and son looking on admiringly by the roadside. The next scene was of more recent vintage, and it showed a father driving his son to school in an expensive sedan, and forcing the schoolteacher, who was riding a decrepit motorcycle, off the road!

The report calls for across the board salary hikes. That would be laudable but prohibitively expensive. Instead Malaysia should have targeted increases to attract those with the most-needed skills: teachers of English, science, and mathematics. With a glut of teachers for Malay and Islamic Studies there is no point in increasing their pay. Even if we reduce it, there will be no shortage of applicants.

The committee is enamored with IT, and calls for bridging the digital divide by 2010. In its infatuation with computers the committee ignores other more glaring divide separating rural from urban schools—poor physical facilities and lack of quality teachers. To me these should be the highest priority, ahead of supplying IT. Many rural schools do not even have electricity, how can they have computers? Many still have double sessions, dilapidated libraries, and inadequate laboratories. I would fix those first.

The committee recommends that schools be provided with a manager to take care of the administrative chores thus freeing the headmaster to pay attention to professional and educational issues. I agree, provided that the manager is answerable to the headmaster and not to some bureaucrat in the ministry.

Another of its recommendations is that teachers at the secondary and upper primary levels be degree holders. I would settle for teachers only at the upper secondary level to be graduates. For others, a good teaching diploma should suffice. I would upgrade the quality of teachers' colleges; this would be better and more cost effective way of enhancing the quality of teaching, rather than insisting that teachers have a degree. This would end up diluting the quality of our universities by diverting them to train the massive number of teachers. Look at America where former teachers' colleges are now universities.

Today a graduate teacher from a local university has less professional skills and knowledge than a diploma-trained teacher from Kirby or Brinsford Lodge of the 1950s. It would be better and more effective to upgrade the teaching diploma than to cheapen a degree.

A major disappointment with the Brains Trust report is that it barely scratches the surface of the monumental problems facing Malaysian education. It does not address the basic problems of our institutions being tightly controlled by the ministry, with no room for them to grow professionally or develop their excellence and expertise.

Reform in Other Countries

Malaysia is not the only nation contemplating reform of its education system. There is a global movement to make education more responsive and accountable. While reforms in the Third World focus on increasing access and availability of basic education, those in the First World are concerned with enhancing the quality and accountability. As Malaysia has successfully passed the stage of providing basic education for all, it has little to learn from the reform efforts in Kenya or Papua New Guinea. Malaysia should instead look to the First World.

I will examine recent reforms in Chile and California. Chile is not in the First World yet, but it is poised to join its ranks. Developmentally it is at the same stage as Malaysia. California on the other hand is fully developed nonetheless it shares many problems with Malaysia, with both having plural societies and large numbers of non-native English-speaking populations.

In 1980 Chile's military government launched a radical reform. Prior to that education in Chile as in most developing nations was highly centralized and controlled by a powerful ministry of the central government. It was the usual top-down command structure patterned after the old Soviet Union and replicated in many Third World countries.

Surprising for a military government, Chile's rulers decentralized education, giving administrative responsibility of schools to local governments ("municipalization"), and ending the state monopoly. The government actively sought private sector participation and vigorously encouraged competition between public and private schools. It changed the financing of schools to that of capitation, based on the number of students and their achievements.

For the military mindset that has central command, rigid controls, and strict regimentation as articles of faith, this was a radical departure. These changes in education were in tandem with other reforms in the economy and society the military was instituting at the time. Essentially it dismantled the massive state structure of the previous socialist government and pushed Chile towards an open market.

The military was advised by a core of competent economists who were graduates of elite American universities, in particular the University of Chicago that had long championed free enterprise and market solutions to socioeconomic problems. These "Chicago Boys," as they were admiringly referred to, had been tutored by the likes of Milton Friedman.

Prior to the reform Chile, like Malaysia, already had a fairly high standard of educational attainment, with an average of 9.7 years of formal schooling. Apart from universal primary schooling, the participation rate at secondary level was a high 87 percent; and tertiary, 26 percent.

Chile's military government dismantled the entire system: administration, financing, and accountability. In the process the government broke the powerful stranglehold of the teachers' union that had grown immensely under the previous socialist administration. Schools were no longer under the control of the central government rather municipalities. The union had to negotiate not with one central ministry but with hundreds of local bargaining units, thereby effectively emasculating the union's power. Remarkably, the government did not meddle with the curriculum, pedagogy, or teaching. It left such professional and technical matters to the teachers and educators.

The previous state monopoly on education was dismantled. Some schools are now entirely private, receiving no state funding whatsoever; others are private-public partnership and get public funding through capitation. National examinations are now used not only to assess the students but also to grade the schools. This information on school performance is made readily available to parents, thus empowering them to make meaningful decisions on where to send their children.

Today Chile's parents truly have meaningful choices, and they are exercising them. By 1998 over 34 percent of the parents chose subsidized private schools, while about 10 percent chose pure private ones.

During the first decade of reform primary enrolment continued at near universal level, with secondary and tertiary enrolments jumping sharply from 65 and 11 percent respectively in 1980, to 87 and 28 percent by 1997. Impressive! The dropout rate too declined dramatically, from a high of 8.0 percent in1981 to 1.6 percent in 1997 at primary level; and from 8.3 percent in 1981 to 5.8 in 1997 for secondary. Even more impressive!

The reforms initiated by the military were dictated from above, with little consultation from the masses–typical of the military mentality. Remarkably when military rule ended in1989, the succeeding civilian government did not dismantle these reforms; instead it refined and enhanced them.

The central lesson from Chile is decentralization. Authority and responsibility are shifted away from the distant central government to the political entity closest to the people. The central government no longer micromanages the schools; it does not dictate what and how to teach nor prescribe the textbooks. Those are left to individual schools and their professionals. The government maintains influence and control through macro levers in the form of capitation funding, open competition, and general market philosophy of openness and accountability. It also uses these elements to bring about changes in the schools. School performances are now monitored and the results released to the public, thus ensuring accountability.

The second lesson is that government can affect profound changes without resorting to micromanagement and other details of control. There are enough macro levers such as the funding mechanism and assessment feedbacks to prod these schools in the desired direction.

Third, equity does not mean the delivery of the same package of goods and services to all rather the system must be flexible and adaptable to respond to the needs of diverse groups. The role of the government should be properly focused on those most vulnerable or left out. For example, the government introduced school meals for the poorest 10 percent of the student population. In the past the central government could not effect these changes as it was involved in running thousands of other institutions that could run themselves very well. By husbanding its resources and focusing its efforts, the ministry was able to help more effectively those who were truly in need.

The Chilean reform shifted the focus of government away from directly managing and controlling the schools to providing general guidelines and broad parameters. The actual administration and running of the schools are left to the local level, accountable directly to the parents.

A similar "top-down" reform was also successfully enacted in California, but within the context of a political system the exact opposite of a military dictatorship. Yet the results were just as profound and effective.

California is the most diverse state in the union. A significant proportion of its children come from families where English is not spoken, a situation similar to Malaysia. Educating and integrating these diverse groups are truly formidable tasks. In the past California like other states used bilingual education to bring these children into the mainstream. Children were first taught in their native language while English was being gradually introduced. As their facility in English improved, other subjects would be taught in English until these students were fully integrated into the mainstream. This philosophy is subscribed to by the American educational establishment, which claims that this is the most effective way to teach and reach these children.

The reality was far different. These children often felt left out and marginalized. They did not learn much; their test scores were atrocious and dropout rates horrendous. When these children grew up they became a burden on society. Their lack of basic educational skills rendered them essentially unemployable. Mostly the burden fell heavily on themselves and their families. They were trapped in a permanent underclass by their lack of quality education. As usual, such social frustrations built up slowly, but once they erupted, they were difficult to contain.

This was what happened in California. Parents, fed up with the poor performance of their children, started a grass-root movement to abolish bilingual education. They were led by leading figures in the immigrant community who had as children successfully opted out of bilingual education to join the mainstream after a brief immersion period of studying English. Employers equally fed up with the poor quality of workers their companies had to contend with, in turn supported these parents.

Their efforts culminated in the passage of Proposition 227 in 1998 that effectively legislated an end to bilingual education in California. Now children with limited English proficiency have to take English immersion class for a maximum of one year, and then they would be placed into regular classes.

The campaign leading to the referendum was highly divisive and rancorous. Opponents of the initiative feared that these children would not be able to cope with the sudden introduction of English and thus would be forced to drop out. Supporters on the other hand were variously labeled as anti-immigrants and racists. They in turn accused the other side of wanting to trap children of immigrants in perpetual mediocrity. All of course professed to have the children's best interest at heart!

The current equally contentious debate on the use of English to teach science and mathematics in Malaysia eerily reminds me of that earlier nasty California experience.

The results of that forced field experiment are now obvious. Within the first few months, teachers immediately began noticing a remarkable transformation. The children were no longer dropping out; their attendance improved markedly and they were learning much more rapidly. Improvements were noted in all age groups. Test scores in one school district jumped from the 11th percentile to the 23rd by the first year. A doubling of improvement! By the third year it had jumped to the 32nd.

Even more remarkable than improved test scores was the progress on the ground level. The students loved speaking English, they actually enjoyed learning. Their teachers were ecstatic! On the playgrounds these children were even more confident and mixed more freely with native English-speaking children. They now had a one-up over their classmates who could speak only English. This tremendously enhanced their self-esteem and confidence, which spilled over to their other classroom performances.

Such dramatic results made converts of those who previously favored bilingual education into boosters of English immersion classes. Did such successes settle the issue once and for all? Far from it!

For one, at the same time the proposition was passed California also mandated class size reduction and introduced phonics teaching of

English (the sounding of letters and syllables). While previously the average class was in excess of 30 students, today they are less than 20, and English was taught using the whole language method. Presumably all three–small classes, phonics teaching, and immersion classes–helped.

Meanwhile proponents of bilingual education in other states also introduced new innovative models. In Texas, the Houston school district in collaboration with Rice University set up a pioneering school using English and Spanish in tandem throughout the school years, a new twist to the old bilingual program. Thus far Rice School/*La Escuela Rice* offers only K-8 levels, and already it is wildly successful such that entry is by lottery, and slots for children of Rice faculty members are limited to 12 percent. The unique features of the school are its small class size, and extensive use of electronics, computers, and the Internet.

In addition to these two major initiatives, there were other small reform movements started by businesses, political activists, parents, and educators. Earlier I alluded to Louis Gerstner's New Century School funded by a private foundation. It gave grants directly to teachers and schools to pursue their own demonstration projects; these would later be shared with others. Not all their projects were successful. Among the successes were Park View Elementary school in Mooresville, NC, that experimented with extended-day and year-round programs; Ortega Elementary School in Austin, TX, a school with predominantly minority students, with its parenting classes to attract greater parental involvement with the school; and another also in North Carolina of creating schools near where the parents work.

The Annenberg Foundation also generously funded a number of demonstration projects nationwide under its Annenberg Challenge. These enabled teachers and educators to pursue their ideas on how best to improve their public schools. Among the lessons learned, as published in its *Lessons and Reflections on Pubic School Reform*, are that every child benefits from high expectations and standards, and that the surest way to improve student achievement is to enhance the skills of teachers. Professional development of teachers is the key to better schools. Additionally schools need strong leadership not only in the classrooms but also at the principal's office, the governing board, and at the ministry. There must also be mechanism to help teachers and pupils get to know each other better. The best and simplest way of achieving this is to make schools small or to divide existing large schools into smaller independent units. One recommendation that is relevant to Malaysian rural schools is that such schools must form networks for mutual support and to learn from each other. Lastly, schools must remain accountable and this accountability must be demonstrated in measurable and tangible ways.

The political activists were involved with charter schools and vouchers to enable poor children to attend good schools outside their neighborhood. One reform movement started by teachers is the Coalition of Essential Schools (CES). This is the most successful in terms of its ideas being accepted nationwide.

I will refer back to these examples in enumerating my reform proposals. The lesson here is that there are many paths to reform and that the different models when carefully thought out and thoughtfully implemented work equally well. We need to start small with few demonstration projects, iron out the kinks, and once they are proven successful, then and then only expand them. Our children are too precious to risk taking part in massive, half-baked social engineering experiments. There must also be a willingness to assess and improve as we go along. A perfect system does not remain so forever. It needs constant improvement and enhancement to meet ever-changing conditions and experiences. The most important lesson of all is that there is no panacea; nor is there a magic wand that one can simply wave and wish the problems away.

Risks To Reform

Changing the status quo is always a formidable challenge; I do not underestimate the power of inertia. Would-be reformers past and present have met less-than-benign fate. Reforming an institution like Malaysian education with its powerful symbolism would be doubly daunting.

The essential ingredients for reform are already there–widespread dissatisfaction with and evident failures of the current system. Society demands that something be done, and the leaders too are recognizing this. While there is general consensus that something must be done, there is no agreement on either what ails the system or what are the objectives of reform. While all agree that the system ought to prepare the young for the increasingly competitive world and simultaneously foster national unity, beyond that there is considerable disagreement.

The divisions are along two broad camps. One side feels that the problem with the current system is that we are not sufficiently commit-ted to its objectives and methods. Their remedy then is simply more of the same, but with more vigorous implementation. The other camp feels just as strongly that there is something radically wrong with the present system both in its objectives and methods that nothing short of a major overhaul would do.

The problem is further compounded by the fact that the primary mission of education is entangled with other societal goals. Language nationalists would like the system to not only maintain the supremacy of Malay but also to suppress the use of other languages, especially English because of its imperial association. These nationalists would not be satisfied until the nation is completely and exclusively monolin-gual. It is this juvenile mindset, ensconced primarily at such places as DBP and Malay Studies departments of public universities, which led to the defacing of non-Malay signs at highways and airports in days of yore. To these insular types, knowing any other language but Malay is tantamount to an act of treason. The good news is that these groups are fast receding into the fringes as more Malaysians, Malays in particular, are becoming more rational.

Few as these dissenters are, I do not estimate their ability to create mischief or grab the headlines. The lead editor of *Dewan Bahasa*, flagship publication of DBP, characterized the recent controversy on using English to teach science and mathematics as "language war!" Meanwhile its director, one Deraman Aziz, was loudly threatening to collect a million signatures to oppose the wider use of English. He quickly disavowed his participation when he was none too subtly reminded of his civil service obligations. Obviously the security of his plush civil service job has priority over his nationalistic zeal.

Malay politicians see education as a huge patronage system. All those juicy building contracts, textbook publishing, and yes, even catering services are viewed less as means of helping the young but more as tunnels to the public trough. Reform education if you must, but keep those spigots flowing! Similarly quotas in education are a security blanket for the less than talented. Again, reform if you must, but disturb the quota at your political peril.

To the Islamists, education is nothing more than to prepare Muslims for the hereafter, the present world be damned.

Malaysian-Chinese meanwhile are obsessed with their self-appointed role as defenders of their mother tongue. Never mind that in China the top universities are now using English or that those most vocal in opposing the extended use of English are sending their children abroad to Anglo Saxon countries. You can bet that those youngsters would not be taking up Chinese Studies there.

With such differing and conflicting perspectives, little wonder that education gets sucked into the maelstrom.

As with any reform, the promised benefits would remain only a potential and be diffused. Meanwhile the casualties and costs would be direct and felt right away, and be concentrated on and borne by a few and definable groups. Emphasizing English would benefit all students together with enhancing the nation's competitiveness, but that is only a potential. Meanwhile the price would be borne by those who have invested heavily in the present system–Malay language nationalists and the current establishment. Those who will bear the pain would be expected to be very vocal in their resistance, and will do their utmost to magnify and amplify the difficulties.

I anticipate the greatest obstacle to come from the current education establishment, especially those in the ministry and the ruling party who have benefited immensely at the expense of young Malaysians. Also included in this group is the entire civil service brought up under the present all-Malay system. These civil servants would be even more emboldened now that their older and English-fluent colleagues are retiring. This Malay-educated establishment would not be kindly disposed to any change. They have done well despite their low English fluency and nonexistent mathematical skills; they see little need for change. Rest assured they would do everything to ensure that any reform would fail.

These obvious resistors would be relatively easy to neutralize, as demonstrated by the now compliant Deraman Aziz. More pernicious and dangerous would be the "stealth" oppositionists. They would be formidable opponents because we cannot identify them. They would be conducting insidious guerilla warfare from within. They would do everything within their power to sabotage any change so as to justify their saying n the end, "I told you so!" These include the politically inclined academics, language activists, and Malay teachers who but for their political leanings would not be where they are today.

The cautionary note in all of these is that to ensure success, the government must be cognizant of the hidden opposition from the establishment. By this I mean not only senior education ministry officials but also the legends of headmasters and heads of universities. The government must deal quickly with those who not only oppose reform but also not sufficiently committed to it. If they were not made to pay the price for their obstinacy, it would only embolden others.

The government has a powerful weapon in that these civil servants and language nationalists have no skills that are valued by the private sector. The mere threat of losing their prized civil service appointments is enough to make them toe the line as pathetically demonstrated by DBP's Deraman Aziz. The government should not hesitate to wield this powerful disciplinary weapon.

There is a hidden yet significant danger to reform that is not widely appreciated or discussed. Education is a powerful symbol in the race politics of Malaysia; reforming it risks rekindling old battles. Many would like nothing more than to take the opportunity to score political points by raising long-settled issues. The danger is that the public, fearful of retracing the divisive path of the past, would simply give up on reform and settle for the mediocre status quo.

The only way to avoid this is to have as wide a debate as possible with public hearings and input from various individuals and organizations. An open debate is healthy. Besides we will never know where the next bright idea might emerge. The solution to the nation's myriad education problems does not lie with some esteemed committee of wise persons deliberating in some air-conditioned office away from the hustle and bustle of the classrooms. As we have seen in Chile, the solution lies not in a monolithic prescribed model rather with trying different forms and adapting and enhancing as we go along. Only in such a fashion could the needs of our nation be met.

In the remaining chapters I put forth my own specific ideas on reform. The purpose is not to enumerate my prescriptions rather to start this much-needed public debate.

7

Strengthening The Schools

*D*uring colonial times the main problem with Malaysian schools was one of access. The English schools then were generally good, some were excellent, but they were not many. They were also necessarily elitist. Education was not for the masses rather for the select and lucky few. Today education has been democratized and made readily available to all. There are many more schools but few are good. Even previously outstanding ones are today a mere shadow of their former glory.

The British perpetuated racial and class divisions with its separate vernacular schools. Its English schools however, succeeded in bringing some segment of the community (primarily the elite and urban dwellers) together. The unity and solidarity of earlier Malaysian leaders could be credited to the fact that they all attended English schools. Today, despite the stated objectives that schools should be a force for bringing the nation together, young Malaysians are growing further apart.

Despite the overall gloom there are islands of excellence. The trick is not to muck up such successes in the zeal for reform rather to enhance and replicate them. In this chapter I will deal exclusively with schools, the next with higher education.

I would not change the total number of school years, but instead of the current format of K-6/7-9/10-11/12-13 (Primary/Lower Secondary/Upper Secondary/Sixth Form), I would substitute primary (K-6), middle (Years 7-9), and high school (Years 10-13). Most of the changes would be at the high school. All students regardless whether they are academically or vocationally oriented would have 13 years of schooling, an improvement over the present. As for the curriculum, there would only be the four mandatory core subjects: Malay, English, science, and mathematics. These subjects would be taught daily at all levels, and in English, except for Malay.

Each school would design its own program to fill the rest of the day. The ministry would provide only general guidelines for the various subjects. Each school would decide what other subjects to offer depending on the availability of teachers and the demand from students and parents. This gives maximum flexibility to the schools and teachers to display their creativity and innovation. Note that the guidelines govern only the *minimum* requirements expected of *all* students. The schools, especially those in the academic streams, are expected to exceed those standards.

Common Issues Affecting All Schools

MOE has a tight leash on schools, and those ministry bureaucrats are control freaks. Nothing gets done without their approval, not even fixing the leaking roof. The ministry controls every minutiae of the curriculum and syllabus, picks the textbooks, and decides who gets promoted. This monopoly must be broken and the private sector be allowed to participate. Schools are also getting too large and overcrowded as to be unmanageable. With headmasters poorly trained as managers, we have the mess today. The physical facilities too are wanting, and stressed with the added burdens of double sessions.

The ministry must relent and grant schools greater freedom. Many of the reforms worldwide are focused on decentralization as we have seen in Chile. In America there is a trend especially in the larger districts of delegating management from the district office down to the individual school–school-based management (SBM).

It would be foolish to let a small primary school in Ulu Kelantan to have its own management. That would only result in it being a pawn of ambitious local politicians and pompous village headmen. But there are schools with a long tradition of excellence and a large pool of distinguished alumni and parents who could guide their institutions to greater heights if only given the chance. I do not mean that the ministry should let go of these schools entirely. Rather it could influence them much more effectively using subtler yet more powerful instruments like the funding mechanism and in approving their trustees' appointments. This would also be less crude but more effective than issuing missives and commands. Schools such as Victoria Institution, Penang Free, and the residential schools should be let free or at least be given the option for self-governance. Give them a global budget based on the enrollment, performance, or any other agreed-upon criteria.

With SBM the headmaster would nominate potential trustees, subject to the minister's approval. The minister thus maintains veto power over such appointments. He should only approve well-qualified and dedicated candidates. As added precaution, there must be sufficient representation on the board from parents, teachers, and alumni. The board would have full authority, including the hiring and firing of staff, and choosing the textbooks. Surely they would be as qualified as those ministry officials. To maintain continuity the board would have staggered appointments, and to prevent entrenched trustees there should be term limits. The ministry would have to draw up model bylaws to govern the board's authority.

Not every school would be capable of or want to have their independence. Thus before any school be granted SBM, there must be a request by the majority of the teachers. There should also be a mechanism to revoke SBM in case of dysfunctional management.

I would anticipate that a few dozen schools would qualify initially for SBM. Later with their success, they would entice others to take that route. Not only would this lighten the load of the ministry so it could concentrate on those schools that truly need its help, it would also empower our schools to seek their own level of excellence.

The second major factor is size. Many schools are too big, way past their optimal size to be effectively managed. I suggest limiting enrollment in primary school to under 400 students; middle school around 500; and high school, 600. Beyond those, students would be lost in the crowd and disciplinary problems become major issues. Studies indicate that smaller schools are not only safer but also more effective. I have seen the world of difference between the massive comprehensive schools where my two older children attended as compared to the smaller one my younger son went.

America is experimenting with dividing its large schools into smaller units, each with its own teachers and administrators but sharing the same campus. At some schools the students stay with the same teacher for two or more consecutive years. The idea is to have as many adults at that school know as many students personally.

There are many other advantages to small schools. Deborah Meier in her book, *The Power of Their Ideas: Lessons for America from a Small School in Harlem*, lists some of them. Meier, a pioneer in American education, feels very strongly that the current huge and factory-like atmosphere of many schools is simply dehumanizing, and takes a severe toll on the students. She has successfully demonstrated her conviction by running a small school in Harlem, the toughest inner city environment. Her students have consistently surpassed the *national* average; if we compare her students to those of other inner city schools the improvement is simply spectacular.

Small schools are more manageable. The teachers know each other and thus are accountable to one another. If someone were slacking, the others would know right away and could gently remind him or her in the common room. The physics teacher knows what the math teacher is doing, and they could coordinate their lesson plans merely by conversing in the hallway. There is no need to have a coordinating committee. Teachers would also know the students better, even those from other classes. When students become exposed to the same few teachers all the time, those adults become valuable role models.

Small schools are not more expensive; in many ways they are cheaper. At large American schools resources are diverted towards crowd control, with metal detectors and policemen. Personnel are consumed with handling disciplinary problems. Small size alone is not enough; it would be meaningless if such schools were not given sufficient autonomy to take advantage of their smallness. Then what we would have are clones of one another, and the mistakes of one get replicated.

My mother was a headmistress of a small primary school in her village during British rule. Because she also lived in the same village, she knew many of the parents. Her pupils were unlikely to bluff their way with her when playing hooky. It would be tough to say you missed school because you were sick when your headmistress saw you climbing the coconut tree that day. Because her school was small she actually taught a class while being a headmistress. I remember many parents bringing gifts of fruits and cakes to my mother during *Hari Raya* and at the end of the year, all very personal touches. Such occasions easily became informal parent-teacher conferences with valuable information on the child being exchanged. I have followed up with that tradition with my own children by giving token gifts to their teachers on the last day of school. No, that was not an attempt at bribing or currying favor as the grades were already out by then.

When Malaysia became independent, Malay schools were "modernized" and the principals had to fill in all the added paperwork to satisfy the new homegrown bureaucrats. My mother was consumed with administrative chores that took her away from her beloved pupils. She finally gave up her headship to return to the classroom. At the time she was bound by the old rules and could do this without any diminution in her pay. My father too was briefly a headmaster, but after one too many meetings with officials at the state office, he decided to come back as a regular teacher until his retirement a decade later.

I believe the effectiveness of traditional religious schools is attributed to the fact that their teachers are intimately involved in the community. The *ustaz* not only teaches in the *madrasahs*, he also leads the prayers at your parents' *khenduri* (feast) and your brother's circumcision rites.

At my son's school the tradition was for the first teacher of the day to greet each student by name and a firm handshake as he or she enters the class, and the process is repeated with the last teacher as the students were leaving. There is nothing more personal than a handshake and looking straight in the eye of a youngster, and perhaps little words of encouragement whispered now and then.

Today's schools are so large that such personal and human touches are gone. Not only are headmasters fully consumed with administrative chores, so are the senior assistants. When principals get far away from the classrooms it is easy for them to become detached from the realities. Ask headmasters to name some students they know well, they would be stumped. Today the administrative types are more likely to be promoted over the born teachers. These bureaucrats look upon their promotions not as opportunities to advance their pedagogical philosophy rather as an escape from the classroom.

Dr. Raymond Orbach, renowned physicist and head of the University of California, Riverside, in an address to incoming freshmen told them that his greatest pleasure was to meet and welcome new students; his second, to teach an honors class. This was his way to get a pulse on the most important segment of the campus community–the students. He does not need to get a detailed report from the dean of undergraduate studies; he meets the students every day in class.

Going back to Mrs. Meier, her program is now widely copied nationwide. In her teaching she tries to instill in her pupils and fellow teachers her school's five broad principles. The first is, "How do we know what we know?" which is simply a way of asking us to weigh and examine the evidence to what we say or hear. The second, "Who is speaking?" that is, whose perspectives? The implication is that there can be multiple viewpoints to be considered. Third is, "What causes what?" a search for relationships, patterns, or connection. Fourth is, "How might things be different?" an opportunity to examine the what-ifs and various suppositions. And lastly, a simple, "Who cares?" not a cynical dismissal rather another way of saying how and in what way do these things matter in the grand scheme, or to wax philosophical.

These five guiding principles are written down and hung in every classroom. I find them so helpful that I cannot help but repeat them here.

At the polar opposite of the large inner city schools that Meier successfully humanized with her small school movement, are the small isolated rural schools. The problems here are of a different order, quantitatively and qualitatively. Their smallness precludes them from offering enriched programs, and their teachers risk professional isolation. One solution suggested by the Annenberg Challenge is for these schools to form networks for support and sharing of resources. Thus small rural schools in one district could join together to share a music teacher or a mobile computer lab and library. Teachers could also get together for joint professional development courses. The areas for such cooperation and learning together are unlimited.

The next important issue with Malaysian schools is double sessions. The top priority must be to end this. I am disappointed that the funds allocated in the 2003 budget to ending double sessions are considerably less than that of providing IT. The government cannot end double sessions by itself; that would bust the budget. But by allowing for private sector participation, the load would be lightened. The government could also achieve more for its money if it cuts down on expensive and unnecessary projects like building residential schools, and by putting its contracts to open bidding and getting the best price instead of limiting them only to Bumiputra contractors.

The last point is parental choice–the freedom to choose the school that best fit the child. To make this a reality all schools must have adequate hostel facilities to cater for students who live far away. I favor limited hostel facilities attached to day schools rather than fully residential schools simply because the former would be considerably cheaper and more manageable.

If we have freedom of choice, how do we prevent self-segregation? One way is by rewarding those schools with a diverse student body. With the added funds they could enrich their academic offerings; this in turn would make their school that much more attractive to all Malaysians. Conversely we should not fund schools that restrict their enrolment to or attract only students from a particular race or religion. Thus exclusively Chinese, Tamil, or Islamic schools would not get any state funding. Most parents genuinely want their children to be exposed to their fellow Malaysians. Those few who resist, then they would have to pay for their children's education. The objective is to have children of the different races study in the same classroom, not necessarily all the time but at least during their core subject classes.

This proposal is far superior to the present Vision School concept where students from national (Malay), Chinese, and Tamil schools share the same campus but study in their segregated classrooms. If we are not careful, these Vision Schools could easily degenerate into hot-beds of race-based gangs.

Inevitably with the freedom of choice, some schools would be per-ceived to be superior than others. Such schools must have clear and transparent admission rules and procedures to prevent favoritism, except for favoring siblings attending the same school.

These common problems disposed off, I return to the essence of my reform.

Preschool And Primary Years (P-6)

Currently the participation rate for preschool in rural and poor neigh-borhoods is near zero. These are the very areas that have the greatest needs. Children of the poor are deprived in many regards. Their pov-erty means that basic health and nutritional needs are often not met. Their parents have limited formal education and thus are not in any position to give intellectual stimulation or help to their children. Schools and education are not their priorities, surviving is. There are many empirical studies linking low educational attainments with poverty and parents' years of formal schooling. This has been observed in many countries and various cultures. Malaysia is no exception.

Fortunately this seemingly intractable cycle can be broken through effective and enlightened policies. In America, successful Head Start programs like the Perry Preschool Project in Michigan showed that early interventions help even those with below normal IQs. In Malaysia special privileges have been remarkably effective in reducing the gap in educational attainment of Malays versus non-Malays. Further, the expected dropout rates between Malays and non-Malays have narrowed considerably directly as a consequence of special privileges. Such findings should embolden policymakers to expand the program aggressively and to enhance its efficacy.

I would not interfere with private preschools. On the contrary I would encourage their growth through tax incentives and facilitating the issuance of permits by minimizing the red tape. Nor should MOE interfere with their curriculum, let each school set its own. This would encourage innovation. MOE should monitor to make sure that it is safe and that no criminals are running the school or that it is being set up near a dumpsite.

I would integrate preschool with primary school and lower the age of entry to four years, especially in poor and rural neighborhoods. These deprived children would then have two years of preschool prior to entering Primary 1, to compensate for their disadvantaged background. I would also integrate nutritional and health services into the schools. Nutritional services include breakfasts, snacks, and lunches similar to America's school lunch program.

Studies in America show that even at the preschool we are already seeing differences in the readiness for learning in these youngsters, and that such differences linger throughout their school years. These differences relate to age, sex, race, ethnicity, and most important, socioeconomic status (SES). The most significant finding is that when SES is kept constant, the differences due to race and ethnicity disappear. Such insights should emboldened our policymakers to ensure that those from disadvantaged backgrounds be given compensatory superior opportunities and facilities.

I would experiment with various demonstration models to deal with the problems of rural and poor schoolchildren. In America, CES, with its emphasis on small schools and group teaching, has been remarkably successful in tough inner cities. Similarly Catholic schools, with their emphasis on strict discipline and the basics, have proved equally successful. A more novel approach is military school. It turns out that for many, strict regimentation is exactly what they need to overcome the frequent lack of authority figure at home. Chicago and Oakland, California, now have such schools and are very successful. The spick and span uniform and sense of belonging are effective antidotes to the unruly and violent gang culture outside the campus. One of these models may well be what children in poor rural Malaysia would need.

I would also have regular visits by the school nurse and dental hygienist. A survey in relatively affluent Santa Clara County, California, revealed a high percentage of school children with visual, medical and dental problems that could potentially interfere with their learning. Imagine what the situation would be in rural Malaysia. Problems like dental cavities and infected gums not only interfere with good health but also learning. As US Surgeon General Jocelyn Elders once remarked, "You can't educate a child who is not healthy, and you can't keep a child healthy who isn't educated."

When I was in primary school during colonial times, there was a special room designated for the dental hygienist and school nurse. I even had one of my teeth pulled out by her! By integrating medical and dental care into the school, problems could be detected much earlier and thus be more effectively treated. Further, these children could be taught simple personal hygiene like brushing teeth daily, washing both hands before eating (Malays eat with the right hand, often that is the only hand washed), and the wearing of footwear at all times to prevent worm infestations. This may not necessarily be a pair of expensive Nike shoes as cheap wooden sandals would be just as effective. Additionally, these children could be taught simple public health rules like sleeping under the mosquito net at night, and simple food hygiene like eating only well-cooked and well-washed foods. Dengue is endemic in Malaysia, and having schoolchildren wear long-sleeve shirts or blouses and long pants or ankle-length skirts and sarongs would reduce the incidence of mosquito bites, the risk factor for the disease. Such a uniform would also satisfy their parents' Islamic sensitivity! These children could also be taught simple rules of road safety. Everyday we read of children being struck down by traffic.

By having trained medical personnel making regular visits, clusters of illnesses with potential public health ramifications like lead poisoning and measles could be detected much earlier.

In poor areas I would introduce the local equivalent of *Bolsa Escola*, where parents would be paid for keeping their children in school. This would be far more effective in reducing rural poverty and simultaneously elevating the educational attainment of the students. It would also send a clear and dramatic message to rural parents on the importance of schooling.

During British rule, bright Malay pupils from poor families were given scholarships in the amount of RM20 to RM40 per month, depending on their grade level. Those were substantial sums, equivalent to the purchasing power today of RM80-160. They had to maintain certain scholastic achievements to receive the money. In addition, if they lived far away from school they also had free room and board at the school's hostel.

The program, as expected, was expensive but the British were smart enough to be selective, targeting only bright but poor pupils. Again because the program was expensive, it was not extensive, so the incentive value was limited. Rural folks thought it was like winning a lottery and not a genuine reward system. Had it been more widespread, more children would work hard to get it.

For incentives to work they must be both sufficiently rewarding and not too difficult to obtain, that is, both expensive and expansive. Too small a reward and people would not be motivated, and too few winners and people will dismiss it as mere luck or crapshoot. Casino operators know this psychology very well.

On the other hand if everyone were rewarded, then the incentive or motivating value would be lost. When I was in Sixth Form every Malay student including children of the rich received a stipend plus free tuition and boarding. This is still the situation with residential schools and *matrikulasi*. Such indiscriminate munificence is not only expensive and wasteful but also loses its motivating allure.

In addition to providing incentives, we must also ensure that schools are attractive, safe, and conducive to learning. They must have adequate and well-trained teachers. To achieve this we must give rural allowances to entice good teachers. We should also provide quarters to encourage them to live in and contribute to the community. Unlike my parents in days of yore, teachers and headmasters posted to rural schools today live away in the towns and commute. They do not have the opportunities to mix and interact with the children and their parents after school hours. This reduces considerably their effectiveness. The community too loses.

These innovations are expensive, but it would be more expensive if these children failed to get quality education because of inadequately trained teachers and poor facilities.

Even seemingly simple items like transportation, uniforms, books, and other supplies can be major burdens for rural families. I would provide free transportation just as in America. Uniforms, textbooks, and other supplies should also be provided free. These miscellaneous items are expensive in their aggregate. The government should not be providing them to all students rather target only the poorest and most deserving, thus maximizing the impact.

I do not quarrel much with the present curriculum. In particular, the teaching of science and mathematics in English is timely. I would go further and have both English and Malay used together in tandem throughout the school years. Doing so would make the pupils learn to read and think in both languages simultaneously. To be considered fluently bilingual one has not only to read and write in both languages but also to dream in both.

I consider myself fluently bilingual. When I read in English I automatically think and respond in English; likewise when I read in Malay, I think and respond in Malay. My brain does not go through a mental translation process; it bypasses that. When I was a surgeon in Malaysia I had no difficulty explaining complex medical issues and procedures to my Malay patients as I had already understood the concepts. I automatically and mentally processed the knowledge and then verbalized it in Malay. What I did not do was plan what I wanted to say in English and then translated into Malay.

The problem with Malaysians today is that because of their limited English, when they want to speak in that language they would first think what they are going to say in their mother tongue and then translate it into English. Not only is this process mentally inefficient, the subsequent English version will sound like the typical "Manglish," literal translations of Malay phrases. We should encourage the young to develop the capacity to absorb knowledge in both languages and then be able to express it in either.

This mental process is equivalent to someone learning the imperial and metric systems. When you are facile with both, you need not mentally convert one to the other. When visiting Tokyo and the temperature is 40 degrees Centigrade, one does not take out a calculator to convert it the more familiar Fahrenheit (104 degrees) and then say, "Wow, it's hot!" One has learned in the metric system to associate 40 degrees with uncomfortably hot; 30, T-shirt beach weather; 20, nice air-conditioned office; and 0, freezing and uncomfortable. Similarly in the Fahrenheit system, 32 degrees is freezing; 70, nice air-conditioned office; 90, beach weather, and over 100 uncomfortably hot. One trains oneself to bypass or eliminate the mental conversion phase.

This is what we should be teaching our students. When they think in English they will speak in English; and in Malay when they think in

Malay, bypassing the mental translation. The younger we start the easier it would be. One of the difficulties in teaching a second language to adults is to break this habit of wanting to translate everything mentally. The purpose of total immersion classes in learning a new language is precisely to eliminate this phase.

That was how I learned Malay and English. Malay is my mother tongue so that is the language I used at home. At school I learned totally in English. So at a very young age I learned both languages simultaneously. A child does not know how to translate, so the brain automatically bypasses that process. I just knew that in speaking to my teachers, I used English; at home, Malay. There was no confusion. You learn right from the beginning to say "beautiful house!" and in Malay, "*rumah cantek*!" (lit. house beautiful). But if you were in the mode of mentally translating what you are going to say, then you would likely say in English, your Malay thought, "House beautiful *lah*!" That of course is how Manglish comes about, literal translations of Malay phrases.

Similarly when I write in English, I gather my thoughts in English and then go ahead and write in it. When I write in Malay I gather my thoughts in Malay and then write in Malay. What I do not do is write my essay in one language and then translate it into the other. I tried it, and it sounded awkward and just not right.

Modern clinical research supports my contention. In one experiment, bilingual subjects were shown blocks of different colors and were asked to state the color in the language in which the question was asked, while their brain activities were monitored by functional MRI or PET scans (imaging techniques of brain activities). Those who were bilingual at a young age showed brain activities in only one spot of their brain when asked in the two languages, while those who were bilingual only as adults showed activities in two areas. That is, those who were bilingual since young treat the two languages as one and use only one part of the brain. Their brain is twice as efficient as those who were bilingual as adults.

Further studies show that young bilingual children learn early that names of objects are arbitrary, so they grasp abstractions early. They are also good at ignoring "noise" or misleading information.

Malaysia should capitalize on these scientific findings and push for bilingual education as early as possible. For Malaysians this would not be a novel experiment, we did it very well 50 years ago under the British.

There are many successful experiments in America on using two languages simultaneously to teach primary school-age children, as exemplified by Rice School described earlier. Likewise in Canada, more and more schools are using this approach.

Malaysia too can experiment along similar lines. In communities with a high background of English and low in Malay (as in urban areas), we could teach more subjects in Malay and fewer in English. Conversely in areas with high Malay but low English usage (rural areas), we should teach more subjects in English. The aim should be that all pupils would be fluently bilingual in Malay and English.

The other major problem with Malaysian schools is the gaping urban-rural divide. The digital divide receives much attention but it is only one manifestation of this quality gap. The dilapidated conditions of rural schools are obvious; they lack even the basics–electricity and potable water. This is one reason they do not attract good teachers. The poor facilities are compounded by double sessions. One of the worst consequences feared by Malay parents on the current proposal to teach science and mathematics in English is that it would further disadvantage rural students; hence their opposition.

The government is embarking on making all schools into single session. I would emphasize rural schools first. With single session the school day could be extended so pupils could spend the afternoon in arts, crafts, and music as well as taking part in sports or "prep" time. With such attractions and varied activities the pupils would be less likely to drop out, especially if we combine this with school lunch programs.

Tamil schools suffer the same fate as rural ones. They are small and remotely located in estates. They attract only Tamil-speaking Indians, not a very large pool. Their dwindling enrollment makes it difficult to justify their continued funding. They would be better off integrated with national schools. Many of these Tamil schools are so dilapidated that they ought to be closed for safety reasons.

National-type Chinese schools do a much better job; they are also increasingly attracting many non-Chinese students, including Malays. That speaks volumes. Their success is primarily because they emphasize the basics, especially mathematics. There is also a high degree of parental and community involvement. They pride themselves for being outside the mainstream, of being "special" and of not being mixed up with the mess that is the national system. Their facilities are also superior; few have double sessions. Apart from the common curriculum mandated by the ministry, they are remarkably free to chart their own course away from the oppressive control of officialdom.

The success of Chinese schools is precisely because the ministry does not pay much attention to them. The oppressiveness of the ministry's control inhibits any innovation, a lesson those bureaucrats have yet to learn.

We should enhance and replicate the successes of Chinese schools. These schools should go out of their way to attract even more non-Chinese, especially Malays. They should have Malay parents serve on the board or otherwise involved with the school, and have many more Malay teachers to serve as role models. They could also make the schools more "Malay friendly" by serving *halal* food and teaching Islamic Studies–in Mandarin. They do that in China; use the same texts. That would definitely sell with Malays.

If these national-type Chinese schools become more Malay friendly and succeed in expanding substantially their enrollment beyond the Chinese community, they would then be viewed less as Chinese schools and more as truly national-type schools that happen to use Mandarin as the language of instruction.

Schools must be involved with the community, and vice versa. A generation ago rural schools were involved in adult literacy classes. This conferred two additional benefits. One, it afforded an opportunity for teachers to supplement their income by teaching these classes, and two, it involved the community with the schools. The community then cared about the conditions of the schools as the adults too were attending classes there. Today there is little need for such classes nonetheless we could still use the facilities for adult education to benefit the villagers. This would also reinforce the concept of lifelong learning and enhance the learning culture in the community. There could be classes for cooking and sewing, child and baby care, and hajj preparation. Or there could be extension classes teaching the basics of business or how to become better farmers. The computer labs could also be used after school hours to teach adults. Likewise with the athletic facilities; in my youth it was quite common to have the village soccer team using the school's playing fields.

Each school should have an adult education division, the *Sekolah Lanjutan* (Continuing School) of years past. In addition to providing personal enrichment and extension classes, such schools could also provide private classes for nontraditional student to take the national examinations. American schools routinely offer such services.

Schools should be more than just for the children; they should be the focus of the community. The government is building expensive multipurpose halls in various communities, a wasteful duplicative effort. Why not build such facilities on the school ground so both school and community could benefit. Similarly many rural communities now have public libraries, again duplicating the school's library. Combine both and you have one excellent library that would benefit both school and community.

When the school becomes the center of the community, the community would likely be more involved with the school, to the mutual benefit of both. The only caution would be that such activities and use should not be that the expense of the school. But there are plenty of time after school hours, weekends, and holidays when the community could use the school's facilities.

Middle School (Years 7, 8 and 9)

My proposal calls for minimal changes to middle school. The same four core subjects would be taught daily. The curriculum could be modified to meet the needs of the students. A school with exceptionally bright students could offer advanced mathematics and special enrichment programs like GATE (Gifted and Talented Education); likewise schools with slower students could offer more remedial classes.

I would introduce electives; letting students choose their own subjects beyond the core. Some electives could be prescribed; for example, at least two years of fine arts or crafts. The student could choose to take the same fine arts or crafts for all the three years or try different one for each year. A long recognized pedagogical wisdom is that arts and crafts should be a basic part of every child's education.

I would make extracurricular activities mandatory. The theme for sports should be, "Athletics for All." Every student should participate; if he or she is not good enough to be on the school team, then there should be house teams for intramural competition. Because everyone takes part in sports there is no need for a special period for physical education.

I would design sports activities around the physical environment. For schools near rivers and the coast, I would provide swimming pools. Every year we read reports of children drowning; these are all preventable. Similarly for schools near golf courses, arrangements could be made so students could use those facilities. For the golf clubs, that would be a splendid opportunity for public relations. After all these clubs received substantial government grants and subsidized land prices, that is the least they could do to be good corporate citizens. These students could be their potential members. Athletic programs need not be expensive. Teams for soccer, *sepak takraw*, basketball, and volleyball do not cost much.

Middle school is qualitatively different from either primary or high school. This difference extends beyond mere differences in age. The middle school years are characterized by raging hormonal changes and tumultuous physical and emotional transition between childhood and adolescent. These students need their own space, away from both the pre-pubertal group as well as the older adolescents. In rural areas where there would be not enough students yes, by all means combine the primary with middle school, but the two should still be separate and independent entities, sharing only the physical campus. Preferably they should have their own separate building at either end of the school ground, and separate teachers and headmasters.

The middle school program should be broadly balanced between basic academics and the fine arts, as well as full participation in extra-curricular activities.

High School (Years 10-13)

High school would see the greatest change. Essentially there would be three streams: academic, regular, and vocational. The academic stream would prepare students for universities; vocational for trade and skilled occupations. The regular stream would prepare students for entering directly into the work force as well those who would end up at non-degree-granting institutions (technical and teachers colleges, nursing schools, and polytechnics).

Students would be streamed based on their performance at middle school, as determined by their overall GPA as well as their PMR scores. The top third would be selected for the academic stream. I would encourage an equal number to opt for the vocational, and the rest would continue in regular schools. There should be no compulsion; students would be free to choose except that entry into the academic stream would, as expected, be competitive.

The word "streaming" is a poor choice here. It connotes a permanent labeling of individuals based on some test scores. What I mean is that some schools would focus on academics and others on vocational.

The rest will continue as regular schools, offering as many subjects as there would be demands by their students. Nothing would prevent a regular school from offering classes that would normally be offered at an academic school (calculus and the pure sciences) or vocational one (woodworking, auto mechanic) if there are demands from the students.

Similarly nothing would prevent the present large schools from transforming themselves into the equivalent of the American comprehensive schools or the German *Gesamtschule* and offering the whole spectrum of subjects from academic to vocational. But instead of having one unmanageable unit I would divide the school into the three smaller components of academic, regular, and vocational, each with its own set of teachers and principals, and located in separate buildings on the same compound. They may share the some common programs for music, fine arts, and sports. In this way students could switch from one stream to the other without having to change campus and the consequent physical and social disruptions.

I would broaden the criteria of those eligible for academic schools to include the top 10 percent of students (as judged by their teachers) from every middle school. Many of them would qualify through the normal selection process, but by making this extra option we would select those bright students who for some reason do not excel in standardized tests because of a variety of reasons. One could be that their particular school was not well equipped with good teachers and facilities. This provision would obviously benefit small rural schools, and rightly so as they should be given preferential treatment. It is not the students' fault that their school is not as well equipped as urban ones. Doing this would also encourage parents to send their children to rural schools as their chance of getting into the academic high school would be greater. This inflow of involved and committed parents would only enhance the caliber of such schools.

This streaming must be flexible to cater for late bloomers as well as those who discover their technical aptitude later. Students should be able to switch in the first two years based on their aptitude, performance, and teachers' recommendations.

There will be the same four core subjects taught daily in all streams. The level or depth would vary. With the academic stream, the science could be offered in greater intensity with individual subjects like physics, chemistry, and biology; in the regular and vocational streams it could be offered simply as general, physical, or life sciences, geared to the students' needs and capabilities. Similarly for mathematics, there could be calculus and statistics for the academic stream; general and "consumer math" in the regular and vocational.

I would pattern the academic schools after the best American prep schools. Local universities could collaborate in designing the syllabus. In this way they would know exactly the academic preparations of their incoming students.

I would model vocational schools along the German Dual System. Industry experts would draw up the curriculum; they would know better than ministry officials the needs of industry. Properly designed the vocational stream could be integrated with apprenticeship programs. Students could spend their mornings in classrooms and afternoons at factories or constructions sites, combining theory and practice. Students could even be paid for working, making the vocational stream even more attractive.

Making the vocational curriculum relevant, meaningful, and with a high degree of practical orientation would greatly reduce the unacceptably high dropout rates for those who lack academic aptitude. America has elaborate remedial programs for "at risk" students, like independent study programs where students are taught less academic subjects but in a personalized fashion. The curriculum is also less rigid. Frankly a good vocational program would be far more effective.

The main purpose of vocational and other non-academic programs is to produce what Robert Reich calls the "routine production services" and "in person services" workers. The former includes factory workers, electricians, and clerical workers; the latter include service industry workers like waiters, tour guides, and childcare personnel.

Many regard these services as menial, thus not requiring full schooling, special training, or deserving high salaries. The reason these workers earn low wages in the Third World is precisely because they are not properly trained. There is a world of difference between a waiter in tuxedo serving an elaborate gourmet dinner in a dining room with tablecloth, fine china, and silver cutlery, to a sweaty Bangladeshi illegal immigrant in his undershirt serving *teh tarik* on a greasy porcelain table. In my student days I used to work in a dining room. It took me over three months before I was promoted to be a waiter, and yes, with my own tuxedo. In the process I learned how to set tables, pamper my customers, take their orders accurately, and such social graces so as to make their experience pleasurable. I was well paid for my services, enough to support my sister in university. I also made a point of saying to my inquisitive guests that I would be going to medical school in the fall. That always prompted more generous tips!

There was nothing demeaning about my job; I enjoyed it immensely. Even today when dining out I cannot help but grade the experience. Once while vacationing in Langkawi my wife and I stayed in a new resort. At dinnertime I began my usual habit of critiquing the service. Unbeknown to me, a foreign gentleman a few tables away was intently listening to my comments. When we finished dinner he stopped by and invited us to his office. He was the manager, and was very interested in my comments! He lamented on the difficulty of getting trained waiters or to have them accept the concept that there are skills and graces they have to learn in order to be good at their jobs. It happened that there was a government vocational school nearby training workers for the hotel industry. I visited it and inquired whether it had a program to train waiters, and received a befuddled look from the man in charge.

Such "menial" jobs may appear to be insulated from global competition. Malaysian waiters may feel that they need not worry about competition from America or Australia. Not true! If our waiters and tour guides cannot make the experience of our tourists pleasant and memorable, they would not return. They will go to Bali or Disneyland instead.

Even clerical workers are not immune to global competition. Many American companies are transferring their back office work to Third World countries like Jamaica. With modern satellite communications it matters not whether the processing is done in Timbuktu or Toledo, Ohio, the data could be flashed back to America instantaneously. The dictations at many American hospitals are transcribed in India. It is first digitized, sent over the Internet to India where it is downloaded, transcribed, and then e-mailed back to America ready for the patient's chart by the next morning. These jobs are done by Indian doctors who find that they could earn more by using their medical knowledge deciphering these dictations rather than treating the sick.

The service calls to American companies are answered not by highly paid American workers rather by Indians in India. They have been trained to get rid of their thick rolling accent and speak like Americans. They even acquire homey American names like Diana and Patty, and learn the minutiae of Americana so that customers at the other end of the line think that they are speaking to someone in Peoria, Illinois, and not Poona, India.

In America the fastest growing service industry is childcare. Childcare workers are tested for health, checked for criminal records, certified for cardiopulmonary resuscitation, and trained for other childcare skills. They are paid well. They are also far different from the illiterate and unskilled maids Malaysia imports by the thousands from Indonesia and Philippines. As Malaysians become more affluent, they too would want their children to be taken care of by competent personnel. Compare the quality (and hence pay) of maids working for expatriates to the Indonesian servants working for local families. Jobs like housekeeping and maid services as well as mechanics, electricians, and plumbers are well paid in America because consumers value those skills and expertise.

Because of these global implications Malaysia cannot afford to ignore the non-academic stream and the education and training for those so-called menial jobs.

The variety of vocational jobs in a modern economy is endless, especially in the service sector. I would boldly say that we should not build any more universities and instead build additional vocational schools and training institutes. This would go a long way in providing skilled workers and artisans, and at the same time give our non-academically oriented students a bright future.

Residential Schools

Residential schools are expensive and consume more than their fair share of the resources. Yet they do not have much to show. Even though they get the best students, the number of their graduates who end up at top universities is far less than that of many private institutions. We should expect more. In my scheme the present residential schools would be in the academic stream.

As these residential schools get the top students, the mission should be to prepare them for elite universities. These students must be prepped for international examinations like SAT, AP, IB, or GCE A level. This means greater emphasis on English. In addition to teaching science and mathematics in English, I would also increase the hours devoted to English classes, as well as the number of subjects taught in that language. I would go even further and make these schools entirely English medium, with Malay taught only as a subject, just like the English schools of yore.

China is converting its top schools and universities into entirely English medium. It is doing so in the conviction that their top students should be exposed to global knowledge and competition. Note, Chinese language is far older and better equipped than Malay, yet Chinese leaders have no qualms in using English. They do not consider such a move as denigrating or in any way dishonoring their language or culture.

I would stop building new residential schools and concentrate on enhancing the output and quality of existing ones. These schools should cater only for the last four years, Forms 4 to 6. It should discontinue the present lower forms. At these levels the pupils are too young to be separated from their families. Further, the predictive value of the tests on which they were selected is not very reliable. Eliminating the lower forms would also effectively increase the output without incurring much additional costs.

Presently admission is based on merit. Unfortunately it is narrowly defined exclusively in terms of examination scores without considering other factors. A doctor's son with an "A" is treated in the same manner as a villager's son with the same score. I would define merit more broadly. Thus a village boy with a B would be favored over a doctor's son with an A. Given the superior environment of the boarding school, we should expect the villager's son to perform even better. The doctor's boy will do well even if he is not admitted to the boarding school; his well-educated parents would ensure that. By admitting the villager's son over the doctor's, we would end up with potentially two well-educated Malays. Left in his regular environment, there would be minimal opportunity for the village boy to shine.

In judging merit we should look at not only the past achievements but also more importantly, the potential. The first part is easy, simply look at the test score–a computer can do that efficiently. The more difficult and judgmental part is to assess the students' total potential.

At present these residential schools are filled with children of the well to do and top civil servants. This is no surprise as they are the ones we would expect to do well at the Primary 6 examinations. But if we do not make a concerted effort to admit children of the less privileged, we would not get the best out of these expensive schools. We should learn from America. Harvard admits many students from disadvantaged background despite their less than sterling test scores because those admission officers look at the potential of these students. Similarly the highly popular Rice University School mentioned earlier purposely limits the slots available for children of its faculty members so as to give others a chance.

In my old village there is a saying, *habis kek orang pangkar* (all the food had been consumed by the servers with none left for the guests–the intended recipients). Meaning, the government's goodies have been gorged by the civil servants and politicians with little left for the people.

Residential schools should primarily be an outreach program, as originally intended. I would reserve 75 percent of the slots for disadvantaged Bumiputras or those who would be the first in their family to enter college. The other 25 percent would be open to all, including non-Bumiputras. They however, would have to pay the full costs. With the extra income thus generated these schools could augment their academic offerings with music classes, better libraries, and well-equipped laboratories instead of having to depend solely on the government for funding.

I would intensify the competition by returning poor performers back to regular schools. This would serve as a lesson to other would-be slackers and ensure that such expensive facilities would not be wasted on the lazy and the mediocre.

One way to cut costs without sacrificing quality and output would be to make these schools not fully residential. Students from nearby areas could be day students, thus sparing the school the added costs of boarding. Having more day students and reducing the need for large hostels could increase the school's capacity without incurring much additional costs. The present practice of sending students all over the country unnecessarily incurs additional transportation costs. Instead, let each school concentrate on students from within the state and nearby areas.

These schools must have stable, strong, and dedicated leadership. It is reprehensible that MCKK has had more headmasters during the last

25 years (since locals took over) than in its first 70. There was an instance when a Malay headmaster stayed barely a few months, just long enough to put an entry on his resume!

The headmastership of these schools must be a terminal appointment and generously paid. The post should not be a stepping-stone for someone on his way to be undersecretary for procurement at the ministry. The last expatriate headmaster at MCKK stayed for over a decade until his retirement. He left a significant legacy. Ask those local headmasters what their legacies are, they would be hard pressed to name any.

Visiting a premier residential recently, I was astounded that the principal could not name his top students, much less the universities they would be attending. Obviously there is minimal personal and professional commitment from these modern day educators. In contrast long after I left MCKK, I was still receiving letters from my teachers and headmaster. And they were not even Malaysians!

To support the headmasters and teachers, these schools must have an equally committed board of trustees. There is no point in appointing luminaries residing in Kuala Lumpur and who makes only occasional visits to the school. We are fortunate in having many outstanding citizens living near these schools. Appoint them! These local engineers, physicians, and lawyers would provide much-needed leadership and valuable mentors to the students. These schools would also be my ideal candidates to be liberated from MOE by having their own school-based management (SBM).

Residential schools have proliferated in the last few years, with many more in the pipeline. They divert resources away from other schools. We must critically evaluate their effectiveness and make the necessary modifications to enhance their results.

Matrikulasi

Matrikulasi was originally meant to supplement Sixth Form but its very success ended up emasculating Sixth Form. Today even leading residential schools have dispensed with Sixth Form.

Matrikulasi is a major and very expensive program. On some universities nearly half of all new enrollees are made up of *matrikulasi* students. It is time to rethink the issue. Our universities are squandering their valuable academic and physical resources doing something that could be done more efficiently and cheaply by schools. Universities should be doing only those academic activities that cannot be done elsewhere, that is, education at the undergraduate, graduate, and professional levels. Under my reform, there would be no need for *matrikulasi*.

The program has acquired an influential constituency especially among the political establishment. Recently UMNO Youth successfully reversed the decision to close UM's *matrikulasi*.

If the authorities insist on maintaining the program, then it should be used strictly as an outreach program and restricted to Bumiputra science students from disadvantaged backgrounds. Students currently attending well-equipped urban or residential schools should not be admitted. By being restrictive in this manner, the center would truly augment the pool of Bumiputra science undergraduates.

In an interview with *Utusan Melayu*, the UM professor in charge of its *matrikulasi* bragged about the center having trained children of many prominent Malays. These are precisely the students the center should not admit. They should be able to take care of themselves and not crowd out those kampong kids who truly need the extra help provided by the center.

Nor should the university use its precious PhDs to teach these classes, instead it should employ those with masters or good honors degrees. Leave the professors to do research and to teach at the degree level. This would optimize the use of valuable and scarce academic resources.

I would also revamp the curriculum, making English compulsory and taught daily. To improve the students' verbal skills, I would have them take part in small group seminars in English where they would participate in class discussions, similar to the freshman seminars at top American colleges. Additionally the students would have to be computer literate.

While I am in favor of closing down *matrikulasi* entirely, I can be persuaded to keep it open if it is used as an outreach program as described.

Islamic Schools

In addition to the national and national-type schools, there is another parallel stream–Islamic Schools. Religious schools have a long history in Malaysia. Learning in traditional Malay society consisted primarily of reading and memorizing the holy Qur'an as well as instructions in performing prayers and other rituals of the faith. These usually took place at the home of the Imam (religious teacher) or at small *suraus* (prayer houses). These later developed into *madrasah*, the village equivalent of the one-room schoolhouse. Some became bigger with living quarters for instructors and students. These schools were usually funded by the community and supplemented by modest contributions from the students.

The pedagogical skills of the teachers are marginal at best. The *madrasah* is no place for the inquisitive mind. Any questioning or otherwise expanding of the thought processes is actively discouraged. Worse, it is regarded as the machination of the devil. I briefly attended one such school; my parents wisely took me out before I would have to spend more time in purgatory. My memory of that experience was the mindless rote recitations and endless memorizations without my understanding any word. About the only kind thing I can say is that it prepared me well for my later years in medical school when I had to memorize all those anatomical terms.

These religious schools were basically neglected and ignored in colonial times. Now the federal government, eager to prove its Islamic credentials and to "out Islam" the opposition PAS, has taken over many of these schools and vastly expanded the system.

Islamic educational institutions run through the entire spectrum, from preschool to graduate and professional schools. Apart from the federal government, state governments (especially those controlled by PAS) as well as Islamic organizations are also actively setting up these schools. These religious organizations have done a significant public service by placing their schools, especially preschools, conveniently in residential areas. There are preschools in the villages as well in urban squatter areas to attract the poor. There is tremendous community support and involvement with these schools. But even in their modern versions, the intellectually oppressive ambience of the old *madrasah* still exists.

This notwithstanding, more and more Malay parents are sending their children to religious schools, both the government as well as private ones. The Islamic cachet, as usual, sells with Malays. While in the past these schools attracted primarily academic dropouts and those unable to afford the regular schools, today this is no longer the case. Often they are the school of first choice. The dropout rates are much lower, in fact non-existent. There is a palpable missionary zeal attached in attending these schools, and this is reflected both in the teachers' as well as the students' attitude. To be absent from school meant not simply playing hooky but also committing a major sin. Besides, Allah is always watching and All Knowing! There is a firm belief that they–teachers and students alike–are doing God's work.

Consequently there are few disciplinary problems. There are certainly no drug problems–a significant accomplishment these days. Teachers have absolute control over their students. Going against the teacher is not just being naughty but going against the representative of God. Awesome! There will hellfire to pay later, if not sooner. Visiting these schools I am always struck with how very well behaved the children are, very polite and dutiful.

Despite the less-than-professionally trained teachers, these students do learn. When visiting my village I am simply amazed of the glowing stories from parents about their children who had done poorly in regular school only to shine when sent to a religious one. One parent in particular boasted how his son was able to read and speak Arabic fluently in only two years. More recently I am hearing these favorable comments from Malay parents I meet in America. These are highly educated Malays who have been exposed to and benefited from Western education.

There are two possible interpretations. One is that the national stream has degenerated to such a level that the previously lowly religious schools have now become highly regarded by comparison. Two, these religious schools have really improved. After visiting both schools, I believe the first.

These religious schools, especially the private ones, have achieved much with their meager resources. There is a lesson here.

All is not well however. The teachers and headmasters may think they are doing God's work and that God is on their side, alas these mortals clearly have been negligent in their worldly responsibilities. Every so often we read of students being killed when their dormitories caught fire. The safety measures on these schools are nonexistent–no fire alarms or extinguishers, and no regular fire drills. Students sleep without mosquito nets, a severe health hazard in view of the endemicity of malaria and dengue. These schools often lack electricity; students study by the old kerosene lamps. And with their loose clothing and flowing headgear, these are dangerous firetraps.

The personal hygiene of the canteen personnel leaves much to be desired. I could hardly contain my professional concerns when I see the kids gulping the canteen food. Newspapers carry almost daily headlines of food poisoning at these schools.

The Islamic stream is an anomaly; its goals are the very opposite of the national aspirations. While the national stream seeks to integrate Malaysians, religious schools purposely keep them apart. While national schools are inclusive (or at least try to), the religious schools are explicitly exclusive. No non-Muslims need apply. While the curriculum of national schools is geared towards equipping Malaysians with relevant skills, religious schools are consumed with seeking rewards in the hereafter. While I criticize the national schools for their narrowly focused curriculum, the religious schools are even worse. One could say that the students are streamed right at preschool to pursue a religious path.

Graduates of the Islamic stream have extremely limited job opportunities outside of government or even within the public sector. Perversely the government implicitly encourages young Malays to pursue religious studies when it expanded the religious establishment. Apart from the vastly expanded religious department, the government also has specialized units like the Institute for the Understanding of Islam. Every government agency, including embassies and consulates, has a resident imam. I fail to see what functions he serves, except as a massive public work scheme to employ these graduates. There is a limit to such expansions and today we have reached the saturation point. Meaning, employment prospects even in government are now significantly reduced.

Part of the difficulty the government is having with the Malay masses is precisely because huge numbers of these Malays with qualifications in Islamic Studies (and liberal arts generally) are unable to find employment. They rightly feel betrayed, and their numbers keep growing. Thus the irony of these graduates being hostile to the very government that champions the cause of Islam.

Recently the government advertised for 100 vacancies for Islamic teachers and was stunned to receive over 4,000 applicants. Imagine the fate of those not successful, and think further that the universities would be producing more of their kind every year. It is finally dawning on the government as to the potentially explosive nature of this mess. Yet to date precious little is being done to reduce the numbers.

To be sure this problem has been building up for years. What surprises me is that it is only now that the government is aware of the problem. As is typical with MOE specifically and of Malaysian officialdom generally, everything has to reach a crisis point and blow up in their faces before they recognize that there is indeed a problem. And then a few more years would elapse before they would begin thinking of a solution. Perhaps a decade later when the problem has become overwhelming would something be done to resolve it.

The narrow curriculum of the religious stream means that its graduates have limited flexibility in employment or furthering their studies. There is also the question of academic rigor. Education Minister Musa Mohamad recently revealed that less than 25 percent of Sixth Formers from religious schools qualify for local universities, compared to over 90 percent for secular schools. This is a national disgrace. To me the more scandalous part is that it took him this long to find out, and then all he did was merely acknowledge the appalling statistics. A national workshop of local academics convened to address the issue was no better. Its deliberations were tediously long on description and woefully short on prescription.

These religious schools must be modernized. They must produce more than just future mullahs; rather they must prepare young Muslims for the modern economy.

America too has many church-based educational institutions, but they produce their share of the nation's scientists, engineers, and managers. Bellarmine, a Catholic school in San Jose, California, routinely sends its students to top colleges. Georgetown University, a Jesuit institution, has outstanding law, medical, and diplomacy schools. Only a tiny fraction of its graduates end up in the clergy. Harvard started out training only ministers, but is now famous for other than its divinity school.

These institutions do not insist that their students and faculty share their faith. Many Muslims enrich these campuses. I find the views of Muslim scholars at such institutions as Georgetown and Emory refreshing and highly enlightening. Countless Muslims have benefited immensely from the superior education afforded by these Christian institutions.

We can begin by modernizing the curriculum of religious schools to include my four core subjects. Islamic Studies should only be one subject, not the consuming curriculum. They would have a third language, Arabic. With their trilingual ability and enhanced science literacy and superior mathematical competency, these graduates would enjoy a premium in the marketplace. Not only would their scope for employment be greatly enhanced, their opportunities for further studies would also be vastly expanded.

There are many advantages in exposing these students to a wider curriculum. Many studies show that proficiency in mathematics correlates well with success at university and in later life. An understanding of biology would make them better appreciate such current dilemmas as transplantation and *in vitro* fertilization. A familiarity with modern economics would make them understand such sophisticated financial instruments as equity funding, bonds, and venture capital, and how these relate to and differ from Islamic financial principles. If these students were exposed to the social and behavioral sciences, they would be better prepared to deal with the ills of our community.

If Islamic students were fluent in English, they would be able to communicate better with and have a greater impact on others, Muslims and non-Muslims alike. Recently, some missionaries from Malaysia's Islamic Institute were preaching (*dakwah*) in America. Unfortunately they could hardly speak a word of English. Some missionaries!

Malay parents value education when couched in Islamic terms. Because of this natural affinity, it is all the more important that we must not fail these students and their parents.

The cause of Islam generally and Malays specifically would be served better if these religious schools were either abolished or integrated into the national stream. That is not a political reality; any politician who dares make that statement would be kissing his career goodbye. Yet there is merit to my argument; it would encourage greater integration. It would do immense good were future *ulamas*, *ustads*, and *ustazahs* to mix with all Malaysians in their formative years instead of being cocooned exclusively within their own kind. It would certainly end their academic and social insularity, and disabuse them of the false dichotomy between worldly and religious knowledge.

Mainstreaming religious studies would ensure that these students get a rigorous education. Islamic Studies is widely perceived as intellectually challenged, an easy way to get a degree. Encouraging it merely emphasizes credentialism–any degree will do–which is already ingrained in Malaysia. With a glut of these graduates, giving out more scholarships is simply stupid.

We should use the rich Islamic scholarly traditions to expand the students' intellectual horizon and stimulate their inquisitiveness. We should de-emphasize rituals and catechism. Sadly indoctrination passes for education at these schools. Critical thinking is discouraged; questions and doubts are not encouraged, while rote memory and conformity are expected and highly valued.

Communication in an Islamic class is strictly a one-way affair. As glorified in some ancient Arabic texts, teaching is akin to water flowing, always from the higher (instructor's) to the lower (students') level. That analogy implies something more destructive: student's mind is but a can to be filled with recycled water, not intellect to be sharpened.

Why cannot there be more rigorous intellectual discussions? How does the Muslim's Allah differ from the Greek and Hindu Gods? Is the Koran to a Muslim comparable to the bible for a Christian? Students could analyze the tithe and how it differs from present day income tax. Would a tax based on wealth (the basis for tithe) be more equitable than an income tax? Similarly, is *zakat* superior to the modern welfare state?

A lively seminar could be had comparing the Day of Judgment with the Hindu reincarnation, and how the concept of heaven and hell in Islam differs from that of other religions. I would give students hypothetical examples. Imagine had Prophet Mohammad (peace be upon him) been an Eskimo, would the imagery of hell be a place of intense scorching heat or a cold frozen dungeon? Would zealous young Malaysians be sporting thick parkas to emulate him? These are the kinds of exciting and stimulating intellectual discussions that could bring the religious class out of its usual slumber. And the answers are not given at the end of the book!

In the decade following *merdeka*, at the height of nationalism and pride in country and culture, a generation was wasted in the relentless pursuit of the national language. The dreams and hopes of thousands of young Malays were crushed when they discovered that their hard-earned certificates were worthless. We are repeating the same colossal mistake today with our zeal and emphasis on Islamic Studies.

By insisting on rigorous standards, Islamic Studies would no longer attract academic loafers, and the nation would get better religious leaders. The cause of Islam would also be considerably enhanced if future *ulamas* have a broad-based liberal education. It gives them a wider and better perspective. They would then be less likely to resort to simplistic recitations of the *hadiths* (sayings of the Prophet) or the Holy Qur'an when confronted with complex problems. Then they would make real and meaningful contributions to their *ummah* (community).

I would discontinue the Islamic High School (STAM—*Sijil Agama Tinggi Malaysia*) certificate. These students should take the regular STP, with Islamic Studies and Arabic as their two non-core subjects.

Religious schools must not be the equivalent of Muslim seminaries. Nor should they be a refuge for Malays who wish to withdraw from the modern world. We must modernize these schools before they waste more Muslim brains. Meanwhile the present students with their useless diplomas must be given supplemental training so they can contribute to society.

If we cannot discontinue the religious stream, then at least we should stop funding them. If parents want to send their children to exclusively religious schools then they would have to pay on their own. What parents do with their money is their right, but the government should not be subsidizing or funding a parallel school system that is at variance with the national aspirations.

I do not underestimate nor minimize the difficulties in reforming religious schools. The religious establishment would not take kindly to any diminution of its role or threat to its power. These people fervently believe that they are doing God's work; anyone attempting reform or in any way perceived to diminish the importance of their mission would face their wrath. But if these schools were left as they are, Islam and Malays in particular would be the losers. Reform must take place, but very carefully and with the greatest trepidation.

The Islamic establishment in Malaysia is as entrenched as the communist party is in Red China today and the Soviet Union in the past. Gorbachev tried to reform the communist system too rapidly, and ended up disintegrating the Soviet empire and getting himself nearly killed. The Red Chinese leadership is much smarter; it reforms itself slowly and surely while ostensibly subscribing to the ideals of communism. As a result China is fast galloping economically past Russia, breeding new millionaires and capitalists every day. Their leaders still extol the virtues of communism and call each other comrades, but their new motto is, "Getting rich is glorious!" China today is only nominally a communist country but in every other respect it is as capitalistic as the West.

In reforming Islamic schools I would choose the Red Chinese strategy, slowly and carefully, giving due deference to the religious establishment while quietly changing the core of the curriculum by gradually introducing modern subjects like science, mathematics, and

English, and reducing the hours devoted to revealed knowledge and prophetic traditions.

To be successful, reform must be sold to the religious establishment as a "win-win" proposition. It should be presented not as an attempt to curb its power and influence rather to enhance them. The aim of reform is not only to produce better and broader educated *ulamas* but also graduates for the secular world who have a core of Islamic belief and faith. I believe that professionals and executives would enhance their effectiveness if they were also well grounded in religious ethics.

Islamic institutions must produce their share of worldly experts and entrepreneurs. Once these institutions do that they would contribute immensely to reducing the socioeconomic gulf separating Muslims from non-Muslims. This would greatly improve race relations and bring the nation closer to its Vision 2020 aspirations.

Charter and Private Schools

Presently there is minimal private sector participation in the school system apart from preschools. Schools are essentially government monopoly, except for some private secular and religious schools. There are few private international schools but Malaysians are specifically excluded except under very unusual circumstances requiring ministerial permission.

Within the last few years MOE is relaxing its prohibition against private schools. Thus far these private schools are operated by or extensions of existing private colleges. They still have to follow the national curriculum, so there is no innovation in that area. The only changes are these schools are less crowded and have better facilities and longer hours. Like the private colleges, these schools are also dangerously segregated racially and socially. MOE does not require that they be more inclusive.

There is a definite role for the private sector. If we have private schools along the lines of international schools it would give Malaysians some choices. These schools would also give public schools much needed competition. To be effective and contribute their fair share, these schools should be more inclusive and not become enclaves of a particular social class or race. They should adhere to certain minimum academic, enrollment, and safety standards.

There are two ways in which the private sector could participate—one as a joint public and private venture in the form of charter schools, and the other as purely private schools receiving no state support.

Charter schools are popular in America. The underlying concept is to empower the ultimate consumers of schools—students and their parents—by taking control away from the central bureaucracy and giving it to the schools. The ministry would be concerned only with monitoring the quality, compliance with rules and regulations, and setting the standards.

Well designed, charter schools would lead to greater integration of students; improve the level of English; involve the private sector in the education system; and most importantly, introduce much-needed competition to the present state monopoly. Such competition would enhance quality and encourage innovation.

To gain their charter such schools would have to meet certain conditions. Their graduates would have to demonstrate competency in the national language. Their curriculum would have the same four core subjects, with the school free to fill in the rest of the day. These schools would have to recognize the uniqueness and special sensitivity of Malaysian society. Their student body must therefore reflect the community. Exceptions would be rare; a school in Ulu Kelantan could have fewer non-Bumiputras.

In return these schools would get state funding—the same amount it would have cost the government to educate these pupils in its present system. Additionally the state would guarantee loans for capital expenses. The actual lending would be done by private sources. Because of the guarantee, the interest rate should be favorable. The schools could also charge additional tuition.

Any entity, local or foreign, could establish such schools provided they meet enrolment requirements stipulated earlier as well as those that would prevent them from becoming either the one-teacher school or the giant educational factories. Further, parents and teachers should constitute the majority of the governing board to ensure that the school's mission would not be subverted. The board would have total control, including choosing the medium of instruction and the setting of fees. The board would be accountable to the students and parents; they would monitor the school better than any government official.

As added precaution, these schools must post performance bonds to repay the government's grants as well as reimburse the students should the school be closed.

Such schools should have clearly stated objectives. They could prepare students for any matriculating examination. Some could emphasize the fine arts, others, foreign languages or the sciences. These schools could look to their leading counterparts abroad as their model. Schools preparing students for American universities could emulate Groton and Exeter. Such schools would also attract foreign students and be a source of valuable foreign earnings.

For the non-college bound, there could be vocational charter schools started by private companies. Proton could have one to train automotive and body mechanics; a consortium of construction companies could start one to train plumbers, electricians, and other skilled workers. A group of hotels could start one to train workers for their industry. Industry, not the ministry, would set the curriculum.

If there is a demand there could be schools preparing students for Arabic and Chinese universities. Such schools must of course meet the enrolment mix stipulated earlier.

Charter schools would lead to greater integration, as students would take classes and do extra curricular activities together, an improvement over the present vision schools or the Pupil Integration Plan.

To prevent such schools from becoming enclaves of the rich, they would have to provide scholarships for the poor. They should also provide hostel facilities so students from rural areas would not be excluded. The schools should also have adequate facilities (playing fields, auditoriums) to preclude their being set up above shop lots.

Private schools on the other hand would not get any state funding. Like charter schools, they would still have to post performance bonds to protect their consumers. To make sure that they play their proper role in nation building and in fostering national unity, these schools should also have a student body that reflects society. The only curricular requirement is that their students must demonstrate competence in Malay and the subject should be taught daily. The students would also have to sit for the same national examination in Malay language as students in national schools.

Private schools would thus have greater autonomy than charter schools, as befits their status in not getting any public funds.

Adopting charter and private schools would require a major shift in thinking and attitude on the part of the education establishment; a paradigm shift, to use the current cliché. They must also disabuse themselves from the ingrained idea that innovations and pedagogical wisdom are the exclusive preserve of ministry bureaucrats or that the government is the only entity that can provide quality education.

Malaysia should start small, by granting charters to about 20-25 primary schools and 10-12 at the secondary level, and the same number for totally private schools. After a few years carefully evaluate the program with a view of enhancing it.

Malaysia benefited immensely by allowing private sector involvement at the tertiary level. It would also benefit by having the private sector be involved in the schools. If Malaysia could reach the stage where Chile is today with nearly half the students opting for non-public schools, imagine the lessening of the load on MOE. It could then pay more attention to those who really need its help.

Testing! Testing!…1, 2, 3!

The bane of testing in Asian schools is that they are being regarded as the end-all and be-all of learning. Even more sinister, we look upon test scores as the only dimension on which to assess an individual. Test scores become means of permanently labeling someone. We should look upon test scores "not as means of confirmation of fate but as clues to improving children's learning," to quote the Annenberg Challenge. Testing is one measure of accountability, serving as an effective feedback for students as well as their teachers and schools.

We all learn at different paces; it is part of the normal curve. We should not infer anything more beyond that. Take learning to read. All too often we label someone who is slow to read or who reads at an older age as a "slow learner," and that tag would be permanently etched on the individual. Parents' and teachers' expectations are now predicated on that label; expectations often becoming fulfilling (Rosenberg phenomenon). Learning to read is like learning to ride a bicycle. Some of us learn it quickly and at a younger age, others take longer and have to be older–the bell curve distribution. We would never make the prediction that because someone learns to ride a bicycle earlier and faster that he or she would later become a champion cyclist. Yet we do that all the time with examination scores. Examinations and tests are an important part of the feedback and accountability process, but we should not be unduly obsessed with them or to presume making unrealistic prediction of someone's potential.

We are now finding that dyslexic children are not slow learners or readers, rather they perceive the written word differently. This particular insight has helped thousands of children become better learners and productive citizens. We certainly would not label such dyslexics as Albert Einstein and Ted Turner (of CNN) as "dumb" or "slow." Some like Winston Churchill and Agatha Christie became great writers.

An appropriate and more realistic perspective on examination and test scores is greatly needed. My reform de-emphasizes national examinations and calls for eliminating SPM (Year 11 examination). With the integration of Islamic schools into the national stream, STAM would also be eliminated.

I would also change the way we assess students and in calculating the final scores on national examinations. Currently Malaysia, like other Asian countries, relies exclusively on the end-of-year assessment. The students' entire career depends on that test. If they are not feeling well that day or if there are interruptions in their personal lives like floods or a family emergency, then they would be doomed. No wonder the heightened anxiety and obsession.

I would limit standardized tests to only the four core subjects. In addition students would be continuously assessed by their teachers on all subjects throughout the year (the GPA), based on their class performance, homework assignments, as well as on regular mini tests. In ranking students for streaming and other purposes, I would use both the GPA as well as the scores on standardized tests, giving equal weight to both. Further I would use the standardized tests to evaluate both the schools and teachers, and to compare their performances with their peers of comparable size and demographic mix. In this way we extend the utility of such examinations. By reducing the number of subjects tested in standardized examinations, we reduce the temptations of teachers to "teach to the test," thus giving them room for individual creativity. More importantly, it would greatly reduce the current obsession parents, teachers, and students have with examinations and test scores–the curse of Asian educational system.

I would modify the scoring of national examinations so that the final test would contribute only 70 percent to the total score; the rest (30 percent) would come from the teachers' evaluation of the students' year-round work (GPA). To correct for interschool variations in GPAs (some teachers are more generous, others more strict) the school's GPA would be correlated with the students' overall performance at the national examinations. There are reliable and valid statistical tools to do this. A school whose students' aggregate GPAs correlate well with scores on the national examination would need no adjustment to their

GPAs. But if the school's aggregate GPAs are much higher than the scores on the national examination, then we know that the school is rather lenient, so the students' GPAs would have to be lowered to factor in this lax grading. Conversely if students with average GPAs score highly on the national examination, then the school is strict with its assessments. To be fair to the students, the school's GPA would have to be adjusted upwards to compensate for this.

There could be further statistical refinements by comparing the GPAs and scores on national examination of the top, middle, and bottom 10 percent of the students.

For the UPSR (Year 6), only the GPAs at Years 5 and 6 would count. They would each contribute 15 points to the 30-point final marks. For the PMR (Year 9), the GPAs for all three years of middle school (7, 8 and 9) would contribute equally (10 percent each) to the final score. For the STP (Year 13), the GPAs for the first two years of high school (Years 10 and 11) would each contribute 5 percent; the GPA for Year 12 would contribute 8; and Years 13, 12 percent to the final score of 30. Thus the students' day-to-day performance during the entire high school years would contribute to the final STP score. This would give a more holistic and thus fairer assessment. It would also have better predictive value.

Such a mechanism would impress upon the students that their work during the whole year is important and contributes directly to the final score. This reinforces the point that studying is a long term and continual affair, not something you cram just before the finals. This would also reduce considerably the anxiety associated with the present system where the students' entire future would be dependent on that few fateful days of testing.

Such a system would give teachers leeway to teach beyond the test. It would also discourage the present end-of-year practice where the class is consumed with "spotting" examination questions–not a particularly useful or educational exercise.

Although I call for eliminating SPM, nonetheless there could still be a national examination in the core subjects but the scores would not count. They would be used only as a trial or yardstick to measure the student's progress as well as an assessment of the school. The school and teachers could then use the information to make the necessary changes or areas to focus on for the next two years.

Although UPSR and PMR would test only the four core subjects, for ranking and streaming purposes, the GPAs of the other subjects not tested by the national examination would also be considered and be given equal weight. This would prevent students from slacking or not paying attention to these non-core subjects. These GPAs would have to be adjusted as per the formula discussed earlier to account for inter-school variability.

The terminal Form 6 examination (STP) would see the most changes. Students would take six (the four core subjects plus two more) instead of the present five subjects. I would eliminate the current use-less General Paper (*Kertas Am*). Those interested in medicine and the life sciences would take biology, physical science (physics combined with chemistry), and an Arts elective, together with the core subjects of mathematics (preferably calculus), English, and Malay. Aspiring engineers would take physics, chemistry, and mathematics, together with an arts elective plus the core subjects of English and Malay. A would-be economist or social science major would also have to take one of the sciences together with mathematics (preferably calculus and or statistics), and of course English and Malay.

Under the present system with the focus on *matrikulasi* and the consequent de-emphasis on Sixth Form, STP is fast losing its popularity. In 1995 there were over 60,000 candidates sitting for STP, in 2001 barely over 40,000. Students are abandoning Sixth Form. The irrelevance of STP can be gauged by the fact that the most popular subjects remain Malay Studies and History, while subjects like mathematics and biology account for only about 10 percent of the total. If we consider the Islamic stream with nearly 29,000 students sitting for STAM, one can see how far detached from the real world the system of education in Malaysia is, especially for Muslims.

My proposal would restore the original primacy of Sixth Form. Having these classes would have a positive ripple effect on the quality of teaching on the lower levels. The laboratory and library facilities would have to be improved and this would benefit the rest of the school. Having better qualified teachers teaching Sixth Form would also enhance the overall standard of teaching at that school.

Eliminating SPM and STAM, and testing only the four core subjects in PMR and USPR would greatly reduce the load of the examination syndicate. The results then could be released much earlier. More specifically, students in Year 6 need not have to sit for their examination in early September. That could now be deferred to late November, thus giving pupils the whole of September, October, and part of November for meaningful class time. By eliminating SPM, students would continue directly into Sixth Form in January instead of having to wait six months for their examination results.

With a reduced load, the examination syndicate could undertake much-needed research to enhance the reliability, validity, and predictability of its tests. It could also present the test scores in a meaningful format so parents could gauge the quality of the schools to help parents make the appropriate selection for their children. Schools could be ranked nationally, by state, with their peers of comparable size, location, and socioeconomic indicators. Schools could also be ranked by their academic strengths. My point is the more information parents have, the more informed would be their decision.

Schools of Second Chance

After discussing examinations, it appropriate to ponder the fate of those who fail and fall through the cracks. No matter how good a system there will always be failures. In the past when opportunities were limited, those who slipped were simply let go; there was no second chance. Many through sheer grit would make something of themselves;

the rest would suffer their fate in silence. If they have learned their bitter lesson they would pass it on to their loved ones in the hope that the mistakes would not be repeated; others would have their children and loved ones repeat them, and the same cycle is repeated.

The remarkable aspect of human capital is this: citizens are either assets or they are by default, liabilities. There is no neutral zone. They are either contributors to or takers from the economy; they either add to or subtract from the wealth of the nation. The contributors are obviously the producers and workers. The takers come in many forms: the young, elderly, and infirm. The young are takers only temporarily; with good education they too would later become contributors and pay back many times more what they had taken from society and what society had invested in them. Likewise, the infirm could be turned into contributors with good medical and rehabilitative care. Even if their infirmities were permanent and irreversible, with appropriate training and ingenuity we could turn those citizens into assets.

In the beautiful poetry of classical Malay literature, the deaf would work in a noisy environment, the blind in the dark, and the mute be entrusted with state secrets! They all have their place. The elderly, well, they had been contributors when they were young, now they deserve to reap their harvest. Increasingly in the West, with better medical care, senior citizens are contributing right into their ripe old age. William Deming, the revered management guru, is still consulting and giving seminars even in his 90's. A number of my colleagues in their 70s are still operating.

America spends an inordinate amount of resources training the intellectually challenged. Visitors may consider this to be a waste. For Third World nations with limited resources it would certainly make more sense to spend them on educating the smart ones first. But for a wealthy country like America that has taken care of the basic needs, spending funds to educate these unfortunate souls is money well spent. These children attend special classes where they are trained to do simple jobs. Then they are placed in a sheltered work environment, not subject to the regular stresses of the normal workplace. All these are attempts at turning them into producers instead of takers, to put them into the asset and away from the liability column.

The obvious societal liabilities apart from the above are criminals, dropouts, and drug addicts. They cost society indirectly by not being producers as well as directly by the damages they inflict and the costs they incur upon society. Criminals cost society directly as a result of their criminal activities, and society in turn has to expend resources to arrest, prosecute, and incarcerate them–all very expensive undertakings. In America it costs about $30,000 a year to keep a prisoner in jail, just about as much to attend Harvard. Drug addicts in addition are a public health menace, harboring such lethal communicable diseases as HIV/AIDS, hepatitis, and tuberculosis. The public will bear the burden for treating them. And if they are not treated, the public will again bear the direct burden of their spreading their deadly diseases.

Thus we must have as good and attractive a school system as possible to minimize dropouts who would enlarge the pool of criminals, addicts, and other takers in the economy. But no matter how excellent and innovative a system, we should still expect failures. As can be surmised from my earlier argument, it is not whether we should provide a second (or even third and fourth) chance for them rather how should we do it to prevent them from slipping into the liability column and costing society.

We would be spending these resources on those who fail anyway. The question is whether we pay that later (and much more expensively) through the criminal justice system and healthcare when they become criminals and addicts, or pay less now by providing effective remedial programs so they can become productive members of society. Malaysia already has a jumbled mess of expensive remedial programs like *Rakan Muda* (Friends of the Young) and more recently, the equally expensive national service. These are run by agencies that have little experience in dealing with the young. *Rakan Muda* is run by the Youth and Sports Ministry, while the proposed national service by the

Defense Ministry. The objectives of these programs are by no means clear, making it difficult to assess their effectiveness. But because they have strong political advocates, rest assured these programs would simply multiply and grow. It is naïve to believe that by simply marching our young under the blazing Malaysian sun would somehow turn them into useful citizens. Instead of spending expensive resources on *Rakan Muda* and national service, use those same resources to provide remedial classes and other enhancement programs in the schools.

The best place for children is still in the school. If regular schools fail them, then we should modify the system. We should allow students to repeat UPSR, PMR, or STM. These repeaters (I would not label them failures, as such pejorative tags tend to stick for life and unfairly burden their bearers) should not be lumped together with the regular students; instead they should have their own special class. Hopefully it would be a small one so their teachers could pay individualized attention. I would also assign the most experienced teachers for that class.

I would offer these students the extra benefit by recording on their final certificate only the better of their two examinations, the first or the repeat. Thus if in the first examination a candidate scored a B in English and a C in science but F in Malay and mathematics, but in the second (repeat) test he or she scores a C in all subjects, then the final transcript would show a B English (last year's better score) and C (this year's same or better score) for the rest. This would guarantee that their second effort would be better (certainly not worse) than the first, giving these students an added incentive.

For the more problematic (or severe) students who cannot be accommodated at regular or vocational schools, I would consider two other options: military and farm (or ranch) school. Both would be completely residential but unlike the regular boarding school, the students would have to do most of the work and earn their keep.

These students would rotate through the kitchen, maintenance yard, and farm. They are not simply doing menial jobs rather they would learn specific skills–how to cook, operate machineries, and raise animals. It is not simply that they would raise chickens or cows like their forefathers did but they would also learn some mathematics and statistics (graphing egg productions, feedings, and weight gain) and animal husbandry so that when they do return to their villages at least they would be better farmers than their parents were. The schools could even contract out the students' services. The ultimate objective is for the students to acquire some usable skills and at the same time get a basic education.

America has experimented with military academies for the problem kids in the inner cities. A similar program would work in Malaysia. Malays in particular have a fascination with uniforms and regimentation, and a military academy may just be the answer for these problem students. The academy I have in mind is very different from the present very expensive Royal Military College. I am certain that the alternatives I am suggesting would not only be cheaper than national service or *Rakan Muda* but also more effective.

These schools could emphasize sports and other extra-curricular activities, as well as vocational subjects and the performing arts. Such varied offerings would ensure that the students would find an activity that would suit their temperament and aptitude. This would also fit with the modern understanding of the multiple facets to human intelligence as conceptualized by Howard Gardner. We should offer different types of schools and teaching styles to cater to those whose talent and intelligence are manifested in different areas.

In custodial characteristics, these schools would be like prisons, with the students' time and whereabouts strictly controlled and regimented, but in philosophy it should be an educational institution. Its mission is learning, not punitive. We are more likely to succeed if we treat these students not as failures rather that we have yet to find a suitable program or teaching niche that would reach and touch them.

We must also be mindful that schools and learning or education are not synonymous. Effective learning can take place outside the classroom, and many a learned and educated man never saw the inside of a classroom. Benjamin Franklin and Thomas Jefferson are two famous examples. In America more and more parents are home schooling their children. In the past when access to schools was severely limited many Malaysians effectively educated themselves through correspondence courses. By offering different models including home, military, and ranch schools we increase the probability that the one of them would meet the particular and unique need of an individual student.

Another remarkable observation is that once students excel in one area they would then transfer their success and confidence into other areas. American schools emphasize sports for this very reason. They found that students who initially do not do well academically but are good at sports or fine arts, develop better self esteem that would help them cope with their studies later. Not to mention that should they excel in those fields, they could potentially have a more rewarding career as professionals in those areas. Many inner city youths managed to climb out of their ghettos through sports and entertainment. Look at Mike Tyson (boxing) and the many rap stars. Apart from entertaining their fans, these individuals contribute millions in income taxes. Given a different scenario, the state would have to expend resources to incarcerate them.

Coming back to military academies, another unanticipated benefit is that they provide excellent recruits for the armed services. Considering that these young men and women could easily have ended in the criminal justice system, that is a definite improvement for themselves as well as their families and society.

Our schools must not give up on any student; those unfortunate enough not to succeed the first time must be given ample opportunities to try again, and again. President Bush's education initiative of 2001 has as its theme, "No Child Left Behind." Malaysia too should have a similar commitment of not leaving any child behind, as well as giving every child all the opportunities that are needed for him or her to become a potential producer.

8

Reforming Higher Education

*U*niversities sit at the apex of the education pyramid. In the past they were a filtering system to select those destined for the elite class. They still do. But in a modern society universities serve far greater functions. They are not only the repositories of the nations' best and brightest but also the critical element and pillar of the modern economy. Universities produce skilled professionals and others that Robert Reich refers to as the "symbolic analytic workers." These are the high value-added workers who will propel a nation into the new K-economy. In the words of the *Economist*, "Universities are the nurseries of the next generation's brains." They and other institutions of higher education are no longer a luxury; they are essential for the economic as well as social growth of a nation.

This chapter contains my proposals for revamping higher education, beginning with the universities.

Public Universities

Public colleges and universities are clearly not meeting the needs of the nation. Consider these facts. Less than 20 percent of high school graduates continue on to post secondary institutions; impressive when compared to Zambia and Papua New Guinea, but not so hot when compared to Japan or South Korea. More and more students, in particular non-Malays, are opting for foreign matriculation examinations, and there is a proliferation of private institutions to cater for this growing market. This is not a reflection of the nation being the "center of educational excellence," as the authorities would like us to believe rather students and their parents lack confidence in public institutions. Where there is a tradition of quality public institutions as in Singapore, private universities and colleges have a tough time competing. Only the likes of Johns Hopkins and the University of Chicago dare enter the market; East London University need not bother.

The most damaging indictment is that employers rate graduates of local public universities poorly. Earlier I noted the plight of over 40,000 local graduates unable to find jobs. That's not all. The performances of public servants, who are mostly products of local universities, leave much to be desired. This last point was highlighted recently by concerns expressed by the Deputy Prime Minister that Malaysian civil servants and diplomats cannot understand much less negotiate effectively treaties and agreements with foreign governments and international bodies. Malaysians abroad who have frequent encounters with our diplomats, especially the younger ones, are not surprised by this revelation. We knew this a long time ago.

In the past, professional qualifications from UM were recognized abroad, thus facilitating the post-graduate studies of local students. The British General Medical Council long ago revoked its recognition of UM's medical degree. Even Anuar Zaini, UM's vice-chancellor and former dean of it's medical faculty, is alarmed at the rapidly declining standard of medical education. The student to instructor ratio in Malaysia, as the good doctor rightly pointed out, is a dangerous 18 to 1; in Singapore and elsewhere in the advanced world, it is 5 to 1 or better.

Few local graduates end up at leading graduate schools abroad, and locally minted PhDs rarely seek or can secure post-doctoral appointments at major centers. The list goes on.

The deficiencies of our public universities are in three major areas: management, academic offerings, and personnel. All three are interrelated, but I will dissect them separately.

The Management

Public universities are functionally administrative units of MOE, with the minister making all the decisions, major and minor. He decides who can be invited to speak on campus or become professors and deans. Universities have supposedly independent Board of Trustees headed by such luminaries as sultans and former kings. I am sure they do make some independent decisions, like what to serve at the convocation pageantry and the design of graduation gowns. On substantive matters, they defer to or await orders from the bureaucrats at the ministry.

As the World Bank noted, government should be supervisors, not directors of higher education. It should set general guidelines and then give the universities the freedom to operate within those parameters. Empower the intellectuals and professionals on campus, trust their judgment; if they are not up to snuff, fire them and get others more competent and talented.

In a feeble attempt at liberalization, MOE embarked on a flurry of "corporatization" exercises aimed at giving public universities greater freedom. In theory the corporate structure would liberate them from the oppressive stranglehold of the ministry. Thus far only UM has been incorporated. Unfortunately only its legal status has changed, everything else including policies and personnel remains the same. MOE still calls the shots.

As state-financed institutions, public universities must remain accountable to the body politic. I am not disputing or challenging that. But this control could be achieved without putting the university on a tight leash and strangulating it. The minister could exert control through the careful selection of trustees. Once you have chosen a group of talented individuals to lead the campus, leave them alone. Let the trustees pick the vice-chancellor and other key personnel. If the vice-chancellor does not perform, frits his time away, or wastes valuable funds on gaudy graduation exercises instead of on the library, let the trustees straighten him or her out. If the trustees are not keeping close tabs, then remove or do not reappoint them.

Unfortunately most trustees of public universities today are either civil servants or discredited politicians. This perpetuates the civil service mentality on campus.

The next time a vice-chancellorship becomes vacant, I suggest the minister should invite the trustees to convene a select committee with representatives from the faculty, students, and alumni to short list the candidates and make a final recommendation. I have no problem with the minister having veto power over the appointment; that would be considerably better than having him directly appointing the candidate.

With representatives from the academic community the committee would more likely select someone highly respected on campus, most likely an accomplished scholar or scientist. Political types usually do not carry much weight among academics. It is important that whoever is selected must have the confidence of the academic community. Civil servants, "has been" politicians, and less than outstanding scholars, the usual staple of ministerial appointments, would have difficulty commanding respect on campus.

The best candidate would be a solid scholar or scientist with exceptional executive talent. But if it were a choice between accomplished scholars with less than capable administrative skills versus capable administrators with no academic bent, I would definitely pick the former. At least then you could provide them with capable administrative assistants.

All too often top campus officials are picked more for their political leanings rather than academic achievements. Ministers rarely seek outside counsel, least of all from academics, in making these senior appointments. Peruse the resume of top campus officials, with rare exceptions they are individuals singularly lacking in scholarly accomplishments. When these academic leaders have not done significant research or published anything original, it is hard for them to appreciate much less respect scholarly pursuits. In my *Malaysia in the Era of*

Globalization I relate the experience of Ungku Aziz, the distinguished former vice-chancellor of UM, in trying to expand the campus library. The senior civil servant at the ministry insisted that all the books then in the library must be read first! It would not surprise me if that civil servant were later promoted to head a new campus.

Ungku Aziz is the rare exception of an accomplished scholar being picked to head a university, but he was of the old era.

The key person on campus is the vice-chancellor. If he (thus far they have all been males) does not value scholarly pursuits, then he is not likely to encourage such activities. Nor would he be supportive of intellectuals, scholars, and researchers. More than likely the creative and the productive would be shunted to some remote corners on campus. The whole academic atmosphere would be destroyed.

By actively involving the entire campus community when making top appointments, the authorities are implicitly expressing their respect for the scholars and professors, and value their input.

What I find reprehensible is the disdain and outright contempt ministers and politicians have for academics. This is especially so when those academics dare criticize the authorities. Earlier I mentioned the cheekiness of a junior UMNO functionary Azalina Othman calling for the resignation of UM's Annuar Zaini. If we want our graduates to be capable of independent and critical thinking, then we must allow their professors some freedom. If we shackle them, one consequence would be that we would attract only the meek and those with a propensity to ingratiate themselves to the powerful. They in turn would transmit those same values to their students. Before long we would have a nation of sheep, waiting to be herded by the shepherd, unable or afraid to venture out on their own. When one bleats, the rest would quickly follow. That is not a recipe for a competitive society; it is a design for disaster. There would be no one to warn the shepherd that they are all heading for the cliff.

I would throw out the highly restrictive elements of the Universities Act. If academics misbehave, there are enough laws to take care of such miscreants. The Act gives undue power to the minister; and he has not hesitated in wielding it. During the haze of 1977 the minister prohibited academic environmentalists from releasing their studies. Now professors have to get the minister's permission to publish. Imagine!

Giving universities autonomy means decentralizing their management. Make each campus an independent administrative entity; the equivalent of SBM, with a global budget based on agreed upon performance criteria. This would be more effective way of exerting control instead of the present crude and oppressive mechanisms.

Let each university decide how to spend its funds. There is no need for prior approval from the Treasury once that budget is allocated. Surely the university's accountants are as competent to track the funds as those of Treasury and MOE. If a vice-chancellor decides to waste the funds on lavish graduation ceremonies and ornate entrance arches, let him. Trust the trustees and the greater university community to keep him in line. If the minister does not like the path the university is taking, be patient. Do not reappoint the trustees, and then be extra careful in selecting their replacements.

Presently academics are bound by the same rules as civil servants, right down to the class of air travels they are entitled. I recently met a dean on a study tour of America and was surprised to find that he was given first class air tickets. External examiners at Malaysian universities are also given similar royal treatment. Heck, even Stanford's deans do not get such cushy perks. On inquiring, I was told that that was the appropriate status per civil service code. The difference between economy and first class return air ticket between Kuala Lumpur and Los Angeles is over US$10,000, enough to double the campus annual library acquisition! But the university is unable to establish its own priorities. If the dean conscientiously opts for economy travel, the money saved would simply revert to MOE or Treasury, for their officials' first class travel. The library would still have to beg.

Decentralizing the management would enable the university to escape the stranglehold of both of MOE as well as Treasury. Today every expense has to be approved by these two authorities, and knowing the pace of the civil service, one can imagine how fast things get done.

Independent management would also free the university to chart its own course. Malaysian universities are essentially clones of one another, with little or no differentiation. They do not even select their own students; the ministry does that.

Being a corporation allows the university to enter into partnership with private entities in providing ancillary campus services. Presently substantial resources are directed merely to feed and house the students. The university could free itself of this onerous burden by contracting it out. Marriott, the company that caters to airlines, provides food services on many American campuses. Similarly private developers could lease campus land to build and operate dormitories and apartments. This would not only alleviate the housing shortages but also free the university from the administrative hassles and headache of running these non-academic services. Those can be more efficiently run by private companies, and become revenue sources instead of cost items. The university could then dispense with the position of deputy vice-chancellor for housing, and send him back to the classroom!

Universities should select their students. The present central application process at MOE should be just a data-gathering and coordinating center, with the students stating their preferences of campus and majors. It does not serve the students or the universities to have the ministry do the selecting. It should act merely as a facilitator to avoid duplication of efforts with students having to file separate applications for every campus they aspire. What I am suggesting is similar to the service run by the University of California System.

This would also encourage competition among the campuses to attract students. We would also get a clear picture of what students think of the various universities. Students too would benefit. A student who wants to be a doctor but his or her test scores are not high enough, would want to apply to the less competitive campus.

MOE has enough responsibilities without having the bother of running the various campuses. These universities have smart people; surely they do not need supervision or control from the ministry. All MOE has to do is issue general guidelines, and then use the more effective mechanism of funding and selection of trustees to exert influence over the universities.

Academic Offerings

The second area needing reform is the academic offerings, specifically undergraduate programs. They are too narrowly focused and rigid. Students are not exposed to a broad-based, liberal education. When they graduate they have little flexibility in the marketplace or in furthering their studies. The problem is compounded by their low English fluency and limited mathematical competency.

Consider the typical liberal arts majors of a local university. The last time they had been exposed to mathematics, science, and English was in Form 5. During Sixth Form or *matrikulasi*, they were not required to take these subjects. Thus they have the mathematical skills of an American Grade 11 student, at best. Considering the low standard of mathematics at most Malaysian schools, I would lower that assessment to that of Grade 10–very minimal and elementary. Islamic Studies graduates are worse as their entire school and undergraduate years consumed with religious studies. Yet these are the graduates who will man the civil service and run such ministries as Treasury and Trade where they will be in charge of billions of ringgit. One of them, Abdullah Badawi, is destined to be the next prime minister.

The sorry caliber of these public servants is best illustrated by an encounter I had recently with a former senior Treasury official. We were discussing interest rates, and he made the comment that an increase of 5 to 6 percent represented *only* a 1 percent increase. One does not need to understand higher mathematics to realize that that represented a massive 20 percent hike (one fifth higher). Similarly, a country with a population growth rate of 2 percent annually is growing twice as fast (100 percent more) as one growing at only 1 percent. The difference is not only 1 percent. If one has a deeper understanding of mathematics and a better grasp at the meaning of numbers, the differences between figures take on entirely different implications.

There are obvious quantitative as well as the more significant qualitative differences between growth rates that are arithmetic, geometric, and exponential. Even with simple arithmetic growth, there is a world of difference between simple and compound rates. A savings account with a simple interest rate of 7 percent will double in about 14 years, with compound interest, in 10. Put differently, $100 at 7 percent compound interest would yield $100 in ten years but only $70 with simple interest. Quite a difference!

Consider the magnitude (or order) of difference between geometric and exponential growth. In the real world different rules apply to entities with such different growth patterns.

On another occasion a senior official of a Malaysian trust company on a business trip to America was showing me his company's cashiers check he was carrying. He was trying to impress me with his heavy responsibilities as the check was for a substantial sum. When I asked him why he bothered with the check instead of wiring the funds, he was perplexed. That would not only have been safer but also save his company the incurred interest during his two-week trip. Had he kept the money in Malaysia and then wired it to America on the day he closed the deal, the amount of interest earned during his travel would more than pay for his travel.

When you are dealing with small sums, a few days of interest matter little. But in dealing with millions and billions, you want the interest rates negotiated to the fourth or fifth decimal point, and days count. On a transaction to buy a 747 jet, nobody carries checks; funds are instantaneously transferred electronically. With such loans the difference between an interest rate of 7.0250% and 7.0275% is worth the tough negotiations.

The greatest show of ignorance for figures was demonstrated by Anwar Ibrahim. As is typical with most Malay politicians, Anwar is a Malay Studies graduate of a local university, but through politics he became Finance Minister. After he was fired as Deputy Prime Minster he made the spectacular accusation that one of his cabinet colleagues had smuggled billions of ringgit out of the country. Anwar related how an airline cabin crew supposedly described to him in graphic details of the minister with his attaché case bulging with smuggled notes. It does not take much imagination to see through the absurdity of that wild claim, yet it was widely disseminated in cyberspace and in the local media controlled by Anwar's supporters. Here is why I scoffed at the ridiculous accusation. Even if the loot had been issued in the highest denomination (RM1,000), the culprit minister would need a few gunny sacks full, not a briefcase. When I posted this simple physical fact on the many pro Anwar websites and chat groups, they sheepishly discontinued carrying that "news" item. Anwar obviously had no conception physically and perhaps even fiscally of a billon ringgit. Yet he was Finance Minister!

Such demonstrations of gross ignorance among ministers and senior civil servants can no longer be hidden. They are too obvious. Earlier I mentioned the Deputy Prime Minister's concerns over the performance of the nation's senior diplomats and officials at foreign conferences. I have been following the highly contentious negotiations with Singapore over the sale of water. While Singapore sends Harvard MBAs to negotiate, we send officials who think that the difference between 1 and 2 percent is only 1 percent! If our officials would only open their eyes and widen their intellectual horizon, they would realize that water, especially clean unpolluted water, is fast becoming a scarce and thus invaluable commodity. In supermarkets a bottle of water costs more than gasoline! Malaysian officials who negotiated long-term contracts without any clause for periodic reviews or automatic increases deserve to be screwed royally.

The last contract negotiated by Malaysia extended Singapore's term to 2060, with no provisions for periodic reviews! Nothing remains constant for such a long period; no one can predict that far ahead. The British managed to get that great deal from the Sultan of Johore early in the last century simply because Britain was an imperial power and could dictate the terms. They did the same thing to the Chinese over Hong Kong.

Unfortunately it is not the civil servants who will pay the price for such incompetence, rather the nation.

These realities are beyond the grasp of our civil servants. Their intellectual horizon is narrow; their reading does not extend beyond the civil service bulletin. They were not encouraged during their student days to be adventurous intellectually. Just read the prescribed texts and remember what had been lectured long enough to regurgitate at examination time.

The examples I describe involve essentially elementary arithmetic where the relationships are linear; nothing sophisticated mathematically. Consider more complicated situations with many more variables to factor in and where the relationships are non-linear. Here you would need an understanding of higher mathematics including calculus and statistics. I do not mean that one has to be able to do the calculations–we have computers that could do that in seconds–rather we should understand the underlying concepts, their meanings, and correlates in real life. I have long forgotten how to solve quadratic equations and how to differentiate and integrate variables, but the concepts still remain clear to me.

There have been some tepid and tentative changes introduced recently to broaden the undergraduate curriculum. Deputy Prime Minister Badawi proposed that Islamic Studies students take one elective outside their major. More recently, UUM and UPM require their students to take the MUET test and some courses in English. These are tentative, very tentative; more needs to be done.

I would restore the undergraduate years back to four. If that cannot be done, than at least make the honors program four years. Broaden the curriculum so students are exposed to a wide variety of disciplines. The present pattern is a hangover of the British system where the emphasis is on depth at the expense of breath. There is plenty of time to go into depth later in the undergraduate years.

Malaysia must emulate top American universities where all undergraduates take at least one year of English, liberal arts, mathematics, and a laboratory science as part of the "general ed" core. They are also expected to have written dozens of term papers by the time they graduate. Some have their senior thesis in addition. All first year students must take a seminar course where the emphasis is on class participation and oral communication. This should be conducted in English and in small groups to enhance the students' verbal skills.

I am baffled that with the nation now emphasizing English, few universities have a Department of English. This "disconnect" between the campus and the outside world is obvious to all except those in charge. The English Department on all campuses must be strengthened in anticipation for the greater emphasis on English.

Additionally all incoming students must be computer literate. They should be able to use word processor, e-mails, and the Internet. The universities need not provide these non-credit courses; students could acquire them through the many proprietary classes available during the hiatus between school and university.

Like the undergraduate program, graduate studies must also be revamped and upgraded. Universities have a mission beyond simply transmitting knowledge–important though that is–to creating and applying knowledge. We cannot simply assume that the principles and assumptions that apply elsewhere are applicable or even relevant locally. They have to be empirically proven within the Malaysian context. If they are not applicable we have to discover why. Research must be an integral component of local universities, and with it, strong graduate programs.

Presently entry into graduate studies is based entirely on having a good undergraduate degree. The problem is, universities vary greatly in quality and there must be another independent yardstick. America has the Graduate Records Examination (GRE) where students are tested on general principles and in broad areas. Malaysia does not have anything comparable. Many Malaysians view the GRE as simply a barrier preventing their entry into American graduate programs. The main reason for this attitude is that Malaysians fare poorly on such tests; thus they prefer doing their graduate studies elsewhere other than America where the GRE is not required.

I would make all potential graduate students take the GRE. Until more data are collected to determine its relevance, I would not base admission decisions on the GRE scores alone. GRE would be yet another yardstick to assess the students and programs. The validity and reliability of that yardstick will be known only after the data are analyzed. In America, in addition to the GRE, all doctoral students undergo at least a year of candidacy where they have to take courses in related fields. Thus social science doctoral candidates would have to take courses in statistics and calculus, as these are two powerful tools for their research. In addition they would have to take formal courses in research methodology, data collection and interpretation, plus in depth courses in their specific and related disciplines. Apart from getting above average scores on the coursework, candidates have to sit for a comprehensive oral (candidacy) examination. All these before they begin their research. It is a rigorous program; hence the high regards American doctorates command worldwide. In contrast, a Malaysian PhD is entirely by research, with no formal course work.

Two specific disciplines deserve special discussion: medicine and law. Today these two are like any other undergraduate programs; students enter directly from high school. In America, medical and law are graduate programs, students must have a baccalaureate degree before pursuing them. Australian medical schools are slowly converting into the America model, with Britain contemplating the same. Singapore is planning its second medical faculty modeled along similar lines.

Medicine is highly specialized and very intense. The curriculum is already crowded with the necessary basic and clinical sciences; there is no time for other studies. If students already have a baccalaureate degree and have taken courses in the basic science and liberal arts, they could then concentrate purely on medicine and the program could be shortened to four instead of the present five years. We would get more broadly trained doctors to boot, instead of the present narrowly focused technicians.

Some of my classmates in medical school had degrees in engineering, history, music, religious studies, and even architecture. This makes for an intellectually stimulating class. It is this hybridization of the various disciplines that makes for the remarkable intellectual vigor of American professional schools.

The training of medical specialists also needs revision. In the past they had to acquire recognized international (usually British or Australian) qualifications like FRCS (Fellow of the Royal College of Surgeons) and MRCP (Membership of the Royal College of Physicians). Unfortunately the local training was haphazard or non-existent; the trainees were left on their own with no formal seminars or teaching. Consequently the pass rate was atrocious; it was the rare candidate who succeeded on the first try. Thus Malaysian academics did away with these foreign examinations and substituted local ones on the pretext that those foreign tests were not valid. Nobody has shown that a Malaysian with an acute appendicitis should be treated differently from an Englishman with the same malady. Unless Malaysian researches can show otherwise, then we should stick with the standard treatment, British or otherwise. The unstated reason to do away with the foreign tests was because local candidates fared poorly.

When I was associated with the General Hospital Kuala Lumpur, I instituted a training program similar to that of an American teaching hospital, with regular teaching rounds and formal seminars. I also assigned each of my medical officers with specific research topics for them to pursue independently. As a result all my trainees passed their FRCS examination, including two who sat for the first time. One is Freda Meah, now a Professor of Surgery at UKM, the other, Zulkifli Laidin, later to become a pediatric surgeon. Further all my trainees managed to publish a paper in refereed journals. My point is, when young Malaysians are rigorously trained and high standards set, they respond.

Today UKM is reverting to its old pattern; trainees now sit for an internal M. Med. examination instead of recognized foreign qualifications. No surprise that I rarely find papers in refereed medical journals emanating from Malaysia.

One reason local academics give for not demanding higher standards or aspiring to greater heights is that doing so would risk losing their graduates to the First World. If the West recognized their qualifications, these graduates would be tempted to emigrate. Forty percent of the graduates from the prestigious Indian Institute of Technology end up in America, likewise their top doctors. Thus by having local graduates fluent only in Malay and their qualifications recognized only locally, they would not be tempted or able to leave. This mentality is akin to that of the ancient Chinese who wrapped the feet of their female infants so that when they grew up they would not run away from their husbands. Trapping by handicapping!

Yes, there would be that danger when you meet or exceed international standards, but the solution to the "Indian problem" is not to downgrade your institutions, rather to treat your valuable and talented graduates accordingly by paying them globally competitive salaries so they would not be tempted to leave.

Would-be lawyers too need broad-based liberal education before pursuing their profession. Law in a modern society is highly complex. How can we expect them to craft contracts involving biogenetic engineering when they have no clue as to what DNA is? Or represent their high tech clients when they do not know the difference between bits and bytes?

Before my daughter entered law school, she had an undergraduate degree in political science, but she also took courses in such seemingly unrelated fields as calculus and genetics. Now as a corporate lawyer and litigator, she finds all this background knowledge immensely helpful.

The other major deficiency of Malaysian universities is their lack of extension and continuing education programs. There are limited opportunities for nontraditional students (those who have left the formal school system) to enter university. Presently they would have to enroll in private colleges first for their matriculation. American universities have extension services catering for these students as well as providing non-certificate enrichment courses. Harvard's extension department offers beginners' level courses as well as those leading to masters' degrees. Many American universities have formal programs for nontraditional students. Columbia's School of General Studies is one such outstanding program. Colleges in my area, from the local community college to Stanford University, offer such courses and I have taken them both for personal enrichment as well as for continuing medical education.

Continuing professional education is big business on American campuses. Georgia Tech has one for business popular with executives because it is so well equipped, complete with hotel and conference facilities. By providing these services, universities would be more directly involved with the community. More importantly the community too would feel connected with the campus. This would ease the perception of the ivory tower isolation and aloofness so common with many Third World institutions.

The university experience is more than just going to lectures and handing in your assignments. It also means learning from your classmates and exposing yourself to those of different views, cultures, and aspirations. I find the segregation of students on campus along racial lines as well as disciplines disappointing. The university must play its role in integrating the students.

I would make the first undergraduate year fully residential, even for students living nearby. Exceptions would be rare and only under the most extenuating circumstances. I would abolish the present separate residential colleges based on faculty. Mix the students; it would do immense good were medical students to share dorms with music majors. I would also intentionally mix the students by race. I would make this explicit to all applicants so that those who would be uncomfortable with such arrangements would know way ahead and not bother to apply. If a Chinese student wants to share a room only with his or her own kind, then he or she would be well advised to apply to a university in Taiwan instead. Similarly if a Muslim student does not want to room with an infidel, then he or she should apply to a university in Saudi Arabia.

Such rules should be flexible. Students who are stuck with a totally incompatible roommate should be allowed to change. This could happen even when sharing a room with a previously good friend or classmate.

Universities should be a place where all ideas are explored, including and especially those currently not popular. There must be an atmosphere of open inquiry and tolerance for differences in viewpoints, and for healthy debate. Unfortunately today universities have to get the minister's permission even to invite outside speakers. It is interesting that in 2001 Johns Hopkins University successfully brought representatives of all Malaysian political parties to a conference. If representatives of Malaysia's wildly divergent political parties could gather and express their views on an American campus without resorting to fist fights or inciting a riot, why cannot such an event be held on a local campus? Of course not even the UMNO representatives would dare approach their superiors back home about planning a similar gathering in Malaysia.

When citizens cannot or are not allowed to sit together to express their differences in an open and civil manner, why, then they would do so on the streets. Recently there was much talk on bridging the increasing polarization of Malays with respect to Islam. Why cannot a Malaysian university convene a seminar and have speakers representing the whole spectrum of opinion similar to what Hopkins did to the politicians? Had local academics taken the initiative, there would not be the charade of the on and off "great debate" between PAS and UMNO that never came about. No one took that initiative because they were all waiting for a directive from the ministry. Such are the negative consequences of too much central control.

Personnel

The two major problems with personnel are how to break down the intellectual insularity, and to retain precious talent on campus.

An example will illustrate this insularity. A senior academic sociologist reviewed my *The Malay Dilemma Revisited*. I was flattered to receive such high level attention, and even more thrilled when the newspaper splashed her review over the entire page, with bold headlines no less. Pleased as I was for the attention, what intrigued me was that she did not address the issues I raised or the validity of my observations. Instead she took me to task for daring to comment on social issues. To her such matters are best left to professional sociologists like herself; us mere mortals should rest our writing quills. To her way of thinking, since I am neither a sociologist nor currently residing in Malaysia to boot, my views have no merit. Would she have been differently disposed had I been a social scientist or living locally?

While artificial boundaries separating the various academic disciplines are fast disappearing in the developed world, in good old Malaysia the academics still think that only sociologists should comment on social issues, and doctors should stick only to medicine!

Such insularities are expressed in other silly and destructive ways. A former colleague, a distinguished cardiologist, was keen to teach and the medical school could have definitely used his expertise. Not surprisingly he did not want to give up his lucrative private practice to go into fulltime academic medicine. He asked the dean for a part-time honorary clinical appointment, but was rebuffed. The dean considered such part-timers as interlopers, trying to get the best of both worlds—a lucrative income and an academic title. "Professorships are not like datukships to be dispensed liberally," he sniffed. Such exclusivity! Never mind that such an appointment would benefit the faculty and students.

I am pleased to note some recent positive changes. UUM has appointed a number of leading industry figures as adjunct professors to its business school. This definitely reduces the silly town-gown rivalry and the attendant destructive "us versus them" mentality, quite apart from reducing the intellectual insularity on campus. UUM however, is a poor learner. Most of its adjunct professors are individuals residing hundreds of miles away; I fail to see how they could contribute effectively to the teaching program. Once a year visit to the campus does not qualify one to be on the faculty. I am surprised that the many universities in Klang Valley do not follow UUM's example, especially considering the wealth of talent in their midst.

I would go further. On American campuses each faculty or department has an advisory committee of major employers, outside experts, and alumni. In this way changes in and the realities of the outside world are quickly communicated to the campus community. As a result of such input, what my wife is teaching today bears little resemblance to what she did a mere five years ago. Today her students do their assignments on computers and submit them on discs or via e-mail.

Yet another way of breaking down the artificial barriers is to encourage interdisciplinary studies and joint academic appointments. An economist studying Islamic financial instruments could have joint appointment with the Islamic Studies department. Likewise, a sociologist studying rural health could seek a joint appointment with the School of Public Health.

The impact of this intellectual insularity is initially subtle, but in the long term the cumulative consequences can be devastating. The decline of the great traditions of Islamic scholarship can be attributed to the insularity of its later scholars. Early Muslim scholars in contrast were open; they learned from the Greeks and Romans, synthesized the knowledge, and then went on to make their own seminal contributions. Much of what we know today as secular knowledge is deeply rooted in the contributions of those early Islamic scholars. But sometime after the 13th century Muslim scholars became insular. They began to differentiate between religious knowledge (*ilm' ain*) from the secular (*ilm kafiyah*). Later Muslim scholars concentrated purely on the religious, leaving Western scholars to pursue secular knowledge, which they did with vigor, armed with inquiring and critical attitudes imbued in them by the early Muslim scholars.

A measure of the insularity of modern Islamic scholars can be gauged by the fact that until recently the oldest Muslim university, Al Azhar in Cairo, had no disciplines outside of religious studies. Only in 1966 did it begin to have other faculties in an attempt to expose the *ulama* to the realities of the modern world.

Knowledge is knowledge; they all ultimately originate with Allah. This artificial division between religious and secular is just that—artificial. The great Malay philosopher and *ulama*, Haji Abdul Malik Karim Amrullah (HAMKA), said it best. Allah gave us two books of revelations: one is open–the Quran–which He revealed to His Chosen Messenger, Mohammad (pbuh); the other is closed–the universe around and within us. We have an obligation to read this second Quran just as much as the first. In pursuing the natural sciences we are doing exactly this.

It is significant that before he was a religious scholar, HAMKA had broad education and experience, very unlike the cloistered upbringing of present-day *ulamas*. He was a journalist, novelist, and even a politician; he brought his vast secular experience and knowledge to bear on his religious studies. This reinforces my earlier point on the importance of broad-based liberal education.

If we keep our scholars tightly in their own literal and intellectual cubbyholes, they too will suffer the fate of later Muslim scholars, and will stagnate and be left behind.

The second problem of retaining talent on campus is more problematic. For one, the pay scale is rigidly tied to the civil service. Promotions too are like the civil service, more on seniority than academic productivity. Additionally, the pay differential between university and private sector, especially for professionals and scientists, is very large. For those with desirable qualifications from elite foreign universities, there is the attraction of academic appointments abroad with their more lucrative pay and far more satisfying work environment.

Malaysian universities can greatly reduce this brain drain by adapting some of the innovative ideas used successfully by Western universities. One, reduce the income disparity by allowing faculty members to supplement their income by doing private consulting work or by providing them with market allowances. Two, supplement the academic staff by appointing private sector experts as Adjunct or Clinical Professors. And three, establish International Tract appointments with globally attractive salaries to attract world-class academics in disciplines that are badly needed.

Before expanding it is helpful to remember that in dealing with highly talented individuals whose skills are in demand worldwide, we must be flexible and accommodating. Simply dismissing those who leave as greedy or unpatriotic does not solve the problem. Let me illustrate this.

A Malaysian with a PhD in engineering from a prestigious American university returned home. He had a number of patents to his credit and needed some protected time to develop them. Instead of capitalizing on his expertise, the dean made him teach introductory calculus–a colossal waste of talent. Without support from the university he soon left. For the university and nation, a lost opportunity.

Contrast that with the experience of another engineer I know here in California. He has a senior appointment with IBM and is also on the faculty at Berkeley. But the National University of Singapore (NUS) was eager to recruit him even though he is not a Singaporean. But he did not want to give up his IBM job or Berkeley ties even though Singapore's remuneration package was more than attractive. In the end NUS agreed to have his service part time. Every three months he would fly to Singapore for two weeks to give lectures, seminars, and supervise the graduate students. Imagine the amazing length and ingenuity NUS went through to secure his service.

Malaysia would need to be not only flexible but also imaginative in trying to entice top talent. Exhortations to patriotism can only go so far.

Market allowances could be used to compensate those academics whose skills are in great demand by the private sector. The advantage of an allowance over a general salary increase is that it is both selective and adjustable. With the present glut of Islamic Studies experts there is no need for special allowances to retain them, but should the situation change in the future, then by all means use the incentive. Meanwhile, why waste money on a problem that does not exist? Universities certainly need incentives to keep their scientists and professionals.

Instead of or even in addition to the market allowance, universities could permit their academics to supplement their income by doing private work. English professors could work with The New Straits Times in improving the writing skills of its journalists; Management professors could consult for private companies. Guidelines would have to be drawn to prevent abuses and conflicts with academic duties. The plan could be modified to benefit the university. One suggestion would be for the income (after expenses) to be shared with the department and university. The community would benefit immensely with this rapid diffusion of expertise from the university. The academics too would enhance their skills and ideas by having them tested in the real world.

Appointing adjunct professors would be one way for the university to acquire the services of experts and yet be spared the expense of paying the full salary. There are many outstanding individuals working at the Rubber Research Institute, Institute of Medical Research, private corporations, and think tanks whose skills and expertise the university could usefully tap. Many are former academics. The university could not afford to offer them their regular salaries but it could get their services for a nominal (compared to their regular income) sum by giving them an adjunct academic title. To be successful, these adjunct and clinical professors must be afforded the usual university privileges lest they feel slighted.

The Governor of Bank Negara could give seminars on monetary policies; and trial lawyers conduct moot courts. For those whose experiences and qualifications do not merit a full professorship, a lesser academic title could be substituted. On many American academic departments, over half of the faculty members are part timers. These outside experts bring much-needed practical perspectives to the academic program.

The present pay scale is attractive only to academics from the Third World. To widen the pool this needs to be substantially increased, but that is not a realistic possibility. The universities can however, have a few selective Distinguished Professorships that would pay globally attractive salaries to bring top talent in disciplines that are desperately needed. By globally attractive I mean at least RM300,000 annually, with matching funding for research.

To the argument that paying top dollar for these talented scholars would be too expensive, consider this. That professor would spend about half of it on housing and living expenses, and a third on income taxes. He would be lucky to have RM30,000 to remit home at the end of the year. Contrast that with the present policy of sending students abroad at an annual cost of RM120,000 each. In 2002 Malaysian students spent RM6 billion abroad, many times the total budget for all the universities in the country. That money is totally lost from the country, with no spillover to the local economy. Had that money been spent in Malaysia, imagine the benefits not only to the local economy but also to the universities and students.

The spin-offs to the nation from such high caliber appointments would be immense. These professors would in effect be our intellectual seeds and catalysts. Taiwan successfully lured a Nobel laureate from UC Berkeley to head its ambitious chemistry program. The economic benefits are also substantial. Singapore's Institute of Molecular and Cell Biology has spawned many successful joint ventures with leading biotech companies.

The university could assign local junior faculty members to be "post doc" fellows to these senior professors. These professors would be our contact with the leading universities where we could send our best students for graduate studies and post-doctoral appointments, or start collaborative academic programs.

These International Tract appointments should be open to all, and if Malaysians qualify, so much the better. Nationality however, should not be the criterion for selection.

The key to success is in the careful selection of candidates. The right scholar, far from creating resentment and envy from his colleagues, would instead inspire them to greater heights. In the 1980's UKM recruited an expatriate professor of surgery, someone complete with his British knighthood. Unfortunately that gentleman was way past his professional prime and thus did not (or could not) contribute much.

The ideal candidate would be someone in his forties, already a full professor at a leading institution. How can we entice such individuals? By appealing to their sense of mission in meeting new challenges, and in helping another nation. More importantly, by assuring them of generous research funding. With their children now grown up and a salary scheme that would not result in a diminution of their living standard, an academic appointment in Malaysia would be an easy sell. Besides, many Western universities have generous leave-of-absence policies so these individuals need not sever their academic ties to their old institutions.

Excellent pay alone is not enough. Apart from supporting their research, we must also give them the freedom to explore wherever their intellect and curiosity lead them. And give them their due respect. When they apply, do not treat them as if they are applying for a peon's job. Treat them royally; remember you are out to entice them. Do not make life difficult for them. And for heaven's sake, do not make them line up at our embassies or the immigration department to secure their visa or working permit.

In addition to these distinguished professorships, the universities could establish less remunerative appointments for lesser-known but on-the-rise academics. America has thousands of these talented PhDs who are languishing from one post-doc position to another, unable to secure a permanent position. With the abolishment of mandatory retirement age, academic vacancies are scarce. Given the appropriate incentives, these individuals could easily be recruited. In Eastern Europe there are thousands of scientists and artists who are poorly paid. The West has already recruited the best, but there are still many capable and talented ones left. To them a Malaysian pay is quite attractive. Many are also fluent in English. Recruit them.

By adopting these innovative schemes and by being flexible, our universities could not only retain their present talent, but also attract many new ones.

Other Post Secondary Institutions

While universities create, disseminate, and apply knowledge, we need other supporting institutions like teachers' and technical colleges to extend these functions. We should not focus only on universities to the detriment of these other equally important institutions. After all for every engineer, we need four or five technicians and draughtsman; for every doctor, a dozen allied health care workers like nurses, technicians and therapists.

To its credit Malaysia has not neglected these other tertiary institutions. Unlike many nations, Malaysia has not succumbed to the fad of "upgrading" its teachers' and technical colleges into universities. The one exception thus far is the recent conversion of SITC into a university.

I will discuss only teachers' colleges, but my underlying theme of trying different models, being flexible, maintaining quality, decentralization, and the importance of industry input apply to all other institutions. I select teachers' colleges for yet another reason. Next to the family, the most important predicator of a child's success in school is the quality to his or her teacher. And quality teachers come from quality institutions.

The teaching profession must not only attract the talented but also provide them with the best training initially, and then regular continuing professional development as well as defined paths for professional growth so as to retain them. Good teaching skills can be taught, and those skills like those of other professions must be periodically updated.

Malaysia has 27 teachers' colleges; most, like the universities, are of recent vintage. A few like the ones in Kota Baru, Malacca, and Tanjong Malim (now a university) have long distinguished histories, having been set up during British rule. They prepare teachers for primary and lower secondary schools. I disagree with the National Brains Trust recommendation that all secondary school teachers have baccalaureate degree. This does not mean that those currently with diploma should not be given every opportunity to pursue their studies towards a degree and to remain teaching at the same level (with added pay of course). At the upper secondary levels however, we must have teachers with a degree, even graduate degrees especially for Sixth Form.

There must be room for innovations and the trying of new models. With the current emphasis on English and the teaching of science and mathematics in English, I propose converting many of these colleges into entirely English medium. These colleges should also specialize to develop greater expertise. Some could concentrate on English, others on science and mathematics, and a few on the performing arts.

Similarly, the current effort to bring IT into the classrooms should begin at the teachers' colleges. Before supplying computers to the classrooms I would first start teaching IT and giving computers to the teacher-trainees. They would then form the nucleus of expertise who will spread IT to the schools. Such a strategy would be slower but more likely to be successful than the present rushed and scattered method.

A major problem with teachers' colleges and teaching generally is that they no longer attract bright and motivated students. Teaching is fast becoming the profession of last resort. This is an unkind statement to make considering the thousands of smart and dedicated teachers out there, but that is the reality. These dedicated teachers too are frustrated in having so many of these less-than-committed colleagues.

One solution to attracting talent would be to raise the pay. Malaysian teachers are grossly underpaid; a hike in the order of 25 percent would be appropriate. There must also be special allowances to entice teachers to rural areas as well as for teaching English, science, and mathematics. Earlier I suggested building teachers' quarters for rural schools. Thus science teachers posted to kampong schools would get double allowances (rural and science), plus living quarters to boot. That ought to spark some interest.

In November 2002 MOE announced that science and mathematics teachers would get a 5 to 10 percent incentive allowance. That's a beginning; to be effective the figure has to be at least 25 percent.

We must recognize that teachers are like members of other professions; some are better and more effective and productive. There must be a mechanism for identifying such superior performers and rewarding them accordingly. Giving the same bonus to everyone or giving undue reverence to seniority would not differentiate or motivate them.

There must be merit pay increases, and I would let the teachers define merit and select their outstanding colleagues.

Others have advocated giving teachers more respect. I agree, and paying them more is one tangible way of showing this respect. I am uncertain of the value of such high profile activities as celebrating teachers' day and having national teachers' awards.

Another way to attract brighter candidates is to broaden their path of advancement. Thus I would provide opportunities for those in teachers' colleges to sit for matriculating examinations like STM and SAT. Of the two, SAT would be more easily accommodated into the curriculum, especially for the colleges that specialize in English and mathematics. Thus when these trainees graduate they would also qualify to enter universities. I would fund a few to go for their degree in return for their returning to teaching.

Teachers' colleges must work closely with universities; indeed there should be formal links. Lecturers at the colleges should be encouraged to take university courses for professional development. Those lecturers with higher degrees could be made adjunct professors at the university. Without those links these colleges risk becoming isolated intellectually.

The consumers of teachers' colleges are MOE and the schools. I would ensure that each college has a board of visitors consisting of headmasters and senior teachers who could give valuable feedback.

Private Colleges and Universities

In a rare display of enlightenment the government amended its Education Act in 1996 to allow for private universities. To be truthful, the government was forced to do this because developments in the industry were fast overtaking the government's ability to regulate it.

The government had always allowed private colleges to cater for students who finished Form 5 but were unable to enter Form 6. Private colleges like Taylor and Stamford prepare students for foreign matriculating examinations like the GCE "A" level. Indeed they offer superior programs, completing them in 12 to 18 months. Further, these colleges use English, a plus for those planning to go abroad.

Until 1996 no private entity could offer a degree. But as is often the case, private sector ingenuity easily overcomes the government's prohibition by developing "twinning" programs with foreign universities where students would spend their first two years locally and then go abroad to the host university for the final two years. Later that was modified to a 3+1 program where they would take the first three years locally. You could see the trend developing where the students would complete their entire education in Malaysia and then go abroad merely to collect their degree, thus effectively circumventing the government's prohibition.

The government had to amend the Act to prevent matters getting out of hand. Unfortunately as is typical of the government's actions, it did so without much thought or scrutiny. Within the first two years it approved nearly 500 applications, about one on every working day! There was no way for the government, given its limited resources and expertise, to adequately monitor the applicants. All too often they were approved without there being firm plans for financing, no key academic personnel selected, and no agreement for a physical site. All that existed were glowing promises and even more grandiose plans. The results were predictable: medical schools approved without laboratories or professors, and universities that exist only on paper or in shopping malls and above shop lots. Such institutions will not lead the nation to educational excellence. Our students and nation deserve better. Malaysia did successfully attract the occasional quality institutions like Monash and the University of Nottingham. Thus far they are the exceptions.

Private Malaysian universities, even local branches of good foreign ones, have a long way to go before they could rightly be considered as truly a university in the traditional sense. Not only do they lack a formal campus and associated amenities, their academic offerings leave much to be desired. None of the private universities have a core of the liberal arts and sciences. Imagine having a university without such basic academic departments as English, history, philosophy, and the basic sciences. Most of the courses offered are the glorified business courses like management and other commercial subjects like accounting and the old standby, law. These subjects can offered cheaply and from the commercial sense, most profitable. In the past these were the core offerings of correspondence schools.

Another popular course is IT. Every private institution on every corner is offering this. The reason? IT sells. Although these colleges and universities may have seemingly impressive IT courses, the contents leave much to be desired. So too are the quality and competence of the graduates. An IT executive for a major company advertised for software engineers. Out of a total of 122 applicants, mostly fresh graduates of local institutions, less than a handful were competent to perform the work required. Many companies still have to recruit expatriates because local graduates lack basic skills, their paper qualifications notwithstanding.

In a competitive academic environment like Singapore these private universities would not stand a chance. Thus while many view the presence of so many private universities in Malaysia as a reflection of academic vigor, to me it means just the opposite. It is a reflection just how bad local public institutions are such that a branch of a provincial British university looks good by comparison.

For models of successful private universities we should look to America. It is unique in that the majority of its elite universities and colleges are private. In the rest of the world private universities are rarely among the best.

Private American universities, like their public counterpart, receive significant governmental funding and tax subsidies, together with student loans and scholarships. In return these private institutions agree to certain public policies, like subscribing to the federal non-discrimination and affirmative action policies.

The prestigious private universities like Harvard are not private in the same mold as IBM or General Motors. They are nonprofit entities. Unlike private companies, they do not declare dividends or are concerned with profits in the commercial sense. The government, recognizing their nonprofit status and the socially beneficial value of their activities, exempts these institutions from taxes and regulatory burdens that apply to proprietary corporations.

There are private, for profit colleges and universities in America; few are good, and none among the elite. In planning for Malaysia's private universities we should emulate the highly successful American nonprofit models, with modifications to suit local circumstances.

Like America, Malaysia should actively support private universities both directly and indirectly. Directly by giving grants; as precedent the government gave grants to foreign institutions for taking in Malaysian students. Indirectly the government could provide loan guarantees for capital expansion. Private lenders would underwrite such loans, the government merely acting as a guarantor, thus ensuring favorable interest rates. For the government, such loans should be safe, secured as they are by the universities' assets.

The government could also exempt them from property and other taxes, and declare gifts to universities as tax deductible. Additionally it could provide scholarships and study loans for the students. In this way the universities could afford a "need blind" admission policy, just like American institutions.

The government provides tax relief and other subsidies to industries, why not to private universities? Like private industry, a university is also a major employer and potential foreign exchange earner through its admission of foreign students. Also like industry, a university would spawn many spin-offs. It is not accidental that Silicon Valley is near Stanford University and the University of California Berkeley. Similarly the Research Triangle of North Carolina is surrounded by Duke sand the University of North Carolina. A quality private university in Malaysia would also spawn similar commercial spin-offs.

In return for governmental support, the university could agree to some mutually beneficial guidelines. One would be for the university's domestic student population to reflect the general society. This sensible policy would not only ensure greater diversity of student body but also prevent the university from becoming the exclusive enclave of a particular ethnic or social group.

Student diversity would have other benefits. What better way to prepare graduates for the global marketplace than to expose them to cultural and social diversities as undergraduates? Besides, in a plural society like Malaysia, it would be extremely unhealthy were local institutions to be segregated racially.

Harvard and Stanford are held in high esteem today in part because children of the rich and poor, whites and blacks, local and foreign can aspire for admission. Harvard could easily fill its slots with bright white kids from the private prep schools as it did before the1950's, yet it aggressively recruits worldwide. Harvard today is much more highly regarded than in the past when it was the exclusive preserve of the White Anglo Saxon Protestant (WASP) crowd.

A student body that reflects society would also create a sense of cohesion and pride between the university and the community. In many Third World countries, the private universities are the first to be attacked by the citizens during an economic crisis because they view such institutions as havens for the rich and privileged.

Malaysia's private institutions, even the excellent ones, are dangerously segregated not only racially but also linguistically and along socioeconomic class. The government could help alleviate this problem by providing study grants for Bumiputras to enroll, and rewarding those institutions that have a diverse student body.

I am terribly disappointed with the latest entry, University Tunku Abdul Rahman (UTAR). It fails utterly in attracting Bumiputras. Before UTAR can aspire to be a great university, it must first be a great *Malaysian* university, meaning it must attract *all* Malaysians. The luminaries on UTAR's Board of Trustees have impressive degrees from prestigious Western universities, but scratch a bit and the trustees' clannishness oozes out. I would have thought that UTAR's trustees would have emulated their great alma maters by having a more inclusive board. Can they not find some capable non-Chinese?

I do not suggest that having few Malays on the board would automatically solve the problem. Many private institutions go out of their way to employ prominent Malays to be on their board, yet those institutions still do not succeed in attracting Malay students. At least then you could not fault the owners, they have tried and made an effort. The blame goes directly to those seemingly distinguished Malay directors. They (their impressive degrees and titles notwithstanding) are content merely in drawing their director's pay. They do not help guide their colleges to be more attractive to Malays. If those directors would visit the residential schools and actively recruit those students, these colleges may well attract more Malays. Not to mention that those directors would then actually earn their keep. Those Malay directors come in handy only when it is time to renew the institution's operating permit. Shame on them! It is sad that these highly educated Malays are behaving just like the typical Ali of Ali Baba partnerships. It proves my point: it is easy to get a PhD; more difficult to eradicate the Ali Baba mentality.

There are other sensible rules that both the university and the government could agree to that would enhance the quality of private institutions. One would be to make a year of Malay Studies compulsory. It would be absurd for one to earn a degree from a Japanese university and yet not speak a word of Japanese. Elite American universities have core curriculum of American history and Western civilization. The American University in Paris as well as the one in Cairo and Beirut use English as the medium of instruction. Yet all students have to take a year of French or Arabic as the case may be.

Our government should rightly insist on certain safeguards. Thus foreign governments or their agencies should not be allowed to set up a university. Because of the particular social and political sensitivity, the same prohibition should also apply to religious bodies.

We should encourage private universities to attract foreign students. Besides contributing valuable foreign exchange, these students would serve as a barometer for the quality of the institution. They would also enhance the educational experiences of all students.

We have to be careful that these student visas are not abused and used as a means for Third World residents to enter Malaysia to work. My suspicion is that many of the visas issued to Chinese and African students are diverted for these illicit purposes. The current daily headlines merely affirm my suspicion. The only way to prevent this is to make sure that these visas are issued only to bona fide students as attested by their having qualifications acceptable to Malaysia. Additionally these students must post performance bonds or somehow demonstrate their ability to finance their study. Malaysia can learn much from Britain and Australia on how to monitor foreign students effectively.

We can extend my earlier concept of charter schools to universities to create joint public/private sector joint ventures. The government could give grants to these charter universities for every Malaysian student they enroll. The amount would be equivalent to what it would cost the government to educate these students at a public university. In return for governmental support, these charter universities should agree to have their domestic student population reflect the greater Malaysian society.

With proper planning and appropriate support, Malaysia too can have fine private universities that are worthy of our pride.

Malaysia has passed the stage of most Third World countries in that it has successfully taken care of the basic need of providing primary and secondary education. To launch into the next trajectory of development, Malaysia must now enhance its tertiary institutions, to make them on par with the developed world. There is no longer a "local standard" for knowledge in a globalized world.

9

Mow Down MOE

The Ministry of Education (MOE), like the rest of the Government of Malaysia, is highly centralized, with strict hierarchal top-down command and a penchant for total control. Nothing happens in the schools, universities, or anywhere else in the vast education land without the ministry and its bureaucrats knowing and approving of it. In character and ambience the ministry resembles the old Soviet system. We all know what happened to it.

The West would like to claim credit for the collapse of the Soviet empire; in reality it would have imploded under its own weight anyway. A similar fate awaits MOE unless it changes. There need to be a radical change in the mindset of the senior personnel. Sadly I do not see this happening.

MOE would not have lasted this long had there been a countervailing force. In communist and socialist countries (they are the only ones with a penchant for an authoritarian state) the government is held in check by a powerful party and workers' union. The natural check for MOE would have been the teachers' unions but they, like the rest of society, are divided along racial lines. They cannot seem to bond professionally; teachers of Chinese schools feel little kinship with those of Malay schools. Consequently the power of teachers is diluted and fragmented. Only the Malay teachers' union is powerful and influential because their members are also the backbone of UMNO. For a long time the ministry (and government) was beholden to this union. The other powerful element that exerts control on MOE is the party–

UMNO. Thus Malay teachers exert their influence doubly: through their union and UMNO.

UMNO has seen better days. In the 1999 general election its wings were severely clipped, with the party losing a state government and many of its prominent ministers. Najib Razak, then Minister of Education, barely squeaked by. That was symbolically significant, both personally and politically. Personally because Najib had only months earlier been returned as one of UMNO's Vice-President, securing the highest number of votes; politically because MOE is very prestigious.

The Malay teachers' union today is leaning towards the opposition, especially since the ousting of its hero, Anwar Ibrahim, who held MOE's portfolio from 1988-1991.

William Roff's *The Origin of Malay Nationalism* chronicles the central role of Malay teachers in the emerging nationalism before and after World War II, in particular the pivotal part played by the teachers' college where they were trained, SITC. The British established SITC at about the same time as MCKK. For many years both institutions took in students from vernacular rural schools, although MCKK was primarily for children of royalty and nobility. Although both began in the same era and catered exclusively to Malays, their products could not have been more different. While SITC graduates were intensely nationalistic and virulently anti-British, those of MCKK were unabashed anglophiles, *Mat Salleh* wannabes. Why the difference, I do not know. At both institutions young Malays came under the direct tutelage and guidance of colonial Britons; in one the Brits managed to make their protégés eager imitators, in the other, loathsome enemies.

As with all generalizations, this one has many exceptions. The brain behind UMNO was no less than Tun Razak, a product of MCKK where he was legendary for his extraordinary brilliance. There were also many anglophiles among SITC graduates, closet ones to be sure, my father being one of them. His high regard for the British dimmed only slightly with their embarrassing performance during the Japanese invasion. In his later years when he noted how well the country had done since independence, he wistfully imagined where Malaysia would have been had it been independent sooner. That gradual realization significantly eroded his earlier admiration for the British.

My father admired the British because of what they were able to accomplish for him at SITC. My father was not good at learning English so he was not able to learn much about history, philosophy, or whatever academic subjects they were teaching him. But he could communicate with his lecturers through music. They successfully introduced this village kid who had never touched a musical instrument in his life (unless you count the handmade rice stem reeds) to the wonderful new and magical world of music. He took to the violin with a vengeance, the only toy he ever had, taking it wherever he went, and learned everything he could from his teachers. They were enthusiastic instructors, he an eager pupil. He was totally consumed with music such that he had to sleep outside his dormitory so he could practice late into the night. During holidays he stayed back on campus to practice his beloved violin. (It belonged to the college, so he could not take it home). Besides, there was nothing to do back at the old kampong anyway. The Brits first taught him the basics and then introduced him to the great works of the masters. He was in complete awe, as anyone would. Through the universal language of music, he bonded with his teachers. He was so consumed with his new passion that he barely passed his other courses. He later confided in me that he may have failed them and would have been kicked out but for the vigorous advocacy of his music lecturers. He was good enough for the British to make him the bandmaster of one of its military units during the war. Such impact and legacy at the personal level did not go away easily or be readily poisoned by the otherwise ugliness of politics and racism of the time.

This British legacy did not end with my father. He in turn brought music to a generation of his village youths. I did not realize his impact until I met a popular musician who told me that he learned all his music from my father. Strangely enough when he was teaching those village kids, he would shove my brothers and me away. He feared that we would be consumed with music to the detriment of our studies, just as he was at college. I dearly wished he had been more generous with us with his talent! As a parenthesis, a generation later when I told him that my daughter, then an aspiring lawyer, was enjoying her choral music in college, he cautiously warned me of the possible dangers lurking. Old habits die hard!

Today it would be hard to find lecturers at our many teachers' colleges with the same kind of passion and dedication demonstrated by those British at SITC.

Some of my father's pro-British sentiments rubbed off on me as a youngster. By the time I went to MCKK in 1961, they had become ingrained in me. But by this time MCKK had changed to become a hotbed of Malay nationalism. And like many who find their faith late, the collegians were exuberant converts to the extent that it negatively impacted their studies. Many felt they had nothing to learn from the British or through English, and thus neglected their studies. I was definitely in a minority in my political conviction, but I had a crude and effective rebuttal for the diehard nationalists. If they think that they could not learn anything from the British or in English, then why not leave MCKK and return to their villages? Of course none took my challenge, which effectively shut them up. At the end of the year, nationalist or not, the chance to go abroad to the English-speaking world was still the most coveted goal. Nationalistic frenzy was one thing, but not if it prevented one from going overseas. This only made those unsuccessful to go abroad even more nationalistic!

Although Malay teachers formed the backbone of UMNO, their Malay education severely handicapped their political careers even though they were the party's workhorses. This frustrated many who thought that they could reach the top merely by being political activists. Few did scale the heights; Ghaffar Baba (an SITC graduate) was briefly the Deputy Prime Minister.

What Malay teachers lacked in education and learning, they more than made it up with their passion. They championed passionately the cause of Malay language and nationalism. One of their leaders, Syed Nasir Ismail, later headed the Dewan Bahasa dan Pustaka (DBP–Language and Literary Agency). A SITC product, Syed Nasir personified that fervor best, albeit misguidedly. He stridently called for Malay language to be used at all levels, including the university. When it was rightly pointed out the practical problems of lack of qualified instructors, Syed Nasir, Ghaffar Baba, and other ardent SITC graduates proudly proclaimed their competence to teach at those lofty heights. Never mind that they had at most only two years of post-*primary* education! Fortunately UMNO's leadership at the time was in the hands of sober men like Tunku Abdul Rahman and Tun Razak. They quietly shot down those silly grandiose pretensions.

My father simply laughed off the claims of the likes of Ghaffar Baba and Syed Nasir. He had good reasons to. When I was in secondary school he always looked over my schoolwork. He did not understand any of it but he was nonetheless very curious what it was I was learning past primary school—the only level he had. He was particularly fascinated with science and mathematics, especially algebra and geometry, subjects totally alien to him. He rightly thought that if what I was learning was the difference between primary and secondary education, imagine the difference between school, university, and postgraduate levels. He remembered only too well the vast gap between the elementary music he learned initially and the great compositions of the masters he would later be exposed. He was understandably more modest in his claims on what he could achieve with his SITC education.

There is a saying in Central Asia that there is a limit to wisdom, but there is no limit to foolishness. This was more than amply demonstrated by the politically minded graduates of SITC.

Back to MOE, events were already overtaking it. Its *Blueprint for Development 2001-2010* was quickly made irrelevant by developments elsewhere. The most significant—the teaching of science and mathematics in English–originated outside the ministry. The minister and his bureaucrats were reduced to mere passive observers in this evolving drama. On another front public universities, which are under the direct control of the ministry, are fast losing their luster. Standards have declined precipitously. To be sure this has been going on for more than a decade but no one noticed it. But with the establishment of private universities, the inadequacies of public institutions quickly became exposed and glaring. With the tightening of the economy and the job market, graduates of local public universities were squeezed out. The market has given its evaluation, and that cannot be ignored any longer.

With globalization Malaysia can no longer insulate itself. Two trends emerge consequent to this. One there is no longer a local standard. Good enough for Malaysia isn't. While in the past local universities may have produced graduates "good enough" for Malaysia, today these graduates are being judged by international standards. Private employers now have a choice, with thousands of Malaysians trained at foreign universities and private local ones that meet international standards. As a result private companies employ graduates of local public universities only as the last resort. As most of these graduates are Malays, it is easy to fall for the old bugaboo of a grand conspiracy against Malays. Before falling for that however, I would submit that there are other more relevant explanations, like their low English proficiency.

The second consequence of globalization is that Malaysians are becoming very much aware of prevailing global standards. While the government may control the local media and other sources of information, the Internet is free of censorship. More and more Malaysians are turning to it as a source of alternative news. Malaysian leaders may yell from the top of the highest coconut tree that the country is the center of excellence for education or health care, but ordinary citizens can judge that for themselves. Education and health care may or may not be superior elsewhere, but what is important is that Malaysians are now free to make that judgment for themselves.

Parents are free to send their children to schools and universities elsewhere if they feel that that is in their best interest. Telling them that it would be unpatriotic or local institutions are just as good would not dissuade them. They have made their own decision based on the information they have–government propaganda be damned!

So instead of the minister declaring ad nauseam that the country is the center of educational excellence, he would do well to spend his time and energy to achieving that goal. Merely wishing it would not do.

To begin with, the ministry must reengineer itself and completely change it mindset from one of total control to mutual consultation. Its leadership style would have to change from that of a drillmaster barking out orders to his raw recruits, to a symphony conductor extracting the best out of his talented musicians. The ministry should move away from the Soviet model to that of a Western democracy, from top-down command and central control to equal participation and consultation with the periphery.

If MOE concentrates on its core mission of education and dispenses with its other extraneous activities, it would more likely do a better job. The ministry has no business doing translations when there are over a dozen universities that can carry out those functions more efficiently and competently. With a robust publishing industry, there is little justification for MOE to have a publishing arm. I can think of many other activities the ministry could discard and leave for the private sector.

In this chapter I will review three activities the ministry could dispense with: its Literary and Language Agency (DBP); the two examination bodies; and its accrediting agency, Lembaga Akreditasi Negara (LAN–National Accreditation Board). Before doing that I will critique the present policy of sponsoring students for studies overseas. This is not the responsibility of MOE rather Jabatan Perkhidmatan Awam

(JPA–Public Service Department) and a number of others including MARA, ministries like Defense and Agriculture, as well as state governments and statutory bodies. This jumbled mess is reflective of the general lack of streamlining and the inefficiency of the entire machinery of government.

Sponsoring Students Overseas

In the heyday of pre-1997 economic crisis, Malaysia sent literally hundreds of thousands of students abroad for further studies. The buoyant economy made an overseas education affordable even to middle class families. The crisis, and the accompanying devaluation of the ringgit, dramatically changed that.

I do not quibble with private students; what they and their parents do with their own precious cash is for them to decide. My focus here is on government-sponsored students, and the overwhelming majority of them are Malays. Most ended up at third-rate universities taking courses which are readily available in Malaysia. I do not see the wisdom of spending precious taxpayers' money on such exercises. Those resources could be better spent improving local universities. I wrote a long letter to the director of JPA describing the tremendous wastage and the poor selection of candidates. I also suggested improvements, but of course did not get a reply. I subsequently published part of the letter as an article in a mainstream paper. Still nothing happened. With the economic crisis the government was forced to downsize the program, sending only the most qualified students and then only to selective institutions. I could not knock any fiduciary sense into our officials, but the harsh economic reality did it for me. The program is now considerably better although it can still be improved.

The various government entities, statutory bodies, and government-owned corporations have their own separate program for sponsoring students. These disparate programs are duplicative, inefficient, and very costly. At one time the consulate in Los Angeles had three student advisors–one for JPA, MARA, and Petronas. The cost of maintaining each one of them is substantial. Despite the numerous advisors we still hear horror stories of students being stranded and stipends missed.

I have met many of these advisors and have yet to be impressed by any of them. They are appointed simply to reward them with a plump overseas posting prior to their retirement. Their typical assignment is for two or three years. The first year is wasted with the officer distracted and consumed with such personal matters as settling their own children in school. By the second year they are already busy buying and accumulating household items to be shipped home. They hardly have time for their primary responsibility–looking after the welfare of the students. To make matters worse, many of the advisors are graduates of Malaysian universities; they have absolutely no clue about education in America, nor are they eager to learn.

Petronas has been remarkably successful in recruiting the brightest students. But even this superior program suffers from many deficiencies. I have talked to many Petronas scholars and it is the rare individual who is pursuing a course of study that is his or her first choice. Many are doing it for the opportunity to go abroad. There are many aspiring engineers taking accountancy; would-be filmmakers taking business, and wannabe lawyers taking engineering simply because those were the scholarships being offered. What a sad mismatch of talent and wasted potential. Imagine had these bright and talented young Malaysians been given the freedom to pursue their own dreams!

An example will illustrate this madness. An aspiring nuclear physicist was given a scholarship to study medicine because it was deemed to be the greatest national need at the time. Of course the young man took it. The following year his sister was also given an award to go abroad, but this hopeful doctor was given one for…biology–the flavor of the year! Again supposedly in the national interest! How could the nation's priorities changed so quickly? I met both of them years later and suggested to the now young doctor that he could still combine his interest in nuclear physics and medicine by becoming a radiation oncologist. And being a bright doctor and a graduate of a top medical school, he was readily accepted to an American program where the hospital would pay him. Guess what? The government would not release him from his bonds! As for his sister, I advised her to come to America, do her graduate work, and then apply to medical school. She found my suggestion incredulous until I told her that it is quite commonly done in America. She may yet become a doctor if only she could also be freed from her bonds. Those bureaucrats have again thwarted the dreams of two bright young people. Of course those officials looked at the situation differently; those students ought to be grateful for what they had been given. Isn't that the Malay way?

I suggest that all publicly funded study awards be disbursed under one agency. We would serve our students best by this consolidation. First, those responsible for selecting the students could enhance their talent-picking skills. They would also become more knowledgeable and familiar with the qualities and requirements of the various universities. Then we would not have the specter of MARA sending its students to unrecognized institutions as had happened previously. As these interviewers develop their skills and expertise, they could hire out their services to private companies and other entities.

Second, with a centralized and computerized office, we could better monitor the students and get accurate follow up data on their performances, thus ensuring that no one would fall through the cracks. Problems could also be spotted earlier and handled more effectively. With their accumulated expertise and experience these experts could then help advise our schools on how best to prepare students for top universities.

The most important reason for consolidation is that students get to choose the field of study that best suits their interest and aptitude, instead of being forced to take one chosen by the sponsoring agency. This alone is reason enough to change the present system.

On completion of their studies, these students could then be matched with the various departments. If a student has done research and is interested to pursue this he could choose to be with the universities or research institutes instead of being forced to teach raw recruits simply because he was sponsored by the Defense Ministry. There was a plight of an honors mathematics graduate (still a rare qualification for a Malay at the time) who was given an opportunity to continue his doctoral studies under a fellowship awarded by his university. Again his sponsor would not relent, he was needed back home, in the "national interest!" The good news was that in the long delays while negotiating with the authorities in Malaysia he managed to extend his stay for a year and completed his masters. On his return however, those bureaucrats got their vengeance. While he was expecting to be seconded to a university or at least posted to RMC or similar institution, he was asked instead to teach raw recruits, a job that could have been done by a graduate of teachers' college. He had to stay within the defense ministry as it sponsored him.

With my proposed consolidation, these changes could easily be accommodated, as would any alterations in the students' plan or departmental needs. If a graduate is not needed by any public agency, he or she could be "auctioned off" to the private sector, enabling the government to recoup some of its costs. Doing this would also circumvent the current popular trick (unbeknown to the bureaucrats) where those with highly marketable skills and desirable qualifications from prestigious universities purposely flunk their Malaysian placement interviews and thus would be rejected and released from their bonds.

This happened to a bright young man I knew in California. He purposefully bombed his Malaysian interview and consequently was rejected. He laughed all the way back to Silicon Valley. He could not help it if his interviewers could not tell the difference between Stanford and Stamford. That young man was smart enough not to play smart!

I propose simplifying the various study awards into three categories: scholarships, grants, and loans. These awards should cover all expenses, and would vary in value with the cost of tuition and living expenses.

Scholarships would be for those accepted to the prestigious universities like the Harvards and Stanfords of America, the Oxbridges of Britain, and the McGills and Torontos of Canada. As these scholarship winners would be our best and brightest, they should be given the freedom to choose their own course of study and career. Surely they would know better than any bureaucrat what is best for themselves. We should also give them the latitude to proceed to graduate work if they so desire, or to work abroad for an extended period of time to gain valuable experience. By granting them these privileges we would encourage others to apply to these outstanding universities.

The grants would be for those accepted into the next tier–but still very selective–universities. They must however pursue courses that are needed by the country (natural and applied sciences, English, business). Unlike scholarships, their parents would have to contribute a portion of their taxable income (I suggest 10 percent) towards the award. For needy students, the grants would have the same value monetarily as scholarships.

The third level of award is study loan. It would be tenable only to the same caliber institutions as the grants. Like grants, parents too would be assessed a similar percentage of their taxable income, but unlike grants the students would have to repay the loans less their parents' contributions. The advantage of loans over grants is that students would be free to choose their own field of study. These loans would have to be repaid in the traditional way, monthly following the student's graduation, with a defined interest rate and amortization period. Alternatively the loan could also be repaid based on the graduate's monthly income for a defined period. I propose 10 percent for a period twice that of his study loan duration. In this way if the candidate chooses a highly lucrative job, the government could conceivably make a tidy profit on its investments. The student would choose the repayment option at the time the loan is being given.

This second novel scheme, the Income Contingent Repayment (ICR) plan, is the brainchild of the American Nobel laureate in economics Milton Friedman. It would free the graduate to choose a career that suits his interest rather than be concerned financially because of the loan. We might be able to attract top talent into teaching with this scheme.

ICR was implemented at Yale in the 1970s by the economist James Tobin, where for every $1,000 the student borrowed from Yale, he or she would commit to repay 0.04 percent of his or her income for 35 years, or when the whole class has paid off its aggregate debt, whichever is sooner. The program was terminated after howling protests from highly successful alumni who complained about having to fork out huge sums of their income to their alma mater. ICR is still an option with the Federal Student Loan in America and has also been adopted in Australia. Canada briefly toyed with the idea but gave up for fear that it would unnecessarily lead to hikes in tuition fees.

We should also have built-in incentives similar to existing ones where if the students excel, their grants could be converted into scholarships and loans to grants.

As the cost of studies abroad is expensive, public funds should only be used to send our brightest students, and then only to the top institutions. We should send them only to the top 50-100 universities in America, and the top half a dozen each in Canada, Britain and Australia. The operating principle should be: Malaysia sends her best, to the best!

In the 1980s and 90s Malaysia had the Top Ten American University program. The sad aspect of that program was that these students had to be sent abroad for their matriculation first. The fact that our schools are not preparing their students for top universities is again another sad reflection of the system.

By streamlining the process, making the rules explicit, and procedures transparent, our students could concentrate on preparing themselves academically instead of busy navigating the bureaucratic maze. Students would assume the responsibility of getting accepted to top universities. They would choose whichever path which best prepares them—Sixth Form, IB, GCE A level, *matrikulasi*, or twinning programs. The sponsoring agency would also be freed from the administrative details of selection, filing applications, choosing the universities, and instead concentrate on giving information, providing guarantors' letters, helping with the applications, and generally being a facilitator and counselor. The government would have a committee of graduates of leading universities to choose the institutions where these awards would be tenable.

By not being involved in the decision, the sponsors protect themselves against charges of favoritism and unfair practices. The decision is open and the process student-driven. Get accepted to Stanford or Princeton, and you will get a scholarship no matter how rich your parents are or what esoteric field of studies you choose. Choose the University of Oregon and you would get a grant if you pursue engineering, a loan if you take sociology. If only Podunk State University accepts you, tough luck, your parents would have to finance your studies.

By being more efficient and selective, we would achieve more with our precious monetary and intellectual resources. And by injecting competition we would ensure that we get only the best students.

Dispense with Dewan

DBP is an independent agency with its own supervising board that answers to MOE. It was established in 1962 to spearhead the development of Malay language. Today DBP has become in addition, a major business monopoly involved in publishing, printing, and distributing textbooks as well as other extraneous activities.

Its first director was the economist Ungku Aziz. His successors were all either politicians of no particular repute or civil servants of the same caliber. Seasoned scholars and able managers they were not. Delays in printing and distributing of textbooks are perennial. Why the government chooses to have its own publishing and other businesses instead of contracting them out to the private sector is beyond me. Even back then there existed a thriving and robust publishing industry. Many of my textbooks in the 1950s were published by such private entities like Sinaran Brothers of Penang. Their books were cheap, well written, and most importantly, available on time. DBP figured that to maintain the status of Malay language, its textbooks must be just as expensive as the English ones that were imported. Dewan could not compete on price, quality, or availability; instead it aggressively and successfully lobbied the government to give BDP the monopoly. Being a typical government agency, DBP cannot deliver, but it is always ready with excuses, from shortage of translators to that of supplies.

My own experience with DBP back in the 1970s was instructive. I frequently gave lectures at the nursing school in Johor Baru and was appalled at the quality of the textbooks translated by DBP. Obviously they were done by individuals with scant knowledge of medicine or nursing. They had translated some ancient British texts, no doubt to save royalty fees. Consequently the pictures were of outdated instruments and equipment. The nursing instructor and I agreed that we could come up with a better text using local materials and examples. We were very excited about this venture if for nothing else that the students would get a more modern text. We contacted DBP, and its representatives too were eager. All went well until I mentioned royalty and copyright. The representative knew nothing of either, or acted as if he did not know. He expected us to write the book gratis and then hand over to the agency the copyright! I demurred, and then began hearing nonsense about "patriotism" and "duty to country and culture."

The incident prompted me to check on some of the books issued by DBP. Sure enough in almost all cases the translators' or writers' name was not prominently displayed. One had to look very hard to find it in the acknowledgment or preface. The one name emblazoned all over is the director's. That episode effectively aborted my career as a textbook writer.

Earlier I visited DBP's headquarters in Kuala Lumpur, located in a high-rent district. It was an impressive building, with an oversized and somewhat gaudy mural at the front. The agency had just finished an extensive and expensive addition. What astounded me was that a huge portion of the new addition was being used for nothing more than warehousing unsold overpriced books. When I suggested to a senior official that those books could be stored more cheaply elsewhere instead of in an expensive downtown office building, he professed not the least concerned. Nor was he impressed with my suggestion that the books be sold at a discount; at least then they would be read. Obviously to those officials, costs and wastage mattered little. Whenever they were short of funds they simply asked the government for more. Malay language was a top priority; no one dared challenge the request. That would be, well, unpatriotic.

DBP also publishes a number of popular periodicals ranging from the quasi-scholarly *Dewan Bahasa* (Language Forum) to the lay *Dewan Masyarakat* (Society's Forum). Apart from providing valuable avenues for new writers, these magazines helped popularize Malay literature and language. It is a reflection of the mentality of DBP that these magazines do not carry advertising for the simple reason that for the agency, money is never a problem. It never occurred to them that advertising would spur interests in other publishing products and that in turn would stimulate the market for published materials in Malay generally. In the same vein, Dewan's magazines and journals rarely carry reviews of books published outside of DBP. To the mindset of these civil servants turned publishers, letting private companies advertise their products would undermine DBP's own books and publications. It did not occur to these officials that by getting advertising revenue they could lower the price of their products and thereby further increase their circulation. It is very hard to erase the ingrained civil service mentality.

I would shutter DBP and use the funds thus saved more productively elsewhere as in building single-session schools. Its publishing business could be contracted out to the private sector or better still, sold out. Textbook publishing is a lucrative business; there would be no shortage of bidders. Those private publishers could produce textbooks much more cheaply especially if we also introduce competition. At present the publishing division is actually a cost item. I would also sell all of DBP's publications. If publishers with far smaller circulation could make a handsome profit, I fail to see why those magazines could not rake in the revenues especially if they accept advertising.

As for the translating activities, that could be done by the legends of new academics. Those experts could do the translating more competently than the civil servants at DBP. Better still, contract out the translations, and to maintain productivity, pay the translators piece meal–no completed translations, no pay. By getting rid of these civil servant translators at DBP and using the saved funds to pay professors and experts at the universities to do the translating or writing, the ministry would get better and cheaper textbooks. This would also provide much-needed extra income for these academics. They are presently so poorly paid that this may well tip the balance to induce them to stay in academia.

As for the research and scholarly component of DBP, this too could be transferred to the universities. All public universities have huge Departments of Malay Studies; let them take over the academic function of DBP. Back in the early days I could see the rationale for having DBP, today it has been made redundant by the multitude of universities. By dispensing entirely with DBP you could then rent out its massive headquarters and use the funds to improve the schools. Transfer all those civil servants back to the Sports or Tourism Ministries, and use the funds thus saved to hire or train more teachers.

I have never seen details of the ministry's budget to see how much DBP consumes, but judging from the number of personnel and size of its headquarters, it must be substantial, expenses the ministry could do without. Getting rid of DBP would send a clear signal that the ministry would now focus its entire resources and personnel on its core mission–improving schools and universities.

Examination Syndicate

The ministry is also involved in the testing business. In the past the private Cambridge Local Examination Syndicate undertook such activi-

ties. Since independence, as a manifestation of the *merdeka*
(independent) spirit, the ministry felt that it could do the job better.
When I took my Form V examination back in 1960, I do not remember the cost but it was certainly not substantial as it did not impose a
particular burden on my parents. And the examination results were
released in late February or early March at the latest. Today we read
stories of school children unable to sit for the test because of lack of
funds, and the results not published until late May (there has been
some improvement in 2002). From late November until the results are
released six months later, students are left in limbo. These are the
youths one sees loitering in the shopping malls or otherwise unoccu-
pied. They have nothing to do but wait. Parents who are smart or can
afford it enroll their children at private institutions. By the time the
examination results are released they would have completed over a
semester's course work.

The Year 6 examination takes place in early September. From then
until the beginning of yearend vacation (early December) these pupils
are essentially wasting their time. No learning takes place; those precious long months are simply wasted away.

The ministry has two examination bodies: Malaysian Examination
Syndicate (*Lembaga Pepereksaan Malaysia*–LPM) that runs the tests for
the end of Years 6, 9, and 11, and the Malaysian Examination Council
(*Majlis Peperkesaan Malaysia*–MPM) that administers the Form 6
examination and the Malaysian Universities English Test (MUET).
Why two entities? My cynical view is that there would then be two
departmental heads and doubling of the establishment. Many more
top jobs for civil servants!

The excuse given for the late release of results is that there are now
so many more candidates. True, but the American College Board
administers SAT to millions worldwide and releases the results in
weeks not months. The delay is due to other more mundane reasons.

Once while vacationing in Malaysia during December, I met a
senior official from the Examination Syndicate who was also on holi-

days. I was surprised as I expected December to be the busiest time for him, being after the school examination season. I inquired why he took the vacation then, and his answer was as direct as it was frank. It was precisely because his department was busy that he took time off. No point taking a vacation when you are not busy at the office, he rationalized! It is such an attitude that accounts for the delays, not lack of staff and money, or too many candidates.

Civil servants staff both bodies; they lack professional training in the psychology of testing, testing methodology, or statistical analysis. There are no studies assessing the reliability, predictability, or even internal consistency of these tests. The general public has little confidence in these tests, with speculations that the results are often tampered, and the authorities have done little to allay those misgivings. The recent scandal over the examination for lawyers (administered by another body) heightens those suspicions. The central figure in that scandal (now awaiting trial) was the former deputy dean of one of the public law faculties. That such a prominent academic could be involved with something so slimy is unnerving.

The rules for examinations too are not without controversy. One is the silly requirement for candidates to state their race and religion. This adds to the general unease and suspicion that such information would be used for sinister purposes. Get rid of that unnecessary data.

These examination bodies have not done any research to validate their tests. There are no longitudinal studies correlating students' performances on these tests and their later college careers. Nor are there studies to validate the internal consistency of the tests, or correlating them with class performance. Similarly there are no detailed analyses of the questions to differentiate between the truly discriminative ones from those that are not. The best questions are obviously those that are answered correctly by the top scorers; the worse or least discriminative are those answered correctly at random. The only way to discover this is to subject each question to statistical analysis. Such analyses would help the examiners get rid of useless, non-discriminative questions and enhance the overall quality of the tests.

Examination bodies can do more than simply grade students and be their gatekeepers. The data they generate could help parents in making their choices; schools in monitoring their performances; and the ministry to guide where to focus its resources.

Land LAN Elsewhere

The National Accreditation Board (*Lembaga Akreditasi Negara*–LAN) was set up in1996 to monitor private institutions of higher learning. It accredits only private institutions; the assumption being that public institutions do not need such monitoring. How that grand leap of faith comes about I do not know.

There were many quality private institutions long before LAN. Colleges like Taylor and Stamford do not need LAN's imprimatur. Parents and students already knew of their quality by their products. Taylor sends more students to elite universities than any other institution in Malaysia, private or public. LAN was established in anticipation of the rash of new private institutions expected with the amendment to the Education Act of 1996.

Despite LAN, newspapers still carry horror stories of colleges and medical schools set up without adequate laboratories and other ancillary facilities. The question arises as to how these institutions were granted permits or accredited in the first place. When you read LAN's mission statement and manual, they are replete with such minutiae as the number of reference books the libraries must have. LANS' board of trustees is filled with former academics.

Even though technically LAN is an independent statutory body under MOE, functionally it is nothing but a department within it. LAN is still bound by the civil service rules and protocol. To complicate matters, there is yet another division within the ministry that regulates private institutions. Precisely where the jurisdiction of one ends and the other begins is not clear. I would have thought that a university or college that is not accredited should not be allowed to operate. Nor should any new institution be given a permit unless it can show that it has the resources–academic, physical, and financial–to meet accreditation requirements. That seems elementary. Similarly an unaccredited institution should not be allowed to admit any students, local or foreign, but then we found out that the authority to grant colleges the authority to recruit foreign students rests not with LAN but with that other agency.

Again when there is duplication of services, matters and responsibilities easily slip between departments.

LAN should be independent, funded entirely by the fees it charges institutions seeking accreditation. All institutions must be accredited. The same standard must apply to both public and private institutions. The public must be assured of quality with all institutions. The government's argument that there are enough regulations to monitor public institutions and thus they do not need to be accredited does not wash.

LAN's governing board must be made up of representatives and experts from the major universities, private and public. It should also invite foreign experts to be among its surveyors. They must not be full time employees rather part-timers contracted from active practitioners in the field. If they become fulltime surveyors and reviewers, they will forget their primary professional expertise as educators. LAN must develop specialized expertise so it could credibly evaluate and accredit professional faculties like business, engineering, law, and medicine. If any institution, private or public, cannot meet those standards, then it should not be allowed to operate.

LAN should learn from the accrediting bodies of advanced countries both on the mechanics of accrediting and also on the more important issue of enhancing quality and standards.

I work in an accredited institution. Months before the survey, the accrediting body would send out a detailed questionnaire to the hospital. These cover basic housekeeping issues as well as policy matters. The actual survey usually takes two or three days, with the surveyors divided into teams to inspect their particular area of expertise. Some would focus on the "hardware" of the hospital (from lights and fire extinguishers in the hallways to the reliability of back-up power systems), others on the "software" (policy manuals dealing with infectious diseases to mechanism of handling public complaints). On the last day of inspection, the surveyors and key hospital personnel would gather in a large hall to listen to the comments and findings, and yes, to challenge those findings if need be. At that summation hearing the hospital would know whether it gets its accreditation. No prolonged waiting or hearing the news through the media. The summation hearing is also a time for both sides to learn from each other. A few weeks later the hospital would get the formal report. If there were to be any bad news, the hospital would hear it first and directly from the surveyors. In Malaysia institutions often become aware that they have failed their accreditation only through the press. This would then be followed by a series of conflicting "clarifying" remarks from officials that resulted in further confusion.

The other pertinent point is that the surveyors and reviewers are made up of working professionals from comparable institutions. There is no point in sending an expert from a university hospital to survey a small community hospital. The problems and issues would be entirely different. Likewise with surveying an educational institution; it would be pointless to send a law professor to survey a technical institute.

Even though the hospital's accrediting body is independent, during the survey there are participants from the state department of hospitals as well as the federal government's Medicare agency. They too perform their own survey in tandem with the accrediting body to avoid duplication of efforts. Likewise LAN could conduct its survey together with representatives of the ministry or even the immigration department, to avoid duplication.

In surveying colleges and universities it is important not only to evaluate their "software" (course offerings, lecturers' qualifications, libraries) but also the "hardware," (lecture facilities, students' amenities, and laboratory capabilities). This idea that you could run a university in a shopping mall or over some empty shop lot is ridiculous. Accrediting agencies in America are now also factoring diversity of students and faculty in recognition of their value in the students' overall college experience.

A good place for LAN to start would be to clarify the definitions of various terms like institute, college, university, or even university-college. Have clear statutory delineations so the public would not be confused.

The other major issue for LAN and the ministry to confront is the plethora of academic offerings of the various institutions. Should an institution be allowed to offer a mechanics certificate right up to a master's or PhD degree? More importantly, can that institution do justice to its various constituents? I seriously question the competence and wisdom of an institution having such a smorgasbord offering of educational diplomas on its menu.

◆   ◆   ◆

By eliminating such ancillary functions as publishing, translating, and testing, MOE could focus on its core mission of taking care of the education of Malaysians. That by itself is a formidable responsibility; there is no need to seek additional ones. Teachers already make up a third of the civil service, and the ministry routinely gets the biggest budget allocation. Thus even after dispensing with these extraneous activities, MOE has enough on its plate and then more. MOE should concentrate on doing only the essentials, and doing them better.

10

Putting It All Together

Educational institutions should educate as well as integrate Malaysians.

It is assumed that national unity would best be achieved through a rigid and uniform school system enforced upon all. This was the basis of the Razak Report. Today the consequences of that premise are obvious. Malaysians remain even more segregated, and these institutions have done a lousy job in their basic mission of educating the young. Malaysians today are severely wanting in their English skills, mathematical competency, and science literacy, severely handicapping them in the modern marketplace.

Malaysia can have a system of education that would both prepare its young for the competitive world and at the same time bring them together. For this we would need a system that is the very opposite of the present. Whereas the current system is rigid and uniform, my proposed system would be flexible and diverse, with just enough core commonality to identify us as Malaysians. Achieving this calls for a Ministry of Education that is radically different from the present form. Whereas today's ministry is highly centralized, with strict top-down command and rigid controls, I call for a more democratized structure with power and responsibilities delegated to lower levels, in some cases right down to the individual institution. The leadership role of the minister is less that of a drill sergeant barking out orders to frightened raw recruits, more of an orchestra conductor coaxing the best from his highly skilled musicians.

This flexible and diverse system would best meet the varied and differing needs of a plural Malaysian society, and at the same time promote greater unity. Getting there does not require major changes in the current basic pattern, more of a shift in attitude and mindset, away from rigid control and regimentation to that of consultation and collaboration between the center and the periphery.

Reform does not occur in the minister's office or with some high profile committee of esteemed citizens. Nor would it be achieved simply with the issuance of some thick glossy reports accompanied by glittering ceremony and pompous speechifying. Rather it takes place in the classrooms, beginning with each child and individual teacher. The central and essential element of a good learning environment is still the skillful teacher who can capture the imagination of his or her pupils. The essence of my reform is to get those teachers and then do everything possible to make their job easier and more enjoyable. This means providing them with an environment conducive to learning, and compensating them adequately.

Reform will fail or succeed in the classrooms. President Bush appropriately named his monumental education reform legislation as the "No Child Left Behind Act Of 2001." The emphasis is rightly on the individual child, and on maximizing his God-given potential. The individual child is the central focus of education, not the politics of language, culture, or race.

When we single-mindedly focus on this basic theme, all the other peripheral elements and goals that are commonly associated with education would fall into place. If we educate our young well, they would become better citizens of not only the nation but also the world. And national unity would be that much easier to achieve. If we burden our schools with extraneous missions, then we dilute and blur that central mission. And when schools fail, that failure would spill over to and be amplified in other arenas.

In his *A Nation At Risk*, David Gardner reaffirms the principle that all, regardless of color, race, or economic status are entitled to a fair and equal chance to develop his or her potential, and when that is done, the benefits would accrue not only to that individual but also to society. The report defines excellence in education from three perspectives. For individuals, it would be to enable them to perform at the boundary of their ability, and then to test and push back those personal limits. For schools and colleges, it would be to set high expectations and goals for all learners, and help them achieve those goals. For society, it is to adopt those policies that would enhance those goals for individuals and institutions. My reform reinforces Gardner's themes.

What I am proposing is not revolutionary or radical, rather evolutionary and incremental. I have not changed the basic premise such as the number of school years, the paramountcy of Malay language, or the basic funding mechanism.

In making my proposals I am guided by the following assumptions.

Recognizing that Malaysia is a diverse nation, there is no "one size fits all" system. We should expect and indeed encourage different models. A school that would be suitable for rural and poor Ulu Kelantan would be grossly inappropriate for urban and affluent Ukay Heights. We must also have parental choice. We cannot force a system down any parents' (or their children's) throat. Give parents the freedom to choose what is best for their children. Parents know (and care about) their children better than any civil servant or politician. We should recognize that educational wisdom is never the exclusive preserve of government officials and bureaucrats. Nor is the government the only entity that can provide quality education. Thus I call for private sector participation in education at all levels.

Amidst the diverse models there must be a core of commonality. All Malaysians must study Malay, English, mathematics, and science, and the student body of all our institutions, private and public, must reflect the greater society. A nation that studies together stays together.

We must encourage schools to achieve this goal. Schools whose student body reflects society must be rewarded with enhanced state support; conversely there should no funding for those catering only to a particular ethnic, racial, or religious group. This applies both to vernacular as well as religious schools unless they open up their enrollment to attract a more diverse student body.

When our institutions enhance their standards and have high expectations, our students will respond. Success depends on continually elevating the bars and challenges, not in lowering them. We must also recognize that success in schools has other correlates outside of education, in particular, parents' socioeconomic status and educational attainment. While we cannot do much to alter these factors, we can, through effective and imaginative policies, intervene and negate their impacts on the children.

My reform seeks to improve the evident weaknesses of the current system and build on the proven successes. I deal only with the broad framework and leave the pedagogical details of what and how to teach to teachers and educators. They are the ones who are trained and qualified to make those decisions. More importantly they are the ones who see the children everyday, not the politicians or policy makers. Those closest to the students–their teachers–should make decisions regarding details of the curriculum, pedagogy, class scheduling, and other educational matters.

I would change the present school years of K-6/3/2/2 (preschool-primary/lower secondary/upper secondary/pre-university) to K-6/3/4 (preschool-primary/middle/high school). I would incorporate preschool with primary school and lower the admission age from the current five years to four. There would not be much change in the curriculum except that there will be only four core subjects: Malay, English, science, and mathematics. These core subjects must be taught daily, and except for Malay, they would be taught in English. Passing them would also be mandatory. Beyond the core, each school is free to choose whatever subjects in whatever language to fill in the rest of the school day.

The sooner pupils are taught multiple languages the better. The benefits would spill over into other intellectual areas like the ability for abstract thinking and to sift the core data from the surrounding noise. There are numerous clinical studies supporting my contention. We should capitalize on this scientific insight.

Students would sit for only three national examinations: at the end of primary 6 (UPSR); middle school (PMR); and high school (STP). The UPSR and PMR would test only the four core subjects. Further these examinations would contribute only 70 percent of the student's final score; the rest would come from the teachers' yearlong evaluation (the students' GPA). For USPR, the student's GPA at Years 5 and 6 would each contribute 15 percent to the final score. For PMR, the students GPA in each of three years of middle school would contribute equally (10 percent each) to the final score.

With the reduced load the examination syndicate could release the results much sooner and there would be no need to have these examinations held so early in the school year and thus taking away valuable teaching time. They could be held in late November with the results out by late December, in time for the students to begin their new school year the following January with minimal interruption.

There would be minimal changes to the present primary national-type Chinese and Tamil schools. They should be viewed less as vernacular schools and more as schools that happen to use Mandarin or Tamil as the medium of instruction. Thus I would make them even more welcoming to others outside their particular racial group. To a certain extent the national-type Chinese schools are already successful in this. More and more Malay parents are sending their children to such schools. More can be done to make these schools Malay-friendly, like offering Islamic classes (taught in Mandarin) and having Malays on the governing board.

After middle school the students would be streamed to enter academic, regular, or vocational stream. This streaming would be based both on the PMR scores as well as the GPAs for all subjects. I envisage the top third to be in the academic stream, and I would encourage a similar number to pursue the vocational, the rest would continue in the regular stream. There should be sufficient flexibility so students could switch during the first two years, based on their performance and teachers' recommendations. The academic schools would prepare students for universities. The regular stream would prepare students to enter directly into the job market or for entry into non-degree granting institutions.

For the Year 13 examination (STP), students would take six instead of the present five subjects. Four would be the core mandatory subjects mentioned earlier. Again, as with the reformed UPSR and PMR, the final examination would contribute only 70 percent to the final score, with the rest coming from the student's GPAs as per the following formula: 5 percent each for the first two years of high school, 8 for the third, and 12 for the last year. My proposal would dispense with both MUET and the General Paper.

The dramatic change from the present is that the student's final grade would not be dependent exclusively on that one final end-of-year examination, rather it factors in the student's year round performance. This would give a better evaluation of the student's true ability and potential. Interschool variations in GPA standards could be adjusted using modern statistical tools.

My reform eliminates the current Year 11 examination (SPM). There are two immediate advantages to this. One, it would eliminate the long hiatus after Form V while waiting for the results, and two, all students would proceed to Form 6 and would thus get 13 years of schooling. My reform also eliminates *matrikulasi*, as Sixth Form would now regain its primacy. *Matrikulasi* is an expensive and wasteful program. Besides, universities should concentrate doing what other institutions could not do, that is education at the undergraduate, graduate, and professional levels. The activities now carried out under *matrikulasi* could cheaply and more effectively be done by schools.

If it were not politically feasible to terminate *matrikulasi*, then I would turn them into an outreach program, restricting its intake to Bumiputra students from disadvantaged backgrounds. Students currently attending residential and good urban schools should not be allowed to enroll.

The professionals at the schools would set the curriculum, choose the textbooks, and assess the students. The ministry's role would be to provide guidelines and to set the minimum standards for the core subjects. The schools would be expected to exceed those standards through their own unique ways. For vocational schools I would expect industry to set up the curriculum so students would learn what would be relevant for the marketplace.

I would revamp the entire Islamic stream, from preschool to university, by integrating it into the mainstream. There is no good reason for segregating Muslim students into their own separate and exclusive schools. If that were not possible, then I would at least integrate their curriculum with the regular stream. That is, Islamic Studies would now be only one subject and not the all-consuming curriculum. These students would still, like all other Malaysians, have to take the four compulsory core subjects. The current Islamic matriculation examination STAM would also be eliminated and students would have to take the regular STP with the four core subjects. Their additional two subjects could be Islamic Studies and Arabic.

The cause of Islam would be better served by having its future scholars and *ulamas* broadly educated and exposed to students of various backgrounds. These Islamic schools must also produce their share of the nation's professionals, scientists, and executives. These schools should not become modern seminaries.

The undergraduate curriculum should be broad-based and liberal along the American tradition. Students pursuing a degree in the natural sciences must take some courses in the humanities; those in the liberal arts must be exposed to laboratory science and mathematics. Additionally, law and medicine ought to be graduate programs, that is, requirements for entry must include a baccalaureate degree.

My proposal calls for private sector participation at all levels. This would not only lighten the load on the public purse but also introduce much needed innovation and competition. There could be purely private institutions or those that are joint public and private sector partnership in the form of charter schools and universities. Charter institutions would receive state funding in the amount equivalent to what it would have cost the state to have those students educated in public schools and universities. Both private and charter institutions must have a student body that reflects the general society. This would be the best way to achieve greater integration and social cohesion. Private schools would have only one required core subject, Malay, while charter schools would have the same four core subjects as in public schools. Beyond that the school is free to chart its own course, including the freedom to choose its language of instruction. Conceivably there could be a school using Swahili if there is enough demand from a broad section of Malaysians. Charter schools would have its managing board made up of mostly parents and teachers.

We must actively discourage segregating the young. It should be a condition for issuing the operating permits of schools and other institutions that their student body must reflect the greater society. The government could encourage this goal by providing scholarships and grants. Having a diverse study body would greatly enhance the learning experience of the students. What better way to prepare them for the diverse global marketplace than to have them exposed to the different cultures during their student days? The remarkable enriching experience of an American undergraduate program is precisely because of this incredibly diverse environment, culturally and academically.

Teachers' colleges deserve special mention. A well-trained teacher is the core of any successful system; hence the importance of these colleges. They should train teachers for preschool to Year 9. At high school, teachers should have a bachelor's degree followed by a year's training in how to teach. I disagree with the proposal of the National Brains Trust to making all teachers have a degree, as in America. Nor do I agree with the American system of training teachers where the emphasis is in the methodology of teaching (pedagogy) at the expense of expertise in a particular subject. I would prefer that teachers first be experts in their chosen subjects and then be trained to teach, at least for the high school level.

In recognition of the importance of English and also with the recent decision to teach science and mathematics in that language, I would convert many of the current teachers' colleges into complete English medium institutions. I would also encourage greater specializations with some emphasizing the performing arts, others science and mathematics.

To attract the talented into teaching we must not only pay them better but also give them clear and varied paths for professional advancement. Teachers colleges' must have opportunities in their curriculum so their trainees could sit for university matriculation examinations. Thus when they finish their training they could also qualify to pursue a degree. With such opportunities we would be able to attract more of the talented into teachers' colleges. This would be far preferable to upgrading all teachers' colleges into universities, as in America. We should instead upgrade the standards of our teachers' colleges.

The experience of the old British teachers' colleges like Brinsford Lodge and Kirby is relevant. They produced high quality teachers; many of their graduates went on to pursue their degrees, including graduate degrees. On many local universities today we see many of these former teachers now with their doctorates. We should be replicating the Kirbys and Brinsford Lodges.

We should improve the pay scale for teachers; an increase of 25 percent would be appropriate. I would also have allowances for those with much-need skills, like teachers of English, science, and mathematics, and another allowance for those teaching in rural areas. Thus a science teacher posted to Ulu Kelantan would enjoy double allowances. With such incentives we would greatly reduce the gaping divide between urban and rural schools.

Additionally I would have incentives for poor parents to keep their children in school. These include paying parents to do so; by incorporating meal and health programs at school; and making the school day longer so these children would do their homework and extra studying at school. I would make their classrooms attractive by air-conditioning them and ending double sessions.

I call for markedly reducing the activities of MOE, specifically dispensing with DBP, LAN, and reducing the scope of the examination syndicates. DBP's translating and scholarly activities could be shifted to the universities, while its publishing and printing arm privatized. Similarly both LAN and the examination syndicate could be made into autonomous bodies and funded solely through the fees they charge. With a major chunk of MOE's activities dispensed, it would become a much slimmer entity and be able to accomplish its core mission more effectively.

I also call for streamlining and consolidating the sponsorship of students studying abroad. We should send only our best, and then only to the top institutions. They should also be given the freedom to choose their own field of study.

The salient feature of my reform is that it does not entail major outlays of expenditures. In fact it would reduce the aggregate costs by more efficient use of present facilities and resources. Nor would my proposals require changes in the law; no new enabling legislations would be required to effect the changes I am advocating. The reforms could be achieved within the current framework. That cannot be said of the other competing proposals.

List of Abbreviations

AP	Advanced Placement
AT	Achievement Test
CES	Coalition of Essential Schools
DEB	Dewan Bahasa dan Pustaka
GCE	General Certificate of Education
GPA	Grade Point Average
IB	International Baccalaureate
IIU	International Islamic University
LAN	Lembaga Akreditasi Malaysia
MARA	Majlis Amanah Rakyat
MCA	Malaysian Chinese Association
MCKK	Malay College Kuala Kangsar
MIC	Malaysian Indian Congress
MOE	Ministry of Education
PMR	Penilaian Menengah Rendah (Year 9 examination)
ROI	Return on Investment
SAT	Scholastic Achievement Test
SBM	School Based Management
SITC	Sultan Idris Training College
SPM	Sijil Persekutuan Malaysia
STAM	Sijil Tinggi Agama Malaysia (Year 13 Islamic examination)

STP	Sijil Tinggi Persekutuan (Year 13 examination)
TIMSS	Third International Mathematics and Science Studies
TKC	Tunku Kurshiah School
UKM	Universiti Kebangsaan Malaysia
UM	Universiti Malaya
UMNO	United Malay National Organization
UPSR	Ujian PenilianRendah Sekolah (Year 6 examination)
UTAR	Universiti Tunku Abdul Rahman
USM	Universiti Sains Malaysia
UUM	Universiti Utara Malaysia

Notes

CHAPTER ONE: A PREEMPTIVE STRIKE

Malaysian students going to Singapore schools: I am unable to get official confirmation of the figures quoted in the media. The papers merely reported the assertion of an UMNO Youth official. The data would be an easy enough to collect, just stand at the causeway on any school morning and start counting. The news item appeared as: "*7000 Pelajar Cina Johor sambung sekolah dalam BI di Singapura.*" (7000 Chinese students in Johore continuing their studies in English at Singapore), *Utusan Melayu* August 23, 2002.

Prime Minister's Mahathir's granddaughter attending foreign boarding school: this was revealed tangentially in his daughter's regular newspaper column, "Musings with Marina." Marina Mahathir (2002),"Too Many Rules." *The Star* August 28, 2002.

The Razak Report (*Penyata Razak*) (1956): *Report of the Education Committee 1956 (The Razak Report).* Government Printing Press, Kuala Lumpur.

MOE's blueprint for education development, see: Ministry of Education Malaysia (2001): *Pembangunan Pendididakan 2001-2010. Rancangan Bersepadu Penjana Cemerlangan Pendidikan.* (Education Development 2001-2010. Plan for Unity Through Educational Excellence.) Ministry of Education Malaysia, Kuala Lumpur, 2001.

The National Brains Trust Report, see: "Knowledge-Based Economy Masterplan." *The Star*, September 12, 2002.

For news report for yet another review of the national schools by Prime Minister Mahathir, see: Firdaus Abdullah and Sajahan Waheed: "School System to be Reviewed." *New Straits Times*, November 29, 2002.

The three pillars of a good education system, see: World Bank Review (1995): *Priorities and Strategies for Education.* World Bank, Washington, DC

People are the real wealth of nations, see: *Human Development Report 2001. Making New Technologies Work for Human Development.* Published by UNDP by Oxford University Press, New York, 2001. Website: **www.undp.org/hdr2001.**

Reform of American medical education: Abraham Flexner (1910): *Medical Education in the United States and Canada. A Report to the Carnegie Foundation for the Advancement of Teaching.* Bulletin No: 4. Merrymount Press, Boston, MA.

MOE's mission statement, see its homepage at: **www.moe.gov.my**

CHAPTER TWO: IT'S MORE THAN JUST EDUCATION

James Wolfensohn quote is from the World Bank Report (2002): *Education and Development.*
www1.worldbank.org/education/pdf/educationbrochure/pdf

Primary education in Indonesia, see: Duflo, Esther (2001): "Schooling and Labor Market: Consequences of school construction in Indonesia." *American Economic Review* 91 (4).

Louis Gerstner's quote from: Gerstner, Louis V, Jr, Roger D Semerad, Dennis Phillip Doyle, William B Johnston (1994): *Reinventing Education. Entrepreneurship in America's Public Schools.* Dutton Books, New York.

Education and Economic Growth: Robert J Barro: "Education and Economic Growth."
www1.oecd.org/els/pdfs/EDSCER/DoCA018.pdf. See also his book cited in the reference.

Impact of education and health: See World Bank Report 2000: *Education and HIV/AIDS. A Window of Hope*. **www1.worldbank.org/ education/pdf/exec%summaryAIDS-Ed-final.pdf**

Nik Safiah Karim's anti-English language sentiment (to think that she is a language expert!), see: "*Pakar Bahasa Bidas Cadangan Pemimpin UMNO*." (Language Expert Condemns UMNO's Leadership." *Harakahdaily* May 24, 2002. **www.harakahdaily.net/article.php?sid=1396**

Goh Keng Swee's remarks on Singapore's parents choosing science and mathematics for their children, quoted in: Daniel Yergin, Joseph Stanislaw, Daniel Tergin: *Commanding Heights: The Battle Between Government and the Marketplace That is Remaking the Modern World*. Simon and Shuster, New York, 1998. This was later made into a three-part PBS TV Series broadcasted on April 3, 10, 17, 2002. **www.pbs.org/wbgh/commandingheights**.

Correlation between earnings and ability in mathematics, see Heather Rose, Julian R Betts (2001): "The Link Between High School Curriculum, College Graduation, and Earnings." California Public Policy Institute, San Francisco, CA.

Differences between wealth and knowledge, see: Ali, Maulana Muhammad (1990): *The Religion of Islam*. Ahmadiyya Anjuman Islam, Lahore, Bookcrafters, Chelsea, MI.

Rosenthal Effect: Rosenthal, Robert and L Jacobsen (1992): *Pygmalion in the Classroom*. Expanded edition. Irvington, New York. Also: Robert T Tauber: "Good or Bad, What Teachers Expect from Students They Generally Get." US Department of Education, ERIC Digest. **www.kidsource.com/education/pygmalion.html**

Stereotype Threat, see Claude Steele (1999): "Thin Ice: Stereotype Threat and the Black College Students." *The Atlantic*, August.

Attitude of Malay students to science and mathematics, see Frank J Swetz, Hassan Langgulung, and Johar Abdul Rasid (1983): "Attitudes toward mathematics and school learning in Malaysia and Indonesia;

Urban-Rural and Male-Female Dichotomies." *Comparative Education Review*, October 1983 (309-402).

The fad of Islamization of knowledge and curriculum, see Farish Noor: "Looking beyond Islamization of Knowledge" **www.intelligensia.com**. Also: Rosnani Hashim (2002): "Islamization of the Curriculum." **www.islam-online.net/10L-English/qadaya/education-1/education1.asp**, and Adi Setia: "Is Islamic Science Obscurantist?" *Education Quarterly*, No:21 March/April 2002.

Returns on investment (ROI) in education. See George Psacharopoulos and Harry Anthony Patrinos (2002): "*Returns to Investment in Education. A Further Update.*" World Bank Education Working Paper No: 2881. **http://econ.worldbank.org/files/18081 wps.2881.pdf**. Also: Psacharopoulus, George (1995): "The profitability of Investments in Education: Concepts and Methods." Human Capital Development and Operations Policy, The World Bank, Washington DC.

Effects of social policy on schools, see: Rosnani Hashim (2002) "Balancing Cultural Plurality and National Unity Through Education." Paper presented at the Ninth International Literary and Education Research Network Conference on Learning. Beijing, People s Republic of China July 16-20, 2002. (Paper provided courtesy of the author, Professor Rosnani Hashim of the International Islamic University.) Also: Suet-Ling Pong: "Ethnicity and schooling in Malaysia: The Role of Policy." **www.cicred.org/education/acters/com-Pong.pdf**; Viswananthan Selvaratnam (1988): "Ethnicity, Inequality and Higher Education in Malaysia." *Comparative Education Review* 32 (2) 173-76; and Kandasamy Maheswari, R Santhiram (2000): "From National Interest to Globalization. The Education of Malaysia." in Kes Mazurek, Margeret A Wizner, Czeslaw Majorek Eds. *Education in a Global Society. A Comparative Perspective.* Allyn Bacon, Boston 385-97.

Computers in Indian villages and Sugata Mitra's "Hole in the Wall" experiment, see: "Frontline World: Hole in the Wall." PBS TV program aired on October 2002. **www.pbs.org/frontlineworld/sories/ India/kids.html**. Also in "A Lesson in Computer Literacy from India's Poorest Kids." *Businessweek* "Minimally Invasive Education." March 2, 2000.

Lee Kuan Yew's comment on air-conditioning, see: "Most important inventions of the last millennium." *Walls Street Journal*, December 31, 1999.

Skeptics on computers in the classrooms, see Stoll, Clifford (1999): *High Tech Heretic. Why Computers Don't Belong in the Classrooms and Other Reflections by a Computer Contrarian*. Double Day, New York, and also Stoll 1995; and Jane M Healy: *Failure to Connect. How Computers Affect our Children's Minds—For Better and Worse*. Simon & Shuster New York, 1998.

Technology and learning: *Improving Learning with Information Technology*. Report of a Workshop 2002. National Academy Press, Washington, DC

Abdullah Badawi's suggestion on teaching IT in schools, see: "IT as an essential subject in school." Speech given at the opening of the Malaysian E-Government Conference, Kuala Lumpur, July 1, 2002. **www.smpke.jpm.my**.

Computer literacy and computational literacy, see: Di Sessa, Andrea A (2000): *Changing Minds. Computers, Learning, and Literacy*. MIT Press, Cambridge.

Boxer, the programming language for educational applications: check its website: **www.soe.berkeley.edu/boxer**

IT in schools: Luis Osin (1998): "Computers in Education in Developing Countries. Why and How." Education and Technology Series Vol 3 No 1. **http://wbln0018.worldbank.org/HDNet/ NDDocs.nsf**; Also Harold Wonglinsky (1998): "Does it Compute? The Relationship Between Educational Technology and Student Achievement in Mathematics. Educational Testing Service's (ETS) Research Policy Information Center, Princeton, NJ **http://ftp.ets.org/ pub/res/technolog.pdf** Effect of

For IT and universities, see: "Impact of Information Technology on the Future of Research Universities." Workshop proceedings sponsored by the National Academies held at Washington, DC on Jan 22-23, 01. Broadcasted on the Research Channel December 27, 2002. **www.researchchannel.org.**

Kerala's superior social indices despite a poor economy, see: Akash Kapur: "Poor but Prosperous." *The Atlantic Monthly*, September 1998.

Malaysia's seventy million population policy, see: "Dasar Pendudukan Malaysia ke Arah 70 Juta Penduduk." (Malaysia's 70 Million Population Policy.) **www.smpke.jpm.my/dasar/pendudok.htm**1997

CHAPTER THREE: THE PRESENT SYSTEM

The state of vernacular schools under British rule, see: The Report from the Commissioner General in South East Asia to the Secretary of State for the Colonies, August 19, 1949. Reprinted in Clive J Christie's (1998) *Southeast Asia in the Twentieth Century. A Reader*. IB Taurus, London.

Pathetic fate of Malay school graduates, see Roff, William R (1967): *The Origin of Malay Nationalism*. Yale U Press, New Haven CT.

Chinese schools holding the government at ransom: see Shaw, William (1976): *Tun Razak. His Life and Times*. Longman Malaysia, Kuala Lumpur.

Education dualism, see the excellent book by Rosnani Hashim (1996): *Education Dualism in Malaysia. Implications for Theory and Practice*. (Southeast Asian Social Studies Monographs), Oxford U Press, Kuala Lumpur.

Suspension of government funding for private religious schools, see: Ainon Mohd and Firdaus Abdullah: "Funding Temporarily Stopped." *The New Straits Times* October 25, 2002.

Graduate school exclusively for Islamic Studies, see: The International Institute of Islamic Thought and Civilization (ISTAC) website: **www5.jarring.my//istac** Also, Adi Setia: "The Many Sides of Islam.

Jihad of the Word." *Education Quarterly* No 19, November/December 2001.

Private higher education in Malaysia: Ahmad Mahdzan Ayob, Noran Fauziah Yaakub (1999): "Development of Graduate Education in Malaysia. Prospects for Centralization." **www.mahdzan.com**. Also Ahmad Mahdzan Ayob (1999): "Business of Higher Education in Malaysia: Development and Prospects in the New Millennium." **http://mhdzan.com/papers/nzpaper99/03growth.shtml**. Also Tan Ai Mei (2001): *Malaysian Private Higher Education. Globalization, Privatization, Transformation and Marketplace.* Asean Academic Press, Kuala Lumpur.

CHAPTER FOUR: WEAKNESSES OF THE CURRENT SYSTEM

TIMSS: Third International Mathematics and Science Studies. **http://isc.bc.edu/timss1999.html**

Research comparing students from *matrikulasi* and Sixth Form, see (for the media report): Zulkifli Bachok: "*Matrikulsai: Pencapaian lebeh rendah berbanding STPM)*" (Matrikulasi: Much lower achievements than Sixth Form). *Utusan Malaysia* May, 11, 2002. For the original paper, visit the researchers' university website: Bidin Yatim, Nor Azdah Ngah, Sharipah Soaad Syed: "*Penilaian Pencapaian Lepasan Matrikulasi.*" (Assessment of the achievements of *matrikulasi* graduates) at: **www.uum.edu.my/ppp/matrikulasi.html**.

Passivity of Malaysian undergraduates, see: G. Silverman: "Silence of the Lambs." Cover story, *Far Eastern Economic Review* November 14, 1996. See also my critique in: "Take Note" Letter to the Editor, *Far Eastern Economic Review*, December 19, 1996.

Survey of Asian universities in: "Asia's Best Universities." *Asiaweek*, June 30, 2000.

CHAPTER FIVE: A LOOK AT OTHER MODELS

The comprehensive large American high schools, see: James B Conant (1967): *The Comprehensive High School. A Second Report to Interested Citizens.* McGraw Hill, New York. Also: Conant, James B (1959): *The American High School Today. A First Report to Interested Citizens.* McGraw-Hill, New York.

A Nation at Risk: David Gardner, *et al* (1983): *A Nation At Risk: The Imperative for Educational Reform. An Open Letter to the American People.* A Report to the nation and the Secretary of Education by the National Commission on Excellence in Education, US Government Printers, Washington, DC. **www.ed.gov/pubs/NatAt Risk/title.html**

Coalition of Essential Schools' website: **www.essentialschools.org**. See also Theodore R Sizer in the reference.

Bard's High School Early College program, see: Abby Goodnough: "Program to Provide a Head Start on College." *The New York Times*, July 7, 2001.

American freshmen having to take remedial courses, see: John Cloud (2002): "Who's Ready For College?" Time Magazine October 14, 2002.

Carnegie Foundation Classification of American colleges and universities, see: Alexandar C McCormack, Ed. (2001): *The Carnegie Classification of Institutions of Higher Education, 2000 Ed.* Menlo Park, CA. It can also be downloaded from its website:
www.carnegiefoundation.org/publications/
classification_2000.htm.

Germany's school system, see: "The German School System."
http://library.thinkquest.org/26576/schoolpage.htm

Education in Germany, see Huib de Priester: "Education in Germany Part 1"
http://www.international-community.de/education.htm

Germany's Dual System, see Indermit Gill and Amit Dar (1996): Germany's Dual System: Lessons for Low and Middle Income Countries." Prepared for the World Bank-ILO Studies on "Constraints and Innovations in Reform of VET" wbln0018.worldbank.org/HDNet/hddocs.nsf/globalview/Germany

Malaysia adopting Germany's Dual system, see: Amit Dar and Indermit Gill: "*Malaysia: Meeting the Demand for Skilled Workers in a Rapidly Growing Economy.*" World Bank Country Report. Malaysia Country Study Summary.

IB as an excellent preparation for taking science and mathematics in college, see: "Learning and Understanding: Improving Advanced Study of mathematics and science in US high schools." **www.nap.edu/books/0309074401.html**

For more details on IB, visit its website: **www.ibo.org**

Mara Junior College's outstanding performance on IB: Roziana Hamsawi: "Mara College scores best IB worldwide exam results...again!" News item, *The News Straits Times*, August 27, 2002.

Brazil's *Bolsa Escola* Program. Silvio Caccia Bava (2001): "*Bolsa-Escola* (School Bursary Program). A Public Policy on Minimum Income and Education." **www.idrc.ca/lacro/foro/seminario/caccia_pb.html**

Bolsa Escola and ATM cards (2002): "ATM cards help nearly 10 million Brazilian children stay in school." *UNDP News* May 2002. **www.undp.org/dpa/frontpagearchive2002/30May02/**

CHAPTER SIX: ATTEMPTS AT REFORMS

Scant media coverage of MOE's *Education Development 2001-2010*, see: "Blueprint for the Future." *Education Quarterly* No:19, November/December 2001.

UMNO's functionary calling for UM Vice-chancellor's resignation over the campus fire: "VC Should Quit, Azlina Reiterates." *The New Straits Times*, July 2, 2001.

Sudden acceptance of meritocracy by the political establishment, see: "Cabinet Supports Meritocracy Move." News item, *The New Straits Times*, August 2, 2002.

Increased Bumiputra student intake into the universities in 2002, see: Saiful Azhar Abdullah and Chot Suat Liong: "Bumi Intake Up In Varsities." News item, *The New Straits Times* October 5, 2002.

Global reform movement (2001), see World Bank Report 2001: *Global Education Reform. Decentralization in Education.* World Bank Report. **www1.worldbank.org/education…Reform/06.01DecenQ&A/ DecenQ&A.htm.**

School reform in Chile, see: Delannoy, Francoise (2000): *Education Reforms in Chile, 1980-98. A Lesson in Pragmatism.* Country Studies: Education Reforms and Management Series, June Vol 1 No 1, World Bank, Washington, DC.

School reforms in America: The current resurgence of voucher and privatization movements for schools date from Milton Friedman's challenge on the "natural monopoly" of government in providing education. See: Milton Friedman (1955): "The Role of Government in Education." In Robert A Solo: *Economics and Public Interest.* Rutgers University Press, NJ

Proponents of bilingual education becoming advocates of English immersion classes, see the interview with Ken Noonan, Superintendent of the Oceanside School District, California at: **www.abc.net.au/rn/ arts/ling/stories/s21671.htm.**

Advocates of bilingual education, see: Krasher, Stephen: "Why Bilingual Education?" **http://gopher.ael.org/~eric/digest/edorc968.html.**

Movement to reform bilingual education in California, see "Los Angeles: Bilingual Charter School Hopes to be a Model in Any Language." *Los Angeles Times* April 9, 2002.

Public school reform, see: Annenberg Challenge, The (2002): *Lessons and Reflections on Public School Reform.* Annenberg Foundation, St

Davids, PA and the Annenberg Institute for School Reform, Brown University, Providence RI. **www.annenbergchallenge.org**

Reference to language war, see the lead editorial: Zulfikifli Salleh: "*Perang Bahasa*" (Language War) *Dewan Bahasa* October 2002.

CHAPTER SEVEN: STRENGTHENING THE SCHOOLS

Clinical studies on the bilingual brain: Kim, KH, NR Relkin, KM Lee, J Hirsch (1997): "Distinct cortical areas associated with native and second languages." *Nature*, July 10; 388 (6638): 171-4. July 1997.

Lay article on bilingual brain, see Judy Foreman: "The Evidence Speaks Well of Bilingual Effects on Kids." *Los Angeles Times* October 7, 2002.

Differences already seen at preschool, see Richard Coley: "An Uneven Start: Indicators of Inequality in School Readiness." Educational testing Services (ETS) Research Policy Information Center, Princeton, NJ.

Dropout rates in rural areas (older reference but the figures have not changed much) see: Azizah Abdul Rahman, Sharifah Md. Nor (1992): "Rural Education in Malaysia." In *Issues in Rural Development in Malaysia*. Victor T King, and Nazaruddin Mohd. Jali Eds. Dewan bahasa danPustaka, Kuala Lumpur.

Movement in America to small schools, see: Anna Mulrina: "Smaller and Better. Move to Small Schools in US" Culture and Ideas. *US News & World Report* June 10, 2002. Also: Meier, Deborah (1995): *The Power of Their Ideas: Lessons for America From a Small School in Harlem*. Beacon Press, Boston, MA

Madrasahs and Islamic schools, see: Abdullah Taib (1973): "The Place of religious education in Malay States with Special Reference to Kelantan." *Akademika* 2.

Lack of interest of Non-Bumiputra students in MARA Junior Colleges: "Poor response for non-Bumiputras to MARA Junior Science College." *Bernama*, November 7, 2002.

Types and classes of workers for the 21st century, see: Reich, Robert B (1991): *The Work of Nations: Preparing Ourselves for the 21st Century Capitalism*. Alfred A Knopf, New York.

American "prep" school: Powell, Arthur G (1996): *Lessons from Privilege. The American Prep School Tradition*. Harvard University Press, Cambridge, MA

Teaching of mathematics and science, see: Martin, Michael O, Ina V S Mullis, Kelvin D Gregory, Craig Hyle, Ce Shen (1998): *Effective Schools in Science and Mathematics*. **www.timss.bcu.edu/timss**

Military schools for American inner city kids, see: Stephanie M Horvath: "Spit-and-Polish schools. Public Military Academies catch on in tough districts. Does 'Yes Sir!' help learning?" *Wall Street Journal* August 2, 2002.

Unemployed religious teachers, see: Pereira, Brendan: "KL worries *ulamas* could foment trouble. The Mahathir government fears jobless teachers could become an unstable fringe group." News item. *The Straits Times* (Singapore) November 29, 2002.

National service as the answer to the failures of schools, see: "National schools failure to boost racial ties prompted National Service." News item, *The New Straits Times* November 23, 2002.

CHAPTER EIGHT: REFORMING HIGHER EDUCATION

Quote from the *The Economist*, see: "British Universities on the Road to Ruin." Leader, *The Economist* November 16, 2002.

Symbolic analytic workers, see Robert Reich, 1991.

Local universities now requiring a pass in English for admission, see: Faiza Zainudin: "*UPM wajibkan ujian Bahasa Inggeris.*" (UOM now mandates a pass in English language) *Berita Minggu* October 13, 2002.

The costs of Malaysian students abroad, see: "Students abroad spent RM6 billion this year." News item, *The New Straits Times* September 17, 2002.

Incentives for science and other specialized teachers, see: "English, Science, Math teachers to get special incentives." News item, *The New Straits Times*, November 9, 2002.

Importance of quality teachers and teacher training, see Joshua D Angrist and Victor Lavy: "Does Teacher Training Affect Pupil Learning? Evidence from Matched Comparisons in Jerusalem Public Schools." National Bureau of Economic Research Working Paper No: 6781. **http://ideas.repec.org/nbr/nberwo/6781.html.**

Indian Institute of Technology graduates emigrating to the West: "India's Whiz Kids. Inside the Indian Institute of Technology's Star Factory." *Businessweek* (International Edition) December 7, 1998.

Inadequacy of local IT graduates, see: Leslie Lau: "Firm Discovers good IT help hard to find. Malaysia's IT graduates cannot string together enough programming code to win a top job. Employers want change." *The Straits Times* (Singapore), November 30, 2002.

For an academic discussion on private higher education, see: Tan Ai Mei (2001): *Malaysian Private Higher Education. Globalization, Privatization, Transformation and Marketplace.* Asean Academic Press, Kuala Lumpur.

CHAPTER NINE: MOW DOWN THE MOE

Malay teachers' role in politics, see: William R Roff (1967): *The Origin of Malay Nationalism.* Yale U Press, New Haven CT.

The Income Contingent Repayment (ICR) student loan scheme was first mooted by Milton Friedman in 1955 (see Robert A Solo: *Economics and Public Interest*).

Dewan Bahasa website: **www.dbp.gov.my**
LAN's accreditation manual See: National Accreditation Board website: **www.lan.gov.my**

CHAPTER TEN: PUTTING IT ALL TOGETHER

President Bush's "No Child Left Behind Act of 2001" Educational Reform website: **www.ed.gov/nclb**

References

Ahmad Mahdzan Ayob, Noran Fauziah Yaakub (1999): "Development of Graduate Education in Malaysia. Prospects for Centralization." **www.mahdzan.com**

Ahmad Mahdzan Ayob (1999): "Business of Higher Education in Malaysia: Development and Prospects in the New Millennium." **http://mhdzan.com/papers/nzpaper99/03growth.shtml**

Akash Kapur (1998): "Poor but Prosperous." *The Atlantic Monthly*, September 1998.

Ali, Maulana Muhammad (1990): *The Religion of Islam*. Ahmadiyya Anjuman Islam, Lahore, Bookcrafters, Chelsea, MI.

Annenberg Challenge, The (2002): *Lessons and Reflections on Public School Reform*. Annenberg Foundation, St Davids, PA and the Annenberg Institute for School Reform, Brown University, Providence RI. **www.annenbergchallenge.org**

Barro, Robert J: "Education and Economic Growth." **www1.oecd.org/els/pdfs/EDSCERIDOCA018.pdf**

Barro, Robert J (1997): *Determinants of Economic Growth: A Cross-Country Empirical Study*. MIT Press, Cambridge, MA.

Bava, Silvio Caccia (2001): "*Bolsa-Escola* (School Bursary Program). A Public Policy on Minimum Income and Education." **www.idrc.ca/lacro/foro/seminario/caccia_pb.html**

Bidin Yatim, Nor Azidah Ngah, Sharipah Soaad Syed Yahya (1996): "*Penilaian Pencapaian Pelajar Lepasan Matrikulasi*." (Assessment of the Achievement of Post Matrikulasi Students.) Abstract. Universiti Utara Malaysia **uum.edu.my/ppp/matrikulasi.html.**

"Blueprint for the Future." *Education Quarterly*, Nov/Dec No: 19, 2001.

Case, Anne (2001): "The Primacy of Education." Research Program in Development Studies, Princeton University, Princeton NJ. **www.wws.princeton.edu/~rpds/downloads/primacy-of-edu.pdf**

Christie, Clive J (1998): *Southeast Asia in the Twentieth Century. A Reader*. IB Taurus, London.

Cloud, John (2002): "Who's Ready For College?" *Time Magazine* October 14, 2002.

Coleman, John S, E Campbell, A Mood, E Weinfeld (1966): *Equality of Education Opportunity*. Government Printing office, Washington, DC.

Coley, Richard: "An Uneven Start: Indicators of Inequality in School Readiness." ETS Research Policy Information Center, Princeton, NJ

Conant, James B (1967): *The Comprehensive High School. A Second Report to Interested Citizens*. McGraw Hill, New York.

Conant, James B (1959): *The American High School Today. A First Report to Interested Citizens*. McGraw-Hill, New York.

Corrales, Javier (1999): *The Politics of Education Reform: Bolstering the Supply and Demand; Overcoming Institutional Blocks*. Education Reform and Management Series, Vol II, No: 1. World Bank Report, Washington, DC.

Delannoy, Francoise (2000): *Education Reforms in Chile, 1980-98. A Lesson in Pragmatism.* Country Studies. Education Reforms and Management Series, June Vol 1 No 1, World Bank Report, Washington, DC.

Di Sessa, Andrea A (2000): *Changing Minds. Computers, Learning, and Literacy.* MIT Press, Cambridge.

Duflo, Esther (2001): "Schooling and Labor Market: Consequences of school construction in Indonesia." *American Economic Review* 91 (4).

Flexner, Abraham (1910): *Medical Education in the United States and Canada. A Report to the Carnegie Foundation for the Advancement of Teaching.* Bulletin No: 4. Merrymount Press, Boston, MA.

Foreman, Judy (2002): "The Evidence Speaks Well of Bilingualism's Effects on Kids." *Los Angeles Times*, Health Section, October 7, 2002.

Fiske, Edward B (1992): *Smart Schools, Smart Kids. Why Do Some Schools Work?* Simon & Schuster, New York.

Freeman, Judy (2002): "The Evidence Speaks Well of Bilingualism's Effect on Kids." *Los Angeles Times*, Health, October 7, 2002.

Gardner, David, *et al* (1983): *A Nation At Risk: The Imperative for Educational Reform. An Open Letter to the American People.* A Report to the nation and the Secretary of Education by the National Commission on Excellence in Education, US Government Printers, Washington, DC. **www.ed.gov/pubs/NatAt Risk/title.html**

Gatto, John Taylor (2001): *A Different Kind Of Teacher. Solving the Crisis of American Schooling.* Berkeley Hills Books, Berkeley, CA

Gatto, John Taylor, Ed (1993): *The Exhausted School. The First National Grassroots Speakout on the Right to School Choice.* Oxford Village Press, Oxford, NY.

Gerstner, Louis V, Jr, Roger D Semerad, Dennis Phillip Doyle, William B Johnston (1994): *Reinventing Education. Entrepreneurship in America's Public Schools.* Dutton Books, New York.

Hassan B Said (2000): "Education in Malaysia: Enhancing Accessibility, Capability and Quality." Presented at the First International Forum on Education Reform in Kuala Lumpur.

Healey, Jane M (1998): *Failure to Connect. How Computers Affect Our Children's Minds–For Better or Worse.* Simon & Schuster, New York.

Horvath, Stephanie M (2002): "Spit-and-Polish Schools: Public Militray Academies Cathc on in Tough Districts. Does 'Yes Sir' Help Learning?" *Wall Street Journal*, August 8, 2002.

Kim, KH, Relkin, NR, KM Lee, J Hirsch (1997): "Distinct Cortical Areas Associated with Native and Second Language." *Nature*, July 10, 388 (6638).

Victor T King, and Nazaruddin Mohd. Jali Eds.(1992): *Issues in Rural Development in Malaysia.* Dewan Bahasa dan Pustaka, Kuala Lumpur.

Kremer, Michael, Syivie Moulin, David Myatt, Robert Namunyu (1997): "The Quality-Quantity Trade Off in Education: Evidence From a Prospective Evaluation in Kenya." Post.economics.Harvard.edu/faculty/kremer/papers.html

Levine, Eliot (2002): *One Kid At A Time. Big Lessons From A Small School.* New York Teachers College Press, NY.

Lezotte, William W (1991): *Correlates of Effective Schools. The First and Second Generation* . Effective School Products Ltd. Okemos, MI. **www.effectiveschools.com/correlates.pdf**

Linden, Toby (2001): "Double-shift Secondary Schools: Possibilities and Issues." World Bank Report, Washington, DC. **www1.worldbank. org/education/secondary/document/linden%20text.pdf**

Martin, Michael O, Ina V S Mullis, Kelvin D Gregory, Craig Hyle, Ce Shen (1998): *Effective Schools in Science and Mathematics*. **www.timss.bcu.edu/timss**

Mazurek, Kes, Margeret A Wizner, Czeslaw Majorek Eds. *Education in a Global Society. A Comparative Perspective*. Allyn Bacon, Boston 385-97

Meier, Deborah (1995): *The Power of Their Ideas: Lessons for America From a Small School in Harlem*. Beacon Press, Boston, MA

Miguel, Edward, Micheal Kramer (2001): "Worms: Education and Health Externalities in Kenya." National Bureau of Economic Research Working Paper 8481. NBER Washington DC. **www.nber.org/papers/w8481.**

Ministry of Education Malaysia (2001): *Pembangunan Pendididakan 2001-2010. Rancangan Bersepadu Penjana Cemerlangan Pendidikan.* (Education Development 2001-2010. Plan for Unity Through Educational Excellence.) Ministry of Education Malaysia, Kuala Lumpur, 2001.

Mulrine, Anna (2002): "Smaller and Better." Culture and Ideas. *US News & World Report*, June 10.

National Academy Press (2002): *Improving Learning with Technology. Report of a Workshop. 2002*. Washington, DC.

"No Child Left Behind. The New Elementary and Secondary Education Act of 2001." Office of the US Secretary of Education, Washington, DC. **www.edu.gov/nclb**

Norain Fauziah Yaakub, Ahmad Mahdzan Ayob (1999): "Higher Education and Socioeconomic Development in Malaysia. A Human Resource Perspective." Paper presented at the Association of Southeast Asian Institute of Higher Learning seminar on "Liberal Arts Education and Socioeconomic Development in the Next Century." In Hong Kong.
www.mahdzan.com/papers/hkpaper99/index.html

Osin, Luis (1998): "Computers in Education in Developing Countries. Why and How." Education and Technology Series Vol 3 No 1.
http://wbln0018.worldbank.org/israel.HDNet/HDDocs.nsf

Perani, D, E Paulesu, N S Galles, et al. (1998): The Bilingual Brain: Proficiency and Age of Acquisition of the Second Language." *Brain*, October, 1841-52.

Powell, Arthur G (1996): *Lessons from Privilege. The American Prep School Tradition*. Harvard University Press, Cambridge, MA

Psacharopoulus, George, Harry Anthony Patrinos (2002): *Returns to Investment in Education. A Further Update*. World Bank Education Report Working Paper No: 2881, Washington DC. **http://econ.worldbank.org/files/18081_wps.2881.pdf**

Psacharopoulus, George (1995): "The profitability of Investments in Education: Concepts and Methods." Human Capital Development and Operations Policy, The World Bank, Washington DC.

Razak Report (1956): *Report of the Education Committee 1956 (The Razak Report)*. Government Printing Press, Kuala Lumpur.

Reich, Robert B (1991): *The Work of Nations: Preparing Ourselves for the 21ˢᵗ Century Capitalism*. Alfred A Knopf, New York.

Roff, William R (1967): *The Origin of Malay Nationalism*. Yale U Press, New Haven CT.

Rosnani Hashim (1996): *Education Dualism in Malaysia. Implications for Theory and Practice*. (Southeast Asian Social Studies Monographs), Oxford U Press, Kuala Lumpur.

Rosnani Hashim (2002): Islamization of the Curriculum. **www.islam-online.net/10L-English/gadaya/educaton-1/education1.asp**

Rosnani Hashim (2002) "Balancing Cultural Plurality and National Unity Through Education." Paper presented at the Ninth International Literary and Education Research Network Conference on Learning. Beijing, People s Republic of China July 16-20, 2002.

Rosnani Hashim (2002): "Islamization of the Curriculum." **www.islam-online.net/10L-English/qadaya/education-1/education1.asp**

Rosnani Hashim (1996): *Educational Dualism in Malaysia. Implications for Theory and Practice*. Southeast Asian Social Science Monographs. Oxford University Press, Kuala Lumpur.

Rosenthal, Robert and L Jacobsen (1992): *Pygmalion in the Classroom*. Expanded edition. Irvington, New York.

Selvaratnam, Viswanathan (1988): "Ethnicity, Inequality, and Higher Education in Malaysia." *Comparative Education Review*, 32 May 173-96.

Shaw, William (1976): *Tun Razak. His Life and Times*. Longman Malaysia, Kuala Lumpur.

Sizer, Theodore R (1996): *Horace's Hope. What Works for the American High School*. Houghton Mifflin, New York.

Solo, Robert A (1955): *Economics and Public Interest*. Rutgers University Press, NJ

Steele, Claude (1999): "Thin Ice: Stereotype Threat and the Black College Students." *The Atlantic*, August 1999.

Stoll, Clifford (1999): *High Tech Heretic. Why Computers Don't Belong in the Classrooms and Other Reflections by a Computer Contrarian*. Double Day, New York.

Stoll, Clifford (1995): *Silicon Snake Oil. Second Thoughts on the Information Highway*. Doubleday, New York.

Suet-Ling Pong (1999): "Ethnicity and Schooling in Malaysia: The Role of Policy." Paper presented at the International Seminar "Educational Strategies, Families, and Population Dynamics." Organized by CICRED and UERD at Ouagadougou, Burkina Faso, Nov 15-19, 1999. **www.cicred.org/education/actes/con_Pong.pdf.**

Suet-Ling Pong)1997): "Sibling Size and Educational Attainment in Peninsular Malaysia. Do Policies Matter?" *Sociological Perspectives* 40(2).

Suet-Ling Pong (1996): "School Participation of Children from Single-Mother Families in Malaysia." *Comparative Education*, 40: August 231-249.

Suet-Ling Pong (1993): "Preferential Policies and secondary School Attainment in Peninsular Malaysia." *Sociology of Education*, 66 Oct 245-261.

Swetz, Frank J, Hassan Langgulung, Abdul Rashid Johar (1983): "Attitudes Toward Mathematics and School learning in Malaysia and Indonesia: Urban-Rural and male-Female Dichotomies." *Comparative Education Review* 27, October 394-402.

Tan Ai Mei (2001): *Malaysian Private Higher Education. Globalization, Privatization, Transformation and Marketplace.* Asean Academic Press, Kuala Lumpur.

Tauber, Robert T: "Good or Bad, What Teachers Expect from Students They Generally Get." US Department of Education, ERIC Digest. **www.kidsource.com/education/pygmalion.html**

United States Dept of Education (1996): *E-Learning. Putting World Class Education at the Finger Tips of All Children.* The National Education Technology Plan. **www.ed.gov/Technology/elearning.**

Wang, Bee-Lan Chan (1980): "Sex and Ethnic Differences in Educational Investment in Malaysia: The Effect of Reward Structures." *Comparative Education Review*, 24, June 5140-59.

Wonglinsky, Harold (1998): "Does it Compute? The Relationship Between Educational Technology and Student Achievement in Mathematics. Educational Testing Service's (ETS) Research Policy Information Center, Princeton, NJ **http://ftp.ets.org/pub/res/technolog.pdf**

World Bank Report (2002): *Education and Development.* **www1. worldbank.org/education/pdf/educationbrochure/pdf**

World Bank Report (2002): *Constructing Knowledge Societies: New Challenges for Tertiary Education.* **www1.worldbank.org/education2002.**

World Bank Report 2000: *Education and HIV/AIDS. A Window of Hope.* **www1.worldbank.org/education/pdf/exec%summaryAIDS-Ed-final.pdf**

World Bank Report (2002): *Education and Development.* **www1.worldbank.org/education/pdf/educationbrochure.pdf**

World Bank Report (2001): Brazil: *An Assessment of the Bolsa Escola Programs.* Report No: 20208-BR.

World Bank Report (2001): "*Global Education Reform. Decentralization in Education.*" **www1.worldbank.org/education…Reform/06.01DecenQ&A/DecenQ&A.htm.**

World Bank Report 2000: *Higher Education in Developing Countries: Perils and Promise.* Task Force on Higher Education and Society. **www1.worldbank.org/education**

World Bank Review (1995): *Priorities and Strategies for Education.* World Bank, Washington, DC

Yergin, Daniel, Joseph Stanislaw, Daniel Tergin (1998): *Commanding Heights: The Battle Between Government and the Marketplace That is Remaking the Modern World.* Simon & Shuster, New York.

Young, Mary Eming, Ed. (2002): *From Early Child Development to Human Development. Investing in our Children.* World Bank, Washington, DC.

Zigler, Edward, Susan Muenchow (1993): *Head Start. The Inside Story of America's Most Successful Educational Experiment.* Basic Books, New York.

Zulkifili Bachok (2001): "*Matrikulasi–Pencapaian Lebih Rendah Berbanding STPM.*" (Matriculation–Lower Achievement as compared to STPM). *Utusan Malaysia* May 11.

About the Author

Malaysian-born Bakri Musa writes frequently on issues affecting his native land. His essays have appeared in the *Far Eastern Economic Review*, *International Herald Tribune*, *Education Quarterly*, *Asiaweek*, *Businessweek*, and *The New Straits Times*, and his commentary aired on National Public Radio's *Marketplace*. His column *Seeing It My Way* appears in *Malaysiakini*.

He is the author of *The Malay Dilemma Revisited: Race Dynamics in Modern Malaysia*, and *Malaysia in the Era of Globalization*.

Bakri's day job (and frequently night time too!) is as a surgeon in private practice in Silicon Valley, California. He and his wife Karen live on a ranch in Morgan Hill.

Index

0-595-26590-1

www.ingramcontent.com/pod-product-compliance
Lightning Source LLC
Chambersburg PA
CBHW032058280526
45784CB00012B/32